1988

REAUTHORIZING JOYCE

REAUTHORIZING JOYCE

VICKI MAHAFFEY

University of Pennsylvania

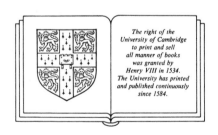

The right of the
University of Cambridge
to print and sell
all manner of books
was granted by
Henry VIII in 1534.
The University has printed
and published continuously
since 1584.

CAMBRIDGE UNIVERSITY PRESS

Cambridge

New York   New Rochelle   Melbourne   Sydney

Published by the Press Syndicate of the University of Cambridge
The Pitt Building, Trumpington Street, Cambridge CB2 1RP
32 East 57th Street, New York, NY 10022, USA
10 Stamford Road, Oakleigh, Melbourne 3166, Australia

First published 1988

Printed in the United States of America

Library of Congress Cataloging-in-Publication Data
Mahaffey, Vicki.
Reauthorizing Joyce / Vicki Mahaffey.
p. cm.
Bibliography: p.
Includes index.
ISBN 0–521–35250–9
1. Joyce, James, 1882–1941 – Criticism and interpretation.
2. Authority in literature.   I. Title.
PR6019.09Z7253   1988
823'.912 – dc19   87–30553
CIP

British Library Cataloguing in Publication Data
Mahaffey, Vicki
Reauthorizing Joyce.
1. Joyce, James, *1882–1941* – Criticism
and interpretation.
I. Title
823'.912 PR5019.092/

ISBN 0 521 35250 9

To my parents, Nancy and Jack Mahaffey

Perhaps there are moments of awakening,
Extreme, fortuitous, personal, in which

We more than awaken, sit on the edge of sleep,
As on an elevation, and behold
The academies like structures in a mist.

Wallace Stevens,
"Notes toward a Supreme Fiction"

CONTENTS

ACKNOWLEDGMENTS

It was not under that the rare birds of Murphy's feather
desired to stand, but by, by themselves with the best of
their attention and by the others of their species with any
that might be left over.

Samuel Beckett, Murphy

THIS book argues that authority may be exercised in ways
that are humorous, celebratory, and unoppressive, using
Joyce's authorial authority as its prime example. In writing
it, I have been fortunate enough to be surrounded by people who
embody the same kind of generosity and honesty I see in Joyce.
My warmest thanks go to "the rare birds of Murphy's feather"
who had little interest in standing over or under what I was trying
to do, but instead stood by, generously offering their reactions and
suggestions when they were needed. The most constant of "by-
standers" were my parents, to whom the book is dedicated, and
my sister, Mindy. A. Walton Litz, in the twelve years that I have
repeatedly tapped his professional experience, never denigrated the
potential of a half-formed argument, nor did he compromise his
criticism of its formal deficiencies, and I owe much to that integrity.
Others who read and commented – often at length – upon various
portions of the manuscript include Ronald Bush, Michael Groden,
Alice Kelley, Marjorie Levinson, Wendy Steiner, and Joseph Val-
ente. My research assistants, Patricia Chu and Robert Mackey, were
invaluable, and special thanks are also due to Marcia Widder, who
helped to ready the final manuscript for the press.

A grant from the American Council of Learned Societies allowed
me to separate the present book from the dissertation that inspired
it. I am also grateful to the University of Pennsylvania for a summer

Acknowledgments

research fellowship and to the University Research Foundation for a grant to cover publication costs.

Three debts remain to be acknowledged: the first is to all those who worked on the manuscript at Cambridge University Press. I would particularly like to thank Terence Moore for his editorial acumen and tact, and Russell Hahn for his professional attention during the production process. My second debt is a public one, to the many readers of Joyce who, through invaluable books and articles, have themselves initiated and reauthorized the continuing process of reauthorization. It is impossible to indicate how much I owe to this generous and committed community, whether my readings accord with or diverge from theirs. My final debt is to my family – to my daughters, Amanda and Laura, and to my husband and colleague, Christopher Dennis, who made available to me the breadth and precision of his knowledge. It is he who taught me that in the wear of daily contact, understanding, however acute, counts less than the more difficult art of bystanding – and standing by.

ABBREVIATIONS

Works cited frequently in the text are identified parenthetically by the following abbreviations:

CW   Joyce, James. *The Critical Writings of James Joyce*, ed. Ellsworth Mason and Richard Ellmann. New York: Viking, 1959.

D   Joyce, James. *Dubliners: Text, Criticism, and Notes*, ed. Robert Scholes and A. Walton Litz. New York: Viking, 1969.

E   Joyce, James. *Exiles: A Play in Three Acts, including Hitherto Unpublished Notes by the Author, Discovered after His Death, and an Introduction by Padraic Colum*. New York: Viking, 1951.

FW   Joyce, James. *Finnegans Wake*. New York: Viking, 1939. References are indicated by the page followed by the line number; for example, 597.22 designates page 597, line 22.

GJ   Joyce, James. *Giacomo Joyce*, ed. Richard Ellmann. New York: Viking, 1968.

JJ II   Ellmann, Richard. *James Joyce*, revised ed. New York and Oxford: Oxford University Press, 1982.

Abbreviations

L I, II, III   Joyce, James. *Letters of James Joyce*. Vol. I, ed. Stuart Gilbert. New York: Viking, 1957, 1966. Vols. II and III, ed. Richard Ellmann. New York: Viking, 1966.

P   Joyce, James. *A Portrait of the Artist as a Young Man: Text, Criticism, and Notes*, ed. Chester G. Anderson. New York: Viking, 1968.

SH   Joyce, James. *Stephen Hero*, ed. Theodore Spencer; revised edition, ed. John J. Slocum and Herbert Cahoon. New York: New Directions, 1944, 1963.

SL   Joyce, James. *Selected Letters of James Joyce*, ed. Richard Ellmann. New York: Viking, 1975.

U   Joyce, James. *Ulysses: The Corrected Text*, ed. Hans Walter Gabler with Wolfhard Steppe and Claus Melchior. New York: Random House, 1986. References are identified by chapter and line number; for example, 5.17 designates line 17 of the fifth chapter ("Lotus Eaters").

INTRODUCTION

WHEN I BEGAN reading Joyce, it was with the expectation that he had developed his vast repertory of stylistic techniques in order to attack the traditional, univocal model of authority reflected in the organizations of Church and State that he had been taught to serve. This is a familiar perspective, cribbed from Joyce himself, who adopts it in *Stephen Hero* and then portrays himself adopting it (with newly attendant ironies) in *A Portrait of the Artist as a Young Man*. Although, like many young readers of Joyce, I was slow to appreciate the complicity of such rebellion with the obedience it claims to displace, I could still imagine that the experience of reading *Ulysses* and *Finnegans Wake* carried me beyond Stephen's dilemma about the preferable response to authority, and into the more subtle question of how authority is constituted and perpetuated. The frustration and boredom occasioned by the *Wake*, spiked with moments of inexplicable laughter or emotion, roused me to a belated but intense recognition of the extent to which convention limits novelty in what we still refer to as the "novel" form. I learned from Joyce what others were learning from contemporary theory, that a reading guided solely by the desire to uncover the author's meaning relies upon the same assumptions about authority – here authorship – that support monotheistic religions and centralized governments, those licensed by representation as well as those established by fiat.

Introduction

The evolving view of authority that I am representing as my own (and also, implicitly, as that of Joyce) bears the trace of what is now a familiar progression of ideas. Outside the frame of Joyce studies, arguments that aim to expose the omnipresence of "patriarchal" or "logocentric" authority have been current for fifteen years, without having substantially changed the picture of Joyce within that frame.[1] The disjunction of attitudes toward authority that separates the mainstream of criticism on Joyce from the mainstream of post-structuralist theory is one of the most interesting cruxes in literary criticism today, partly because *Ulysses* in particular and the whole of Joyce's corpus in general constitute a reading of such differences and their relationship to one another. What I've called – respectfully – mainstream criticism of Joyce is firmly rooted in the epistemology of *Dubliners*; post-structuralist criticism of Joyce is as strongly rooted in the epistemology of the *Wake*. The difficulty, and the challenge, is to engineer a point of contact between critics with such opposite orientations; and a model for such a bridge may be found in *Ulysses*.

Ulysses, as Joyce's most attentive readers have always known, is authorized by the two apparently incompatible points of view represented in the extreme by *Dubliners* and *Finnegans Wake*. The point of view elaborated in the *Wake* is, among other things, an immensely subtle critique, or "reading," of the limitations of monological authority that anticipates many of the arguments advanced on different theoretical and political fronts over the last twenty years.[2] It counters the much more wide-

1   Exceptions include Attridge and Ferrer's *Post-Structuralist Joyce*; Maud Ellmann's "Disremembering Dedalus," in *Untying the Text: A Post-Structuralist Reader*, ed. Robert Young; Cheryl Herr, *Joyce's Anatomy of Culture*; Jennifer Levine's "Originality and Repetition in *Finnegans Wake* and *Ulysses*"; Colin MacCabe's *James Joyce and the Revolution of the Word* and the collection he edited, *James Joyce: New Perspectives*; John Paul Riquelme's *Teller and Tale in Joyce's Fiction*; and of course Margot Norris' *The Decentered Universe of Finnegans Wake*. In relation to the large body of work on Joyce, these exceptions are few. Moreover, I do not as a rule include criticism of the *Wake* as part of what I am calling "mainstream" criticism of Joyce; readers of the *Wake* comprise an atypical subcategory of Joyce criticism that is often far from "mainstream."

2   Although it is relatively easy to cite examples of such arguments –

2

spread assumption, licensed by the relative accessibility of *Dubliners* and the frequency with which it is taught, that Joyce epitomizes institutional authority. *Ulysses*, however, maps out the difficult route that connects such points of view, a route that becomes accessible when the reader refuses to pledge fidelity to only one of the two opposing possibilities. *Ulysses* insists, more subtly than the *Wake*, that these opposites are part of the same contradictory reality, a fact that makes fidelity to one extreme both unnatural and impossible. If, as Lynch's cap taunts Stephen in "Circe," "extremes meet" (*U* 15.2098), betrayal is not only inevitable, but implicit in the very decision to pledge fidelity to only half of an arbitrarily partitioned reality. Joyce traces the phenomena of oppression, destructive conflict, and even violence to such institutionalized divisions of reality, and to the favoritism and prejudice that protect our choices.

Unlike some of his more doctrinaire descendents in the twin worlds of theory and practical criticism, Joyce is constantly alert to the potential as well as to the limitations and humorous possibilities of several different kinds of "logic," or ways of organizing and authorizing perception, including what we now call logocentric or patriarchal logic. In the deeply divided world of literary studies as it is now constituted, that makes him almost unique. Instead of proposing to abandon the monological model of authority, he instigates a dialogue between "traditional" or logocentric methods of interpretation and those that have been excluded; between rational, scholastic logic and the unschooled apprehension of complex interconnection; between an ethos of individualism and an ethos of community; between the world defined as "male" and its "female"

those of Mikhail Bakhtin about monological versus dialogical discourse; those in philosophical linguistics, spearheaded by Jacques Derrida and disseminated by the so-called "Yale" school; those in French feminism, informing the works of Hélène Cixous and Luce Irigaray, among others; those that produced Marxist revisionists such as Terry Eagleton and Fredric Jameson – it is more difficult to indicate how widespread such critiques have become, and how various are their ramifications. The best general introduction to post-structuralist theory is still that of Jonathan Culler, *On Deconstruction*, which concentrates on feminism, reader response criticism, psychoanalytic criticism, and deconstruction, but not on Marxism or on Russian critics such as Bakhtin.

complement; between the referentiality of language and its materiality; between conscious and unconscious desire.

While it would be misleading to define Joyce's project wholly in deconstructionist or feminist terms, it would be equally dangerous to deny the intersection of the different approaches. Joyce's work, like that of many deconstructionists and feminists, reflects a deep interest in the dynamic processes of polarization and reunion that allow systems such as society and language to change, and a serious concern with the pressure to stabilize – and paralyze – such change by hardening the distinction between opposites in order to privilege one term over its counterpart. Joyce's resistance to the unnatural stabilization of language and of value begins with a more general criticism of society in *Dubliners*; but it becomes increasingly more specific as he moves his primary focus to an individual in *Portrait*, to narrative style in *Ulysses*, and finally to individual words and letters in *Finnegans Wake*. All of these works may be seen to accord with the theory that opposites are always and necessarily identical as well as different, a theory that posits value, not in one term of an opposition at the expense of the other, but in the continuing process of separation and reunion. Identifying the theoretical underpinning of Joyce's lifelong project, however, does little to explain its special appeal. That appeal lies in the ingenious consistency with which precept governs practice and practice recomplicates precept throughout Joyce's works.

It is of course much easier to give assent to a proposition in theory than it is to restructure our way of thinking, speaking, writing, and acting so as to embody that truth. As Joyce remarks of himself in the "Portrait" essay, "It was indeed a long time before this boy understood the nature of the most marketable goodness which makes it possible to give comfortable assent to propositions without ordering one's life in accordance with them" ("A Portrait of the Artist," *P* 258). Such restructuring is particularly difficult when twenty centuries of ethical imperatives and precedents regarding the use of language direct us to interpret the fact of opposition in a prejudicial way. In order to see opposites as truly equal and self-reversing, we have to give up the assumption that we ever do one thing and one thing only, since any one objective will implicitly call its opposite into play, whether or not we choose to admit the duplicity that the act of division necessarily produces. The ease with which the interdependence of contraries may be forgotten or denied in practice can be illustrated through a hypothetical – although not unfamiliar – argument about Joyce. If, for example, we decide to value Joyce as a model of comprehensiveness because his work both demands and resists familiar labels, we might enlist in support of such a claim Stephen's argument about Shakespeare in "Scylla and Charybdis," arguing that Joyce, like Shakespeare, chose to play all the parts. However, to aggrandize Joyce by celebrating his comprehensiveness is partial in both senses of the word: it sets him up as a mastermind, a model of authority who invites and defies imitation, thus dividing him from his admirers. The author who is everybody is the authority whom nobody can be. This is an irony Joyce learned from Homer, who presents Odysseus as an everyman who also, as he tells the Cyclops, bears the name of "Noman"; and its traces are apparent in "Scylla and Charybdis" as well. What Best and Eglinton fail to understand is that the Shakespeare Stephen is constructing is both all of his characters and none of them, a ghost whose only vitality is in the characters who produced, represented, and outlasted the conflicts of the man.

Stephen recognizes what his interlocutors cannot, that at a certain point even praise folds over on itself, and while we may believe ourselves to be celebrating wholeness, a closer look will reveal that we are also, perhaps inadvertently, cheering emptiness. The entire endeavor to privilege through categorization has become comically hypocritical, as beneath the realm of consciousness "whole" drops its silent "w" and turns into an opposite that is also, phonetically and philosophically, identical.

Any assertion about Joyce's comprehensiveness can only maintain its integrity if its proponent is as quick as Stephen to deny his or her own theory. Then Joyce, like Shakespeare as Stephen presents him, may be seen as what he has become, an imaginary figure who is both everywhere and nowhere, alive through the forms he has created and dead, a ghost imprecating his half-dead progeny to "List, list, O list" to the wrongs of the past. His authority is provisional, his world both full and empty, his every point contingent upon its ability to engage readers – living in one sense and unliving in another, like Joyce himself – in a mutually animating dialogue.

The argument that is emerging about the doubleness and variability of Joyce's authorities should still sound familiar, even if we are aware of how easily its dicta may be violated in critical practice.

Introduction

The assertion that Joyce insists on the equality and interdependence of binary oppositions – writer/reader, man/woman, fact/fiction, theory/practice – and celebrates the humor and instruction implicit in their self-reversals is hardly a novel suggestion, whether one's authorities are Derrida, Barthes, and Kristeva, or Giordano Bruno and Nicholas of Cusa, whose theories of the coincidence of contraries come to life as the Shem and Shaun of *Finnegans Wake*.[3] As long as we can name the field, theorists and Joyce critics can play the same game. An equally familiar problem, however, is that readers can seldom be sure of their ground (or *grounds*) for reading. Reading is both a conscious and an unconscious activity, guided partly by new models and partly by habits of mind acquired before reading became self-conscious. A reader's experience of language is subject to different kinds of authority, some of which exceed the reader's conscious control and approval, and more than one kind can be operating at any given moment. The most vital challenge, whether in reading Joyce or in articulating what we do when we read, is to remain open to the knowledge of what conflicting forces may be governing us at any given moment, and to learn to arrest our thought at the point where self-contradiction inevitably begins. Such a challenge demands both practical and theoretical awareness of the potency and variability of the major forms of authority, whether or not we approve of them. It is easiest to develop our awareness of the different ways that we become subject to various authorities (and authors) by reading books that do not pander to our illusions, but instead interfere with our assumptions chapter by chapter, sentence by sentence, word by word, or even letter by letter, like the works of Joyce. As a voice reminds us in *Finnegans Wake*, language is the food of the mind, and the only way to forestall choking is by taking the time to chew: "some may seek to dodge the gobbet for its quantity of quality but who wants to cheat the choker's got to learn to chew the cud" (*FW* 277.26–278.3).

For over ten years, the trend has been to divide *Ulysses* into two parts, with the last part reversing the emphases of the first, a division

---

3 The presuppositions of post-structuralist theory are not new – Joyce found them in the banned works of "heretics" – but the fact that similar presuppositions structure *Finnegans Wake* explains why critics schooled in the *Wake*, such as Hugh Kenner and Fritz Senn, can enter so easily into post-structuralist discourse.

that accents the book's hospitality to post-structuralist authority.[4] The two-part division has yielded several valuable insights into the book's structure, but the casualty of a loosely deconstructive reading is the "Penelope" episode, which fits comfortably into neither of the two parts. It makes sense, for this reason, to reinstate the more obvious tripartite structure, reading the first and third parts, associated with Stephen and Molly, as extremes that meet and disperse in the middle section, associated with Bloom.

Ulysses, then, represents a model of three kinds of authority derived from different combinations of two positions. Like Shem and Shaun, who can unexpectedly combine to form three in the *Wake*, the three forms of authority are composed of two opposites and, between them, a third possibility that is not a synthesis of the other two, but instead marks their simultaneous presence and absence. The pattern that emerges is not dialectical for three reasons: (1) there is no temporal or rational progression towards a higher, more synthetic consciousness – the same knowledge must be repeatedly relearned in reference to new oppositions; (2) the "third" possibility, while positioned midway between the other two, is not a compromise between them or a product of them; and (3) the relationship between the middle term and the two that bound it entails, paradoxically, both inclusion and exclusion: the middle term marks both the absence of the other two and their simultaneous presence. A perceiver positioned between two extremes will, according to Joyce's model, neither try to work out a compromise between them nor choose one at the expense of the other, but will instead try to appreciate their simultaneous identity and difference, an effort that momentarily reconstitutes and deconstitutes the perceiver.

Of the three kinds of authority that structure *Ulysses*, the first is the patriarchal (Stephen might call it patristic), transcendent authority which Stephen recognizes. The second kind of authority is binary and paradoxical, an authority embodied in Bloom. The two authorities that authorize Bloom are represented by Stephen and Molly; most of what we know about Bloom we know through these two characters. The third mode of authority is collective,

---

4 Michael Groden's *Ulysses in Progress* gave evidence to support such a division, and Karen Lawrence in *The Odyssey of Style in Ulysses* took the logic of a two-part *Ulysses* one step further.

immanent, and largely unconscious, and it is associated most fully with Molly. The three kinds of authority seem to differ primarily in number: single, double, and multiple. However, each version of authority is defined not only by one of Joyce's characters, but by a figure or image from the *Odyssey*, and this doubling of text and context makes it clear that although the three kinds of authority form a spectrum of values bounded by individuality and plurality, all are defined by analogous contradictions. Stephen, like Telemachus, begins his odyssey by looking for a substitute father who can tell him about his real father. The ideal of the Father seems to be unitary, but it is embodied in alternative ways: the spiritual father opposes the biological one, and in the reading of the *Odyssey* reflected in *Ulysses*, the false father opposes the helpful one. Stephen, like Telemachus, appeals not to one but to two "spiritual" fathers – Nestor (whose self-contradictions are masked by the complacency of his trust in his own authority) and Proteus (whose variability gradually reveals itself as the most trustworthy form of guidance). Bloom's doubleness is reflected in what Joyce called the "splendid parable" of "Scylla and Charybdis,"[5] which figures, in the relationship between rock and whirlpool, the structural identity and inversion of extremes, while fabling the danger of choosing one instead of both/neither. Molly's interconnective, materialistic authority is represented by Penelope's web, the shroud that she weaves by day and unpicks by night to forestall her own entrapment. The web, like the image of the father that represents Stephen's authority, seems to be a one-sided image – of plurality rather than individuality, of democracy as opposed to autocracy – but when examined more closely, it, too, emerges as a double image that illustrates the interdependence of freedom and entrapment, material multiplicity and the here-unacknowledged unity of design. Overall, Joyce's treatment of these three forms of authority suggests that each responds to a different aspect of the same contradictory reality, a reality that is both singular and plural, and neither singular nor plural.

The simplest formulation of an argument with ramifications that can be quite complex is that contradiction is inevitable; discourse ambivalent; the body bilateral; authority double. By the dictates of

5   Georges Borach, "Conversations with James Joyce," in Potts, *Portraits of the Artist in Exile*, p. 70.

the Church, such a view is heresy, and more specifically, it has strong affinities with the gnostic heresy, which is defined partly by its philosophical dualism, partly by its syncretism, and partly by its roots in Hellenic philosophy.[6] Stephen seems to be a champion of individual authority, but his theory of Shakespeare shows that he has begun to break down the distinction between individual and collective identity, without having realized the implications of his theories in practical, material terms. Molly illustrates the realization of Stephen's theories in her openness to the interconnective potential of a wide range of material things, but she has no awareness of the individual pattern into which her apparent "randomness" resolves itself; she lacks Stephen's analytical self-consciousness. Stephen "knows" the world in an abstract sense, Molly knows it in the carnal one; and Bloom knows, or comes to intuit, the interdependence of both perspectives.

In a work as conscious of the verbal condition of its existence as *Ulysses*, it is not surprising to find that Joyce's three kinds of authority call into play three complementary modes of reading. A reading presided over by a mind like Stephen's tends either toward the theoretical or the biographical (Stephen unexpectedly combines the two in his theory of Shakespeare). Biographical and theoretical readings are alike in their hunger for a meaning extrinsic to the work, whether that meaning is displaced onto a philosophical or linguistic system or anthropomorphized into an author: despite their many differences, theoretical and biographical readings are equally *authoritative* in orientation. Conversely, the mode of reading associated with Molly might be described as a post-structuralist approach unhampered (and unaided) by the post-structuralist's self-conscious awareness of the way language operates. On the surface, Molly's mode of reading is the opposite and complement of Stephen's, since it is oriented towards the reader rather than the author, and since it registers not purpose or intention but effect, playing

6 The best overall account of gnosticism is that of Hans Jonas, *The Gnostic Religion: The Message of the Alien God and the Beginnings of Christianity* (Boston: Beacon Press, 1958; second edition 1963). Joyce was certainly well versed in gnosticism, from Epiphanius of Salamis – who may have had something to do with Joyce's early interest in "epiphany" – through Origen and Valentinus, an arch-heresiarch mentioned in *Ulysses* (U 1.658), to the Manicheans battled by Augustine.

on our subconscious sensitivity to the networks of association set up by the way words look and sound. If a reader like Stephen has a stake in the extent to which meaning can be controlled by an author via the rules of definition, logic, and structure, a reader like Molly is equally invested in the ease with which language can escape conscious control, establishing and dissolving rival systems of interrelationship. Molly's mental world is unconsciously structured by the interconnective "logic" of puns; she understands, in an intuitive rather than a self-conscious way, that puns are not always as isolated and accidental as we tend to assume, but combine to form implied narratives, networks of underground, illegitimate "meaning." The sensual and sensory logic of Molly's subconscious is the logic that expands into *Finnegans Wake*, Joyce's most sustained attempt to exhume the buried life of language. Although the dreams in the *Wake* seem to be governed by a male mind, the project of attending to the sensuality of language is one that Joyce associates with women, tracing the taboos against puns to the original sin, to woman's hunger and plea for a more tangible, metaphorical, and etymological rather than strictly denotative "sense": "so please-kindly communicake with the original sinse" (*FW* 239. 1–2).

It is possible to classify and schematize tendencies toward different kinds of authority, as Joyce does through his treatment of character in *Ulysses*, but as the structure of *Ulysses* suggests, the three main tendencies are interrelated; they are separable, but we need not experience them independently. The interdependence of alternative authorities is especially clear in the relationship between the authority acknowledged by Stephen and the plural authorities that govern Molly: whereas Stephen's authority is a transcendent and primarily spiritual one, Molly's authorities are immanent and physical; whereas his is sanctioned by his past but oriented toward the future, hers are nostalgic but sanctioned by a future that has recently come to pass. In political terms, Stephen's authority is capitalist and Molly's communist in the etymological senses of those words; in terms of sexual politics, his is a male authority and hers its female complement. Most significantly, his authority is institutionally recognized, hers disenfranchised, so that whatever authority Molly's perspective may have is latent rather than generally accepted, or even acceptable. Stephen and Molly represent the boundaries of human moral authority as they have been culturally defined, the margins of "good" and "evil." What is most striking about the opposition between such extremes is the ease with which their values may be reversed; in fact, certain strands of feminism may be defined as an attempt to effect such a reversal, whereby the values characteristic of Molly become "good" and those respected by Stephen "evil." Joyce's point seems to be that such reversals are already implicit in the very posture of opposition: Stephen and Molly contain one another through the logic that makes it possible to define them as mutually exclusive. What defines both Stephen and Molly is their partiality to contrasting halves of human and verbal experience, but both their authorities are equally "partial." What makes Bloom whole, and hollow, by contrast, is his partiality to both Stephen and Molly, despite the apparent incompatibility of the positions they represent. They mark his limits, even while they signal his limitlessness as a subject who has paradoxically allowed himself to be "framed."

The reading practices of Stephen and Molly are more clearly reciprocal and potentially one-sided than are the paradoxical inconsistencies of Bloom, but both Stephen and Molly are exceptional because they instinctively compensate for the one-sidedness of their approaches. Stephen offsets the rhetorical power of argumentation with an acute awareness of its dangers: its teleological emphasis, and its power to convert listeners, to abort rather than engender the process of questioning. By emphasizing the eccentricities of his argument about Shakespeare, by denying any belief in it, and by offering on more than one occasion to sell it, Stephen dissociates himself from the authority that his mode of suasion has granted him; instead of belief, he requests money, a substitution that underlines the kinship of the two kinds of currency. Moreover, by demanding a return that is inappropriate to the situation, he effectively undermines the expectation that any counteroffer – whether of money or of belief – is necessary, thereby devaluing the rhetorical objective of his argument and highlighting the intricacies of its progress. Molly, in contrast, eschews the rational power of logical sequence altogether, yet her language has a seductive authority of its own, the illogical symmetries of a labyrinth, or a web. She spins a web of thoughts that seem threateningly present and impossibly inconsistent until the reader uncovers the principle of interconnection – spatial rather than temporal, material rather than conceptual – that guides her discourse, whereupon her web of words yields up a confession of loss, of emptiness, and of love for the idea and ideal of bloom that complicates and offsets her aggressively sensual power.

Willful complacency, of the sort that makes self-defense – and self-pretense – necessary, is one of the few targets of attack that Joyce never abandons, although he lampoons it more humorously in the *Wake* than in earlier works. The following argument is undoubtedly complacent and one-sided in places, but it is never willfully so. It is divided into three parts, which correspond to the three views of authority represented in *Ulysses*. The first is devoted to monological authority, and to the obedient and rebellious offspring who ensure its perpetuity. Since Stephen plays by turns both of the roles offered to children in a patriarchal system, and since the humor of his inability to free himself from the presuppositions that bind him to an unknown "father" is the subject of *A Portrait of the Artist as a Young Man*, the *Portrait* already implies the need for a different authority, the two-sided Bloom of *Ulysses*. Even two-sidedness, however, can be reduced to one-sidedness by the application of prejudice, unless the disfavored side be represented and loved in turn. Molly plays a collection of culturally suspect roles: she is the unfaithful wife, the assertive woman, the materialist, the reader who refuses to acknowledge the rules of grammar and logic that produce authorized "meanings," the producer and destroyer of illegitimate and largely unconscious networks of meaning. The last part of this book is devoted to her.

My methodology is simply an attempt to apply what I've learned from Joyce: to be attentive to slight shifts in context, to change authorities as lightly as necessary to preserve the tension of discovery and recovery, to remember that influence is both retrospective and prospective, and to respect the reciprocity between a given verbal center and the margins that define and confine it, since every center is, with respect to some other figure, marginal, and every margin potentially central. I have tried to bound my discussions with brief accounts of how each book has been read, and how each book rereads the works it builds on. At every stage, I have tried to show how consistently Joyce exposes the hidden contradictions within whatever we tend to regard as unitary and uniform. Finally, my goal has been to highlight new particulars of Joyce's work, what Wallace Stevens in "Notes toward a Supreme Fiction" calls the "particulars of rapture," by detailing his double, meta-phorically "sexual" method of engendering them, a method that emphasizes the equality of two participants in any productive exchange. As far as my own authority is concerned, I can only say that it is as provisional and self-consuming as that of any author over any reader: the "privilege" of the author is the privilege of age, which is both experience and obsolescence.

The experience of reading *Reauthorizing Joyce* may be unsettling precisely because the authorities that govern it keep shifting. I have tried to minimize confusion by labeling the major shifts, but the quieter fluctuations of phrasing and nuance are difficult to control, and impossible to tag. I can only hope to emphasize one or two points at the outset: first, that I have tried to commit myself, like Stephen, to an analytical, discursive method but not to its telos. This means that an argument can only be taken so far before it becomes necessary to deny the conclusion toward which the argument points as an "end." Second, the shape of the overall argument is as significant, and possibly more significant, than its direction. I argue that Joyce represents authority as inherently double, a doubleness that takes as its two poles an individualistic model of authority on the one hand, and a communal model on the other; but the sequential progression from individual authority to communal authority is represented here, as in *Ulysses*, as a redundancy as well as a discovery. This book, like *Ulysses*, seems to progress from a critical analysis of individual solipsism to a celebration of connectedness, but the dream of connection pulls with it the nightmare of entrapment, a nightmare that renews appreciation of the value of individuation that we began by criticizing. The end of this book, like the last work in Joyce's corpus, inevitably entails a reevaluation of its beginning, because the processes that it examines are all Odyssean ones designed to allow us to traverse an uncanny world, alien yet oddly familiar. In Stephen's words, we are "walking through ourselves," discovering that the self-involvement we begin by experiencing is a communal experience – it is common to everyone – and that the interpersonal awareness that comes with maturity is not only a celebration of relationship, but also an exodus, a choral preparation for the isolation of death. All Joyce's works chart a progression that is also an inverted regression, like the mime of Nick, Mick, and the Maggies, which proposes to begin with "a community prayer, everyone for himself, and to conclude with as an exodus, we think it well to add, a chorale in canon, good for us all for us all us all all" (*FW* 222.4–6).

One of the most exciting aspects of Joyce's lifelong analysis of different modes of authority, and of the ways of reading that prove the power, conscious and unconscious, of such authorities, is that although derivable from Joyce's fiction, they extend far beyond the borders of that fiction. Some of the most interesting implications of Joyce's way of reading are notably absent from the argument that follows, although I've tried to allude in passing to different interpretive possibilities. For example, Molly would be quick to hear and to respond to the "doubling" in "Dublin," and the "Ire" in "Ireland," and if she were more analytically inclined, she could see the relationship between Joyce's fascination with binarism and the long and bloody history of a country riven by intolerance and anger. The history of Ireland, its divisions and its continuing violence, is deeply implicated in Joyce's relentless investigation of authority, until it finally erupts in competing narratives of invasion and assimilation in *Finnegans Wake*. There is an important book yet to be written on the charged relationship between Irish politics and literature written by Irishmen, such as Joyce and Beckett, that seems to present itself as more European than Irish; but that subject deserves fuller treatment than I could give it here. Similarly, the section on Molly's materialism and its relationship to what I've called a communal system of value deserves to be considered within the framework of Marxist and neo-Marxist theory, and Molly's unconscious perspicacity to be read across Freud's theories of humor, particularly *Jokes and Their Relation to the Unconscious*. The coincidence of Marxist and Freudian tendencies in what we would now characterize as a post-structuralist mode of reading suggests a variety of ways in which Molly might serve as a controversial locus that draws together and contextualizes major currents in twentieth-century thought.

Joyce's view of authority was emotionally charged by his sensitivity to historical and sociopolitical realities and informed by his taste for theoretical argument of all kinds, but it was exemplified most immediately in the various and flexible operations of his language, which is why language and literature provide the major focus of the argument that follows. In *Finnegans Wake*, Joyce suggests that every writing encodes the readings (or "raidings") that preceded and inspired it: "The prouts who will invent a writing there ultimately is the poeta, still more learned, who discovered the raiding there originally. That's the point of eschatology our book of kills reaches for now in soandso many counterpoint words. What can't be coded can be decorded if an ear aye sieze what no eye ere grieved for" (*FW* 482.31–36). One way to illustrate the three kinds of authority that animate *Ulysses* is simply to pinpoint their relationship to something as apparently uncontroversial (except in the context of the *Wake*) as the time of day. The following reading condenses an argument that is developed more fully, and over a longer period of time, in the body of the book.

STEPHEN: SUN IN MORNING

To someone who reads "normally," automatically translating sounds into the socially constituted meanings that make sense in terms of (1) the way the word is spelled and (2) the conventional context of the sentence in which it occurs, Stephen at the beginning of *Ulysses* is, among other things, a son in mourning. Such a reading of Stephen's situation is sufficient unto itself, or "singular," and it certainly represents some part of the author's intended meaning. However, when read against Molly's authority, the unauthorized aural connections that link words with other words, the terms in which we think of Stephen also make sense of a different, more humorous kind. The image of Stephen as a "sun in morning" is appropriate not only to the time of day of Stephen's section, but also to the reading of Stephen implicit in his identification with Christ and Lucifer in *A Portrait of the Artist as a Young Man*.

Most readers of *Portrait* realize that Stephen alternates between the roles of Christ and Lucifer. Read in a doctrinal way (which is how Stephen reads), Christ and Lucifer mark the antipodes of "good" and "evil" filial behavior. However, when read against the sound of the words that denominate them, the differences between Christ and Lucifer recede before the identification of both with light. Christ is the "son" (evoking a now-familiar pun), and the name "Lucifer," as Joyce reminds us throughout his fiction, means "Lightbringer" (see Stephen's identification in "Circe" of fallen matches: "Lucifer" [15.3595–9]). If a reader recognizes homonyms as indications of real, if unsuspected, relationships, "son" and "sun" have more than an accidental connection (a possibility suggested in

Ulysses by the title of one of Bloom's books – *Is Jesus a Sun Myth?*).
Christ as "sun" is indistinguishable from Lucifer who brings light;
what is devalued as "evil" is the *fall* of the lightbringer, a fall which
is offset by the *rise* of the Son/sun.

The point that such an analysis brings to the fore is that Christ
and Lucifer, when analyzed "poetically," or in terms of the language
that constructs them, represent the same phenomenon: light. They
are not two sons, but the same "sun," moving in different directions. And lest we forget what values are being denigrated, we are
presented with an alternate version of the fall, this time perpetrated
by a woman with the significant name of "Eve," which repeats
through its association with a time of day the theme that the falling
of the sun is evil.

If Molly were more analytically inclined, she could propose a
reading of Stephen as the "morning sun," and she could justify it
as a reading authorized not by the legitimate conventions of definition, but by the "illegitimate" sensual congress of verbal sights
and sounds that we all react to subconsciously, and in dreams. Such
a reading is essential to an understanding of Stephen's one-sidedness: Stephen thinks that Christ and Lucifer map out the only two
possible responses to an authoritative father, but what he cannot
see is that those two responses are also the *same* response. Stephen
is struggling to discover which of the two possibilities best suits
him as an individual; he cannot see the comedy of *A Portrait*, which
shows that he cannot be *either* without being both, since there can
be no rise without a fall, and vice versa. Stephen's dilemma is a
common one: how can we arrive at an alternative interpretation of
an authorized story if we refuse to consider the relevance of logically
incompatible ways of establishing meaning? The twin stories of the
"fall" recount not only an event, but a way of interpreting the
moral of that event, a moral that darkness – along with the sensuality and disobedience associated with it – is "wrong."

BLOOM: NIGHT AND DAY

Once the interdependence of Christ and Lucifer, rise and fall, man
and woman, morning and evening, has been established, it becomes
possible to position Christianity relative to Greek mythology,
which Joyce implicitly does in *Ulysses*. If a great proportion of
Greek myths grew out of stories about constellations in the night

sky, Christianity is a complementary celebration of the sun in the guise of a Son. Both Christianity and Judaism, however, define genesis as an encounter with a darkness that is evil. A fuller view of the relationship between religion, on the one hand, and light or darkness, on the other, can engender a philosophic dualism that commonsensically accepts their interdependence. The "Bloomian" attitude that results might be described as a kind of comic Manicheanism, comic because it doesn't regard the conflict between dark and light as an ethical issue, but as a natural cycle that has been used as an expedient means of validating a specific interpretation of "right" behavior.

One of the most concise and moving accounts of the freedom and the isolation of taking a truly egalitarian view of light and dark, the mental and the physical, is found not in Joyce's work but in that of his disciple Samuel Beckett. Beckett's Murphy is a less optimistic counterpart to Bloom – less heroic, more pathetic, more subject to the black comedy of circumstance, less an epitome of epic endurance – but despite the differences, Murphy consciously tries to recreate the evenness of mind that Bloom restores to the universe of *Ulysses*. In the sixth chapter of *Murphy*, the narrator's description of Murphy's mind is furnished with a reading of Christianity as subject both to "the idealist tar" and "the ethical yoyo," both of which Murphy has managed – not without some absurdity – to elude:

Murphy's mind pictured itself as a large hollow sphere, hermetically closed to the universe without. This was not an impoverishment, for it excluded nothing that it did not itself contain. Nothing ever had been, was or would be in the universe outside it but was already present as virtual, or actual, or virtual rising into actual, or actual falling into virtual, in the universe inside it.

This did not involve Murphy in the idealist tar. There was the mental fact and there was the physical fact, equally real if not equally pleasant.

He distinguished between the actual and the virtual of his mind, not as between form and the formless yearning for form, but as between that of which he had both mental and physical experience and that of which he had mental experience only. Thus the form of kick was actual, that of caress virtual.

The mind felt its actual part to be above and bright, its virtual beneath and fading into dark, without however connecting this with the ethical yoyo. The mental experience was cut off from the physical experience, its criteria were not those of the physical experience, the agreement of part of its content with physical fact did not confer worth on that part. It did not function and could not be disposed according to a principle of worth. It was made up of light fading into dark, of above and beneath, but not of good and bad. It contained forms with parallel in another mode and forms without, but not right forms and wrong forms. It felt no issue between its light and dark, no need for its light to devour its dark. The need was now to be in the light, now in the half light, now in the dark. That was all.[7]

Murphy understands and needs the kind of binary authority embodied by Bloom: he, like Bloom, has intuited and appreciates the "evenness" in "evening," and prefers it to a mode of feeling that requires the mind's light "to devour its dark."

Murphy is shot through with the effects of Joyce's reading of light and darkness: Murphy is in love with Celia, whose name means "sky," recalling Murphy to the light and darkness, heaven and hell, of creation.[8] Murphy is only at peace when he rocks, his gaze arrested looking down, then looking up: "Slowly he felt better, astir in his mind, in the freedom of that light and dark that did not clash, nor alternate, nor fade nor lighten except to their communion."[9] Murphy is a Stephen Dedalus who never has and never will realize the values Bloom represents, except as dark "virtual" forms in his mind.[10]

7   Samuel Beckett, *Murphy* (New York: Grove Press, 1957), pp. 107–8.
8   Ibid., p. 176.
9   Ibid., p. 252.
10 It is interesting to see how the "artist" poems of Tennyson and Browning respect the "evenness" of dawn and dusk as a condition of self-awareness: see "Ulysses," "Tithonus," "Andrea del Sarto," and "Fra Lippo Lippi."

MOLLY: EVE

Molly's realm, like that of Eve (and Eveline), is darkness: darkness of the sky, the body, and the mind. Women in *Ulysses* become prominent only from dusk – when Bloom encounters Gerty – to dawn, when Molly weaves and unweaves her thoughts. The important point about the obscurity associated with Molly, though, is its relationship to enlightenment: knowledge of good and evil is only accessible through a taste of the carnal and material world that Molly revels in. Stephen's one-sidedness cannot fully be conceived unless the reader adopts a mode of reading antithetical to the one Stephen authorizes in *A Portrait*, a habit of mind that takes puns seriously, approaching them not as isolated coincidences of two similar sounds but as clues to underground networks of meaning, the hidden coherency of unconscious relation.

What is most surprising about even a cursory examination of the interrelationship of words that look and sound alike is that the connections so frequently combine to create alternative narratives. Seen in such a light, language is not only a material construct, but one which owes its density to a constant crossing of opposites, a meshing of warp and woof that creates a paradoxical but strongly interconnective logic. The last half of *Ulysses* and much of *Finnegans Wake* play on the implicit relationship between texts and textiles, and on the interdependence of male and female styles. A look at language from what Joyce presents as a "female" perspective demands an appreciation, not so much for any individual author, but for the millions of "authors" who have shaped the language over time simply by using it, listening to it, and unconsciously adjusting its similar sounds and images to reflect a poetic rightness of relation that counterbalances the authorized, and the intentional, meaning. If, as St. John asserted, God is the Word, that word is double: it is both abstract and material, transcendent and immanent, authorized from without by an individual author and from within by the multiple crisscrossing of the sights and sounds of words as they weave and unweave the material network of language.

PART I

"UNITARY" AUTHORITY

1

THE MYTH OF A MASTERMIND

Never suppose an inventing mind as source
Of this idea nor for that mind compose
A voluminous master folded in his fire.
                    Wallace Stevens,
            "Notes toward a Supreme Fiction"

IT IS NO LONGER controversial to say that authority is a predominantly "male" concept; the terms "patriarchy," "logocentrism," and "phallocentrism" have entered critical discourse as alternative names for the monological pattern that has shaped much of Western thought and many of its most powerful institutions. However, as numerous commentators have discovered, a serious problem plagues those who would criticize authority as unilaterally male: it is virtually impossible to criticize such authority without usurping it or reproducing its negative image, and both alternatives perpetuate the very system the critique was designed to uproot. The theory of "deconstruction" is designed to describe and contextualize the inevitability of contradiction, but deconstruction, as the name implies, has pessimistic implications that (deliberately) undermine the point of the entire enterprise. In contrast to Derrida, who entertains the one-sidedness of logocentric thought in order to expose its contradictions, Luce Irigaray attempts to boycott patriarchal uses of language whenever possible. She protests the objectification and commerce of a male economy by refusing to commit herself to hard-and-fast answers that can be traded, gesturing instead toward female fluidity and indefiniteness.[1]

---

1   See *This Sex Which Is Not One*, trans. Catherine Porter, and Jane Gallop's discussion of Irigaray in *The Daughter's Seduction*, especially pp. 63–79.

Irigaray's strategy, although it doesn't cancel itself out like Derrida's, is "negative" in another sense: the one-sidedness of a female response repeats, as well as reverses, the exclusivity of its male counterpart.

The problem with any criticism of authority is that self-contradiction is inevitable: if the inevitability of self-contradiction is emphasized, the critical project seems futile, and if it is not, the project becomes hypocritical. If Derrida and Irigaray illustrate the eventual futility of play, on the one hand, and opposition, on the other, Barthes and Foucault, in their well-known manifestoes against "the author," provide relevant examples of the inadvertent hypocrisy implicit in more polemical approaches.

Barthes' solution to the problems posed by authorship is to propose an altered view of writing, not as the product of individual creation, but as a corrosive activity that eats away all human sources and ends in "the destruction of every voice, of every point of origin. Writing is that neutral, composite, oblique space where our subject slips away, the negative where all identity is lost."[2] Barthes celebrates such writing as anticapitalist and antitheological, penned not by an authority but by a "scriptor":

> We know now that a text is not a line of words releasing a single 'theological' meaning (the 'message' of the Author-God) but a multi-dimensional space in which a variety of writings, none of them original, blend and clash. The text is a tissue of quotations drawn from the innumerable centres of culture... Succeeding the Author, the scriptor no longer bears within him passions, humours, feelings, impressions, but rather this immense dictionary from which he draws a writing that can know no halt: life never does more than imitate the book, and the book itself is only a tissue of signs, an imitation that is lost, infinitely deferred.[3]

The problem with Barthes' analysis, as Christopher Butler has shown, is that it seeks a solution in the very design Barthes professes to reject: to replace the author's authority with the reader's is to

2 Roland Barthes, "The Death of the Author," in *Image–Music–Text*, trans. Stephen Heath, p. 142.
3 Ibid., pp. 146–7.

change "dictators" while leaving the structure of authority unchanged.[4] Although suspicious of univocal authority in principle, in practice Barthes affirms it by crediting the view that author and reader play unequal roles, so that the reader must be either subordinate or rebellious. Instead of regarding author and reader as equals engaged in a changing, polysemous dialogue, Barthes retains the notion that author and reader are engaged in a struggle for authority which one or the other must win.

Foucault's treatment of the author restores some of the complexity that Barthes discards, since he admits that the author has, from the outset, a double function: an author is not only an individual designated by a proper name, but a mask for the reader:

> a projection... of the operations that we force texts to undergo, the connections that we make, the traits that we establish as pertinent, the continuities that we recognize, or the exclusions that we practice.[5]

In the end, however, Foucault too argues for a reversal of "the traditional idea of the author" rather than an appreciation of its contradictory nature and potential. He would have us reject our accustomed view of the author as "the genial creator of a work in which he deposits, with infinite wealth and generosity, an inexhaustible world of significations," replacing it with an awareness that the author embodies the principle of exclusion. The author, according to Foucault, is "the ideological figure by which one marks the manner in which we fear the proliferation of meaning."[6]

Although both Barthes and Foucault successfully disseminated a broader awareness of the religious and political implications of authorial privilege, the solutions they proposed involve the same exclusivity that they associate with authors. Both writers urge us not to accept but to deny certain attributes of the authorial position: Barthes denies the author's power and Foucault his comprehen-

---

4 Butler, "Joyce and the Displaced Author," in *James Joyce and Modern Literature*, ed. W. J. McCormack and Alistair Stead, pp. 67–71.

5 Foucault, "What Is an Author?" in *The Foucault Reader*, ed. Paul Rabinow, p. 110; rpt. from Josué V. Harari, ed. and trans., *Textual Strategies: Perspectives in Post-Structuralist Criticism*.

6 Ibid., p. 119.

130, 102

25

siveness, which is also our willingness to comprehend the burgeoning ramifications of words. Together, what they show is that whether we see authority as single, like Barthes, or double, like Foucault, we are equally involved in contradiction: Barthes criticizes and assumes the author's power; Foucault condemns and echoes the proclivity of writer and reader to deny abundant meaning. A more fruitful course might be to admit that "monological" authority paradoxically manifests itself in two forms, but to specify that such authority is double in a way that lodges a second division within the first: one of its two sides is unitary, but the other is dualistic, which is to say that the figure of authority is triangular.

The hidden "doubleness," or contradictory nature, of authority is apparent when we consider Joyce's own authority, which takes two logically incompatible forms. On the one hand, Joyce is a canonical writer who possesses immense authority within the academic institution; on the other, he is an iconoclastic rebel who eludes or spurns institutional authority at every opportunity. The authoritative Joyce is the incarnation of the artist as Stephen once conceived him, who, "like the God of the creation, remains within or behind or beyond or above his handiwork, invisible, refined out of existence, indifferent, paring his fingernails" (*P* 215). However, the image of Joyce as divinely indifferent dissipates when he is examined, not as a hidden hand, but as a human being practically interested in the circumstances of his environment. As a nonviolent revolutionary who boycotted the institution of marriage, and who escaped the fetters of nationalism through exile and the Church through apostasy, Joyce demonstrates a serious respect for the repressive power of social institutions as well as an exceptional determination to distance himself from them.

Both versions of the author are, in their incompleteness, fictions; more interestingly, they are Joyce's own fictions, plucked from the subtle contexts he devised for them and used to sustain the mythos of his reputation. To present Joyce as a priest of mysterious prose is to present him as Father Flynn rinsed clean of the ugly ironies of *Dubliners*; to cast him as a rebel against external authority is to preserve him forever in callow youth, a Stephen Dedalus sentenced without parole to a world comprised paradoxically of words. Joyce presents Father Flynn and Stephen Dedalus as alternative portraits of the artist: he christens Father Flynn with his own first name, an authorial gesture that Stephen in *Ulysses* warns us not to disregard

(U 9.920–28), and he introduces Stephen as a self-portrait of "the artist" in his youth. Between them, Father Flynn and Stephen Dedalus define the possible extremes of male authority: simoniac worldliness and naive idealism, empty faith and faithful rebellion.

Father Flynn and Stephen Dedalus represent the interdependent limits of a patriarchal authority that Joyce subsequently attempted to circumscribe. That Joyce continues to be identified with one or the other of their images – portraits that he devoted half his career to "framing" – testifies to the accuracy of his analysis, as well as to the power and longevity of the authority he sought to reconfigure. How many times has Joyce been eulogized as a "priest of the imagination," despite the clear implication throughout Joyce's fiction that the transformative power of priests is as paralyzing as it is magical? How many times have other readers countered such praise by charging that Joyce's real business (like that of Father Flynn) is drapery: to drape simple communication in mystery, until readers are as bemused and stifled as the boy at the beginning of *Dubliners?*

The argument against Joyce runs mechanically in the grooves of Joyce's critique of Father Flynn: the typical charges are that James Joyce (like James Flynn) greets eternity with an idle chalice; he performs mysterious offices of communication without any faith in their efficacy. His writings, like holy scriptures, seem to require reams of patristic commentary, "books as thick as the *Post Office Directory* and as closely printed as the law notices in the newspaper" (D 13) to elucidate his intricate questions.[7] Like Father Flynn, the canonized Joyce is vulnerable to a charge of literary simony, of trafficking in words. At his worst, he enters history as an enigma-monger, coldly indifferent to harsh political realities, packing his works full of empty riddles designed to "keep the professors busy for centuries arguing over what [he] meant,"[8] while Austria-Hungary crumbles and the Third Reich gains support.

Critics of Joyce's difficult style, by painting a portrait *of* the artist that matches a portrait *by* the artist, fall into the gap that opens *Dubliners*, the gap between judgment and practice. By disapproving

---

7 The portrait of Joyce as Father Flynn authorizes much of the disdain for the "Joyce industry."

8 These are Joyce's own words, according to Jacques Benoît-Méchin (cited in *JJ* II, 521).

of Joyce's techniques, we put ourselves in the position of inadvertently imitating them, of criticizing in him the paralyzing authority he criticized in Father Flynn. If in *Dubliners* Joyce traps his detractors in the act of disdaining an authority that mirrors their own, he proffers his admirers a more honeyed temptation in *A Portrait of the Artist as a Young Man*. Sympathetic readers of *Portrait* find it easy to applaud Stephen's growing iconoclasm, and to interpret it as a reflection of Joyce's independence and an affirmation of their own. The irony of this particular stance is that in order to assume it, we have to belie the very independence we profess to appreciate; to see Stephen as a true iconoclast is to accept his authority on the subject of himself with unquestioning obedience.

The view of Stephen as a proud revolutionary furnishes a complementary view of Joyce as a conscientious critic of institutional authority. The romantic image of Stephen Dedalus crying *"non serviam,"* vowing to fly by the nets that threaten to ensnare him, eschewing all weapons except those of "silence, exile and cunning" (*P* 117, 203, 247), is the view of himself that Stephen most relishes, but it should not be attributed to the mature Joyce. Joyce presents Stephen's perspective as engaging but naive, marked by the same idealism and futility that marks the monasticism Stephen rejects. As an Irishman branded with a national history of failed uprising, Joyce is as attuned to the double meaning of revolution – rotation as well as rebellion – as to the paradox of celibate fatherhood. *A Portrait of the Artist as a Young Man* focuses on the appeal as well as the comedy of Stephen's inability to see that his obedient and his rebellious gestures are alternative, as well as alternating, movements within a single epistemological and political system.

Interestingly, those who paint Joyce as Father Flynn and Stephen Dedalus aren't painting a portrait of Joyce, but of themselves; they usurp the role of artist through the act of creating an image of him. The artist whose image the reader would capture thereby becomes a sitter, and the reader becomes the artist; the image that results is a portrait, not of Joyce, but of the reader-as-artist. (As Basil remarks in Wilde's *The Picture of Dorian Gray*, "every portrait that is painted with feeling is a portrait of the artist, not that of the sitter.") When the reader's image of the artist resembles the artist's own characters, the ironies multiply, and it becomes imperative to reexamine the likenesses between the self-image that the reader projects onto the author and the more deliberate self-images the author has provided.

Such comparisons illustrate the ease with which readers, like Stephen and Father Flynn, may fall into inadvertent hypocrisy – grotesque in the case of Father Flynn, comic in the case of Stephen – because they refuse to admit the possibility that the authority they alternately worship and reject might invite both responses by being contradictory in itself. It is common, but odd, to deny Joyce's contradictory authority in practice by painting him as *either* Father Flynn *or* Stephen Dedalus. Such polarization among Joyce's readers makes it more difficult to appreciate how deeply duplicitous authority in *Dubliners* actually is, not only in the way it is represented, but in the way it operates: its duplicity works on the reader in a strikingly subtle way, by encouraging us to condemn Father Flynn's mode of exercising power without seeing the relationship between his authority, Joyce's, and our own.

DUBLINERS: LESSONS THAT LESSEN

The duplicity of the word "gnomon" represents, in miniature, the duplicity of authority itself throughout *Dubliners*. Most readers will eventually attach "gnomon," the word that the boy puzzles over at the beginning of the story, to Father Flynn. By the end of the story he is literally a figure with something missing, or figuratively, "the part of a parallelogram which remains after a similar parallelogram is taken away from one of its corners" (*OED*). The suspicion that Father Flynn is lacking something – faith, and perhaps his reason – encourages us to damn him as a fraudulent father; but Joyce's authorial technique throughout the story, and throughout the volume, might be described as equally "gnomic" (or "gnomonic"). Joyce's stories themselves are initially difficult to understand because the very piece that would make the design of the story apparent is invariably "missing," which forces the reader to choose between giving up in disgust and reconstituting the entire design in order to "complete" the story.

How is it that we can admire Joyce's "gnomic" technique and at the same time disdain Father Flynn as a "gnomon"? In terms of the homonyms that "gnomon" evokes, and which commentators have occasionally called into play for different purposes, what is our authority for differentiating between the author and his authoritarian character, treating one as a "know-man" and the other as "no-man," when phonically, and perhaps philosophically, the two are the same? The unsettling answer is the familiar truism that something is inevitably missing from our own reading: our authority to admire or condemn derives from the selectivity with which we read, the "holes" in our perception that allow us to reshape a story in accordance with our unconscious desires. The source of authoritarian power – whether that of the author, the priest, or the reader – is its mystery, its gaps, its selectivity.

Father Flynn and the young boy – who bears a strong resemblance to Stephen Dedalus – are Joyce's earliest representations of teacher and pupil, author (or authority) and reader; and the way that "The Sisters" evolved illustrates Joyce's growing awareness of their reciprocity – their power to produce and reproduce one another, thereby perpetuating the same model of authority. Father Flynn has the authority to teach the boy "scripture," and what he teaches him is to ignore its simplicity in favor of its "grave" mysteries. The gross embodiment of a paralyzed, sterile, and dying order, Father Flynn at first seems repulsive but harmless, until we realize that "The Sisters" is a ghost story on the order of *Hamlet*, and that the dead father lives on in the mind of the boy he instructed so well. The boy's observation of the sisters reveals the subtle efficacy of the priest's influence: Father Flynn, like other "ghostly fathers," has reproduced himself spiritually through the patterns of exegesis he has communicated to the boy. As his thoughts about the sisters reveal, the boy has unconsciously absorbed his master's fastidious contempt for commonness, and when he is distracted from his own attempts to pray by Nannie's mutterings – his attention deflected to her clumsily hooked skirt and downtrodden boots – he imagines that his tutor is smiling in his coffin (*D* 14). The poverty and ignorance of the sisters imprint themselves more sharply on his mind than their goodness, which he registers almost as impropriety, like Nannie's offer of cream crackers, which he refuses to avoid making noise (*D* 15). In "The Sisters," as in "An Encounter," the boy holds himself superior to others, only to be shown his own image in a faithless priest and an onanistic passer-by. "The Sisters" is more chilling in its effect than "An Encounter," however, because the boy lacks any awareness of his "learned" condescension. Although his dream that the priest is trying to confess something to him and receive his absolution clearly indicates that he has taken over the role of dead Father, he doesn't understand the implication, and the suspicion that the priest has wronged him remains buried in his dreams.

The boy's sharp awareness of the sisters' lack of money and education conceals his own lack of compassion, and his tutor's lack of appreciation for the women who had devoted their lives to him. For all his learning, Father Flynn never taught his sisters anything; the priest's return for his sisters' service was neglect, but when the boy sees the signs of such neglect, he reads them as inferiority – his scrupulousness is "mean." Neglect and scrupulousness go hand in hand in "The Sisters." The epithet of "scrupulous meanness" that Joyce used to describe his style in his 1906 letter to Grant Richards (*L* II, 134) could also be applied to the boy, the priest ("He was too scrupulous always, she said," *D* 17), and even to the discerning and critical reader. Neglect, scrupulousness, and meanness are all the products of habit: it is easy to see why Joyce asked his brother Stanislaus if a priest could be buried in a "habit" (*L* II, 109). The elusive target of "The Sisters" is not the sisters, but habit, and particularly the comfortable habit of evaluation. And evaluation leads us back to the authority with which we began, to "gnomon," which has another, obsolete meaning which is as important to "The Sisters" as any of the others: "A rule, canon of belief or action" (*OED*) – in short, a habit of interpretation.[9]

"The Sisters" suggests that those who read by gnomon, write by gnomon, and live as a gnomon – as to varying extents we all do – are linked by a standard that privileges vacancy. Moreover, a refusal to acknowledge the source of such authority perpetuates it; the "father" produces a pupil who is apt to reproduce him. Father Flynn creates a boy much like Stephen Dedalus, and in the version of "The Sisters" printed in *The Irish Homestead* (13 August 1904, pp. 676–77), Stephen Daedalus is listed as the first "author" of Father Flynn. An acute critical reading of the composition of "The Sisters" anticipates the outlines of Stephen's theory of *Hamlet*: the boy becomes the priest's father, paradoxically and redundantly fathering a Father. Stephen's artistic creation, or "son," is Father Flynn, who has "fathered" the young boy who so closely resembles Ste-

---

9 This obsolete meaning is not listed in Don Gifford's *Joyce Annotated: Notes for Dubliners and Portrait* (Berkeley: University of California Press, 1982).

phen by teaching him his own mode of reading. Stephen fathers a Father who produces a "son" who will grow up to perpetuate the process: authorship, in this view, can never do more than recreate its own authority. Characters and their authorial "father" produce one another, just as we continue to produce and be produced by the fictional characters we have rechristened "James Joyce."

In the opening stories of *Dubliners*, it is the reader who is apt to be involved in contradiction if he or she attempts to divide authority by privileging one of its sides over the other. Evaluation, if it intervenes too early in the analytical process, stops that process and impels the self-designated authority toward an encounter with the very values he or she professes to condemn. Joyce suggests that the problem begins with the authoritative practice of imprinting a system of values onto an impressionable reader, rather than teaching readers to uncover and question the implied figures that authorize such systems. Joyce's analysis of authority in *Dubliners* identifies power as a figure of incompleteness, a gnomon, but in *Finnegans Wake*, authority is reconfigured as the figurative process itself, which draws all knowledge from the outlines of the human body.

FINNEGANS WAKE: FULLER FIGURES

The assertion that *Dubliners* traces authority to emptiness, to the missing piece that turns a parallelogram into a gnomon, limns an image of authority that in anatomical terms is "female" rather than "male." Initially, this may seem surprising given the emphasis on patriarchal transmissions of power throughout *Dubliners*. Why present a patriarchal model of authority as more womblike than phallic? Why did Joyce take care to substitute an empty chalice for the cross the priest was holding in the first version of "The Sisters"? Evidently, Joyce took the un-Freudian view that the womb is an image of authority just as powerful as the more familiar image of the phallus. They are equally unitary images – one linear and the other round – which represent two different modes in which authoritarian power operates, one overt and potentially intrusive, the other covert and enveloping.[10] In the "Night Lessons" section of *Finnegans Wake*,

---

10 In *Finnegans Wake*, one of the recurring figures for HCE and ALP are 1 and 0, respectively, who wed to form a "10": "Ainsoph, this upright one, with that noughty besighed him zeroine" (*FW* 261.23–4).

Joyce suggests that although he appreciates the impulse to organize thought through organs, the categories implied by either a phallus or a womb are incomplete; they are, in a sense, "gnomons." Both male and female sexual organs are, like Joyce's view of authority, double as well as single, and to deny that doubleness through privileging only the unitary organs of the reproductive system is equivalent to performing a castration/hysterectomy on the sexual figures that generate both life and thought.[11]

Joyce, in his last treatments of male authority, short-circuits theoretical discussions of authority by redirecting attention to the parts of the body that authorize it. What emerges from his treatment is figurative evidence that critiques of what Cixous calls "phallogocentrism" may be based on an overly partial conception of the way that sexual and cognitive processes operate.[12] Although we tend to think of phallic authority as unitary and single, it is paradoxically not single when regarded in terms of the entire male figure: the head, as a unitary and protruding part, has always been treated as a counterpart to the phallus, which explains why "reason" has been traditionally regarded as a male attribute, and why logocentrism and phallocentrism may serve the same ends. Sexual and capital images of authority, which represent the main instrument and the source of male power respectively, are related in a way that emphasizes the complex potential of the body as a figure of thought. However, there is also a significant difference between the two parts of the body: the power of the head is internal, or mental, whereas the power of the phallus as a symbol resides in its external shape: it is instrumental.

"Phallogocentric" authority is based on not one but two parts of the body that might seem to reflect one another, the head and the phallus – a doubleness of relation that is reproduced in the operations of each. Even when considered separately, neither the head nor the phallus can be effective alone: if the source (or head)

11 In 1969, Margaret Solomon claimed that the major symbols of *Finnegans Wake* are "the male and female sexual organs of the human body," arguing that "every facet of the book can be (and in my opinion, should be) related to this microcosm" (*Eternal Geomater: The Sexual Universe of Finnegans Wake*, pp. vii-viii). The argument that follows is, in part, an extension of Solomon's premise.

12 Cixous, "Sorties," in Cixous and Catherine Clément, *La Jeune Née*, pp. 116–19. See also Culler, *On Deconstruction*, pp. 165–7.

33

is single, its tools (hands) are double, and if the tool (penis) is single, its source (testicles) is double. Such a view of the male body necessarily changes the emphasis in theories of sexual difference: the female body, like the male one, is similarly single and double, with ovaries instead of testicles and a womb instead of a penis. The differences between male and female sexuality reconfigure the difference between the penis and the head on a male body: the female sexual organs – which are internal and comprehensive rather than external and intrusive – are the deprivileged counterparts to the internal world of the mind, conceived as male.

The technique of noting the figurative repetitions and inversions, unities and symmetries that define the individual body, on the one hand, and the relationship between male and female bodies, on the other, illustrates the logic behind assumptions of male superiority, inviting us to reinterpret the relationships within and between figures in a more equitable way. Female sexual organs, because they are internal, become the dominant power source for the woman, comparable to the mind of a man. The head of a woman is important, not for what is inside it, but for its external appearance; it is an instrument of woman's sexual power, as man's phallus is an instrument of his thought.

The relationship between male and female power, as it is culturally defined, may be represented as a simple inversion of top and bottom: the source of a man's power is his head, and the source of a woman's the region of her bottom. Joyce illustrates the inverse relationship between the head of the male and the female "end" as early as *Ulysses*, in the image of Molly and Bloom in bed: their position of unconscious relation – his head to her feet, and vice versa – refigures the strangely inverted relationship of man to woman.

Molly and Bloom are literally opposed, but Joyce's most extended treatment of opposition – between the sexes and between the top and bottom halves of the body – is in the tenth section of the *Wake*. In the center of the "Night Lessons" episode, he illustrates the view of opposites reflected in the writings of Giordano Bruno and Giambattista Vico as the two (identical) banks that define a stream. The metaphor, preserved in a dead language that aptly represents the language of the dead, is at once a figure of sexual opposition, since rivers are presented as female and protrusions of earth as male throughout *Finnegans Wake*, and a figure of male rivalry, represented by the twin banks. (Female rivalry is always, in the context of the *Wake*, the conflict of a woman with herself – with her own appearance, or with an older or younger incarnation of herself.) In this passage, opposition within and between the sexes is presented in terms of the self-recognition and eventual union that it makes possible:

> *antiquissimam flaminum amborium Jordani et Jambaptistae mentibus revolvamus sapientiam: totum tute fluvii modo mundo fluere, eadem quae exaggere fututa fuere iterum inter alveum fore futura, quodlibet sese ipsum per aliudpiam agnoscere contrarium, omnem demun amnem ripis rivalibus amplecti (FW 287.23–28).*

Let us . . . turn over in our minds that most ancient wisdom of both the priests Giordano and Giambattista: the fact that the whole of the river flows safely, with a clear stream, and that those things which were to have been on the bank would later be in the bed; finally, that everything recognises itself through something opposite and that the stream is embraced by rival banks[13]

The image of opposites as rivals embracing the same stream neutralizes any preference we might have for one or the other "bank," giving us a natural illustration of the identity of extremes.

The parenthetical center of the tenth episode is concerned primarily with the fact of opposition, which the structure of the episode – divided into two parts, elaborated through two opposed sets of marginal commentary that exchange places midway through the episode, with cryptic footnotes that *never* give the bottom line – continues to elaborate, focusing on points of intersection between opposed lines of inquiry, the cruxes of a geometrically opposed and divided world. The nature of this world – its history and tendency – is summed up in all of its contradictoriness in the geometrical figure that becomes the focus of the children's learning, and a condensed representation of Joyce's own thought.

The diagram that the children draw in the tenth section of *Finnegans Wake* represents both sexual and intellectual knowledge, mapping both their point of origin and their desired destination. The diagram and the children's interest in it is represented as a

---

13 McHugh, *Annotations*, p. 287.

version of the original sin: knowledge of the figures that generate life as we know it is forbidden. Here, the "forebitten fruit" (*FW* 303.16–17) of the knowledge of good and evil serves to introduce the children not only to the mysteries of their mother's loins, but also to the history of metaphysics, and its figurative, or geometrical, basis.

The double history/hystera begins with Euclid's challenge to construct an equilateral triangle ("Problem ye ferst, construct ann aquilittoral dryankle [an equilateral triangle; Anna's aqua littoral – water on the shore – dry ankle: see image of two banks above] Probe loom!" *FW* 286.19–20). The children meet the challenge by drawing two overlapping circles with the same radius, so that the circumference of each circle bisects the center of its counterpart (see *FW* 287, 294, 295). In the area enclosed by the arcs, the children construct not one but two triangles with the same base and opposite vertices (*FW* 296) to complete the following figure:

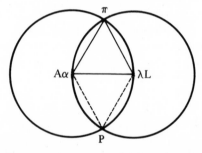

(*FW* 293)

As the surrounding commentary indicates, this figure imparts carnal knowledge to the children, a knowledge of their own bodily origins. Shem presents it as a figure of the female body, with the vertex of the bold triangle marking an omphalos, or navel, perfectly balanced by a more lightly traced nether vertex at the genitals (*FW* 293). When the figure is completed, Shem tells Shaun, "I'll make you to see figuratleavely the whome of your eternal geomater" (*FW* 296.30–297.1), inviting him to lift "the maidsapron of our A.L.P., fearfully! till its nether nadir is vortically where . . . its naval's napex will have to beandbe" (*FW* 297.11–14). Shaun, directed as he is by euphemistic cultural imperatives, looks at the wrong "p" – the pi rather than the capital "P," the navel rather than the genitals – but Shem contemptuously redirects his gaze: "you're holy mooxed and gaping up the wrong palce . . . Her trunk's not her brainbox . . . See her good" (*FW* 299.13–20). By chiding that her trunk's not her brainbox, Shem implies that her genitals, to which he is pointing, do constitute a kind of "brainbox," a figurative equivalent to the head of a man.

The triangular figure of ALP's pubic area, "first of all usquiluteral threeingles" (*FW* 297.27), is only one view of her hidden power – a frontal view. However, the children's exclamations prompt us to see that this is a cubist portrait, designed to reveal the many-sidedness of the human figure, as we can see when we realize that the two spheres give the corresponding view from the rear: "me elementator joyclid, son of a Butt!" (302.12–13). Another perspective emerges from beneath when Shem relates that from these buttocks stem a "parilegs" (pair of legs) that, when open, create an obtuse angle that it is HCE's challenge to bisect: "Show that the median, hce che ech, interecting at royde angles the parilegs of a given obtuse one biscuts both the arcs that are in curveachord behind" (*FW* 283.32–284.4).

"Parilegs" unpacks to produce both "pair of legs" and "parallax," and the concept of parallax, familiar from *Ulysses*, prompts us to relate the double spheres we are viewing to the visual organs used to perceive them: the eyeballs. The spheres represent both the object of perception and the means of perception, which undermines the entire subject–object, male–female distinction as well. When Shem tells Shaun to "lens your dappled yeye [double eye] here" (*FW* 293.23–294.1), his language continues to resonate with implications that visual perception and sexual knowledge are interrelated. He calls the spheres "The doubleviewed seeds," weaving a verbal relationship between "W.C.," viewing, and the generative potential of male testicles, and deftly underscoring the verbal and figurative relationship between two kinds of "balls." (In *Ulysses*, Joyce finds a similar symmetry between eyes and sexual power in the female body, in which breasts rather than testicles double as sightless eyes. See "Circe," when Mrs. Yelverton Barry reminds Bloom of the time that he gazed at her "peerless globes" [breasts, blind eyes] in the *Theatre Royal* [*U* 15.1019].) Two pupils are studying two circles only to find that among other things, those circles represent the pupils of the eye: their study is a contemplation of themselves, of the mechanism of perception as well as the constitution of what is perceived.

"Night Lessons" is a chapter about studying which illustrates the self-referentiality of all learning, no matter how abstruse or foreign the object of study may seem to be. The distinction between subject and object collapses because any objective form, or shape, that we might uncover is already adumbrated in the figure of the human body. Shem illustrates the identity of voyeurism and narcissism when he points to the "p"s where the two circles meet. His language suggests a desire to observe female micturition that recalls his father's, but the "tricklesome" waste he longs to see between bicirculars blends with the image produced through binoculars; once again the "end" of viewing is entangled with its beginning, buttocks with eyes: "there's tew tricklesome poinds where our twain of doubling bicirculars [also binoculars], mating approxemetely in their suite poi and poi, dunloop into eath the ocher. Lucihere.!" (*FW* 295.30–33) The points where the bicirculars meet are the "p"s, but the point where binoculars "mate" is also the image, and the fact that both viewer and viewed are represented in the same plane reinforces the suggestion that they constitute a single interdependent reality. Doubleness, as a condition of reproduction and depth perception, is the prerequisite for a unified image; the unified image is only possible "Outer serpumstances beiug ekewilled" (*FW* 297.7).

Viewed anatomically, Shem's diagram can represent either the front or the rear, viewer or viewed, with a facility that stresses the interchangeability of both. However, the diagram is double in yet another way: it represents a "first cause" that is both material and rational. If, on the one hand, the text traces human genesis to "our anmal matter" (animal matter, alma mater/fostering mother; *FW* 294 n. 5), it also represents that first cause as a logical reconstruction performed by a "geometer" in the tradition of ancient philosophy. The first cause, as represented by this figure of knowledge, is alternately material and immaterial; the drawing is at once a figure of flesh and a figure of thought. But since the children are more interested in carnal knowledge than in its conceptual counterpart, the philosophical relevance of the figure is suggested in a marginal way.

At the very outset of the "lesson" the right margin, with its straight, bold type, announces an "IMAGINABLE ITINERARY THROUGH THE PARTICULAR UNIVERSAL" (*FW* 260), repeating shortly thereafter that this is a "PROBA–POSSIBLE PROLEGOMENA TO IDEAREAL HISTORY" (*FW* 262). After the diagram has been introduced and interpreted, the same voice (now coming from the opposite margin) indexes the subject at hand as *"Destiny, Influence of Design upon"* (*FW* 297). Glancing references to Kierkegaard ("Enten eller, either or" 281.26–27) and Descartes ("you make me a reborn of the cards," a literal translation of "René Descartes" 304.27–28) reinforce the suggestion that this is a lesson in philosophy as well as in sexual anatomy. But the nature and significance of Joyce's comic metaphysical commentary is only apparent when it is juxtaposed against Aristotle's treatise on "the first causes and principles of things," his *Metaphysics*.

Aristotle's overriding concern in the *Metaphysics* is to investigate the nature and number of "the first causes and principles of things" (981b),[14] and to this end he analyzes the philosophies of those who believe that the first principles are material, as well as those who believe that they are ideal Forms, or the objects of mathematics. But the problem that he is concerned with throughout is how to reconcile contrariety with unity in our experience of being, and his solution is essentially to triangulate the notion of being. He argues that each of the oppositions that different philosophers have identified are, like being and unity, "one thing in the sense that they are implied in one another . . . , not in the sense that they are explained by the same definition" (1003b). He points out that in any list of contraries, "one of the two columns is privative" (1004b), which suggests that both opposites make reference to a single concept that serves as an implicit point of reference, just as "healthy" and "unhealthy" both refer to a state of the body that is potentially either. The distinction between potentiality, or "potency," and actuality is crucial in explaining why triangulation occurs, since, as Aristotle argues in the ninth book,

> Everything of which we say that it can do something, is alike
> capable of contraries, e.g. that of which we say that it can be
> well is the same as that which can be ill, and has both potencies
> at once; for the same potency is a potency of health and illness,
> of rest and motion, of building and throwing down, of being
> built and being thrown down. The capacity for contraries,

14 The translation of Aristotle used throughout is that of Richard
    McKeon, in *The Basic Works of Aristotle* (New York: Random House,
    1941). I have followed the usual practice of referring to specific pas-
    sages by work (*Metaphysics*), section (986), and subsection (a or b).

then, is present at the same time; but contraries cannot be present at the same time, and the actualities also cannot be present at the same time, e.g. health and illness. (1051a)

Potency precedes actuality, but "potentially existing constructions are discovered by being brought to actuality," which means that in practice we reconstruct the one potency from the conflicting actualities.

Although he prefers to trace his thought to Empedocles, who took the natural elements rather than the abstract notion of "number" as a first principle, Aristotle's argument about the process of being, like Plato's, is also indebted to the views held by the Pythagoreans. As Aristotle relates in the first book, the Pythagoreans "supposed the elements of numbers to be the elements of all things" (986a), which are contrary. As a recent commentator emphasizes, however, the Pythagoreans were not real dualists:

> All thinkers felt themselves bound to "give an account" of the opposites. None erects them into first principles as the *physis* of our world, so creating a real dualism of first principles. As on Olympus, for all its dissensions and conflicts, there was one ruler and one only, so in Presocratic thought there is one *physis*. The importance given by Aristotle to the opposites in his account of the Pythagoreans must not mislead us into thinking that their opposites were the first principles of a dualistic cosmos.[15]

The Pythagoreans derive all contraries and their modifications from the laws of number, much as Aristotle derives them from a potent meaning.

The most useful contribution of the Pythagoreans, however, was to declare "both how many and which their contrarieties are" (986b). Some members of the Pythagorean school identified ten specific principles, arranged as cognates, which Aristotle (986a) lists as:

15 J. A. Philip, *Pythagoras and Early Pythagoreanism*, suppl. vol. VII of *Phoenix: Journal of the Classical Association of Canada*, p. 46.

[Number]

Limit	Unlimited
Odd	Even
One	Plurality
Right	Left
Male	Female
Resting	Moving
Straight	Curved
Light	Darkness
Good	Bad
Square	Oblong

What is most revealing about this list is that it implicitly designates one term of every opposition as undesirable: plurality, femaleness, darkness, motion are all classed together with evil. Metaphysics has been crossed with ethics, and the result is an implicit disruption of the balance between equal possibilities. In a purely descriptive sense, the Pythagorean model of being is triangular, but as a figure of value, it is one-sided. Moreover, the identification of one principle as a directional one defined by the extremes of "right" and "left" suggests that the implicit model of this metaphysical geometry isn't metaphysical at all, but corporeal, and that the triangular structure being represented is the bilateral symmetry of the top half of a human body: hands (the contrarieties) dominated by a head (the *physis*, here "Number"). The mind represents potency, whereas actuality is represented by the instrumentality of opposed hands.

Joyce, as is well known, bred a hybrid thought by crossing his reading of Aristotle with a study of medieval Christian theology.[16]

16 From the beginning, Stephen's aesthetic theories were, like those of Anaxagoras and Aristotle, concerned with that "principle of things which is at the same time the cause of beauty" (*Metaphysics* 984b). In *Portrait*, Stephen tells the dean of studies that he has resolved to "work on at present by the light of one or two ideas of Aristotle and Aquinas" (*P* 187); and in *Ulysses*, Mulligan objects to a matutinal recital of Stephen's theory of *Hamlet* by shouting, "No, no... I'm not equal to Thomas Aquinas and the fiftyfive reasons he has made out to prop it up" (*U* 1.46–7). Just as Aristotle created fifty-five celestial spheres in the *Metaphysics* to prop up his theory of God as "eternal and immovable and separate from sensible things" (1073–1074), Stephen cre-

But even a cursory comparison of Aristotelian philosophy, as illuminated by his discussion of the earlier Pythagoreans, with Christian doctrine shows that the two are related. The doctrine of the trinity, like Aristotle's theory of a single potency that can split into two opposed actualities – although not at the same time – represents metaphysical reality as fundamentally "triangular." Moreover, the triangle as a figure of ethics modelled on the relationship between head and opposed hands emerges in the representation of Christ separating the saved from the damned on the last day:

> When the Son of man shall . . . sit upon the throne of his glory . . . before him shall be gathered all nations: and he shall separate them one from another, as a shepherd divideth his sheep from the goats: and he shall set the sheep on his right hand, but the goats on the left. (Matthew 25:31–33)

The saved and the damned are positioned at the right and the left hands of Christ, so that evil occupies a designated place in an implicitly triangular figure, as it also did for the Pythagoreans.

In a "triangular" structure of value, authority is represented by the apex, or head, although the right hand is designated to execute its dictates as a dexterous representative of the higher authority. Even the meanings of "right" and "left" reinforce the view that

ated a theory of Shakespeare through a theory of Aquinas furnished with Aristotelian reasoning. (See also Stephen's thoughts on Aristotle in "Proteus" [*U* 3.1–28], and the importance of the conflict between Aristotle and Plato in "Scylla and Charybdis.") Stephen's interest in both Aristotle and Aquinas is clearly modelled on that of Joyce, who was immersed in the study of Aristotle as early as 1903: his Paris notebook includes notes on Aristotle's psychology and his *Metaphysics* (Gorman, 95–96; *CW* 141–146; Richard F. Peterson, "More Aristotelian Grist for the Joycean Mill," *JJQ* 17: 427–33), and he reviewed *Aristotle on Education* for the *Daily Express* in September 1903 (*CW* 109–10). Not surprisingly, however, Joyce's understanding of Aristotle goes far beyond Stephen's, as even a cursory examination of "Night Lessons" in the light of Aristotle's *Metaphysics* makes clear. Joyce, after Aristotle, presents metaphysics as fundamentally figural or geometrical, for as a narrator comments during the Wakean geometry lesson, "you must, how, in undivided reawlity draw the line somewhawre" (*FW* 292.31–2).

the body is a figure of value that represents the privilege of the strong over the weak: "left," from middle and old English, actually means "weak," and "right" is a "power and privilege." Joyce's treatment of authority in all his works, from *Dubliners* through *Finnegans Wake*, reflects a belief that this structure dominates not only the institutions of Church and State, but also our methods of argumentation and interpretation, which are governed by "authorities" and their representatives who teach us to differentiate between different halves of a single human whole, and to set them in conflict as "good" and "bad." The "body politic," as we have constructed it, is doubly sundered by shame: the mind's shame at contemplating the body, its "lower half," and the shame of the right half of the body at its reversed image on the left. The left half of the body, by such a logic, deserves to be "left," or abandoned; if it isn't right or righteous, it must be sinister and wrong. In the Recorso of *Finnegans Wake*, Joyce "rights" (and writes) the wrong of such a formulation through a simple, commonsensical substitution: "there are two signs to turn to, the yest and the ist, the wright side and the wronged side, feeling aslip and wauking up, so an, so farth" (*FW* 597.10–12). The adjectives "wrong" and "wronged" are interchangeable, depending on which side is speaking.

In a system that counts on the resistance of the "wronged" half, no change can be effected simply by championing causes attributed to the "left."[17] Joyce's response was more ambitious: he attempted to analyze and recontextualize the history and implications of a triangular structure of value. The diagram at the center of *Finnegans Wake* represents the fruit of that analysis. Instead of using a triangle to represent the upper half of a male body, Joyce uses it and its inverted double to depict the lower half of a female one, thereby equalizing the relationship between physical and intellectual genesis. Instead of seeding conflict by favoring one side of the figure over the other, Joyce emphasizes both sides of the entire figure as seen from any angle: the symmetry of navel and genitals, on the front surface; the bilateral symmetry of buttocks, on the rear one; and the relationship of front and rear, represented in a single plane. Circumscribed by double spheres, two inverted triangles serve not

17 See Ellmann, *JJ II*, on Joyce's early interest in socialism, especially pp. 87, 142, and 197–8.

only as traditional symbols of logical necessity, but as deltas, figures of the kind of change that previous trinities have tried to stabilize, or arrest.

Joyce's diagram is an affirmation of "hidden" human doubleness, and the potential that such doubleness represents. He suggests that triangular relationships are created *by* intersecting doubles, just as the children must draw two circles before they can construct an equilateral triangle within them. Contextually, if not formally, triangular systems owe their existence to the double reality that they teach us to deny. Aristotle recognized this doubleness; his triangles are dynamic, always producing contraries out of unity and unity out of contraries, even if he posits unity as the first principle. Conflict and oppression occur when the *difference* between opposites is allowed to outweigh their reciprocity.

Authority, when it takes the form of a single triangle authorized by the top half of a human body and maintained by the power of the "right," owes both its weakness and its strength to its self-division and resistance to change. Many of Joyce's contemporaries were acutely aware of both the divisiveness and the sameness of Western culture: as early as "Sunday Morning," Wallace Stevens calls for a more physical and human vision of meaning to replace the anthropomorphic ideas of the Roman Jove and the more human Christ, arguing that

> The sky will be much friendlier then than now,
> A part of labor and a part of pain,
> And next in glory to enduring love,
> Not this dividing and indifferent blue.

Stevens' desire to reunite creation with creator, the human community with the idea that authorizes it, is still shaping caveats to the reader in "Notes Toward a Supreme Fiction," where he warns, "Never suppose an inventing mind as source / Of this idea nor for that mind compose / A voluminous master folded in his fire."

Later in "Notes toward a Supreme Fiction," contemplating the predictability of a man-made culture, Stevens proposes, "Perhaps, / The man-hero is not the exceptional monster, / But he that of repetition is most master." If that is true, the narrator speculates, "It means the distaste we feel for this withered scene / Is that it has not changed enough. It remains, / It is a repetition." In a meditative way, Stevens reasons that reproduction through mastery is simply a re-presentation of the same reality under a different guise. Luce Irigaray has more recently made the same point in the context of a feminist argument against patriarchal culture:

> If we continue to speak the same language to each other, we will reproduce the same story. Begin the same stories all over again. Don't you feel it? Listen: men and women around us all sound the same. Same arguments, same quarrels, same scenes. Same attractions and separations. Same difficulties, the impossibility of reaching each other. Same... same... Always the same.[18]

More insistently than Stevens, Irigaray condemns the divisiveness and staleness of "authoritative" language and of the entire ethos of representation on which it is allegedly based, proposing instead, rather impractically, that we "do without models, standards, examples" altogether.[19]

Irigaray traces the sterility and sameness of patriarchal culture to its denial of sexual difference: "Female sexuality has always been theorized within masculine parameters."[20] The same argument, in terms of Joyce's figures, can be made by noting that all authority stems from a single source: the apex of the triangle, its "head." The source of authority is always single (never double, as in a biological model) and the options of response are limited to two, represented by the two remaining angles of the figure. For women, the two options tend to be defined in terms of sexual experience – they may be virgins or whores – and for men, the same options are defined in terms of loyalty to the "head" – they may be obedient or disobedient. The authoritarian model reproduces and multiplies itself not through a meeting of opposites, but via the mind's power to impose its will on a larger body, which then divides itself into those working for and those working against that will. The aim of authority is not change (the kind of change that characterizes bi-

18 "When Our Lips Speak Together," trans. Carolyn Burke, *Signs: Journal of Women in Culture and Society* 6 (1980): 69.
19 Ibid., p. 78.
20 "This Sex Which Is Not One," in *This Sex Which Is Not One*, trans. Porter, p. 23.

ological evolution), but increase ("author" stems from the past participle of the Latin *augere*, to increase). Authority is the principle of increase writ large; the status of the author is literally increased through the number of disciples he can remake in his own image. Any author, or authority, may therefore be defined as the single "head" of a divided body of followers, one who is also "ahead" of them in time.[21] In literary terms, an author is a writer cast in the mold of religious, familial, and political authorities; a disembodied, omniscient voice; a putatively original mind that can literally imprint readers with its own type.

Sexuality is doubly denied by the privilege of the top half of the human body over the lower, or sexual, half, and by the privilege of the right side over the left, or "female" side. Such a figure perpetuates itself, not by a mating of opposites, but by the mental power that the (dead) father is able to exert over the son, his right hand. The most familiar example of the way that such power operates is Christian; and in *Ulysses*, Stephen's thoughts reflect an unusually precise awareness of the repetitiveness and self-referentiality in the account of God's self-perpetuation through Christ given in the Apostle's Creed:

21 The power of mastery is fueled by a respect for originality, an insight that Walter Benjamin uses to bridge art and politics. In "The Work of Art in an Age of Mechanical Reproduction," Benjamin sees in the proliferation enabled by mechanical reproduction the possibility that the power of authority, and the myth of originality that supports it, might crumble. Mass production might therefore have the egalitarian political implications that its name implies – production by and for the masses. He argues that traditional notions of authority – originality, authenticity – facilitate "a processing of data in the Fascist sense" (*Illuminations*, p. 220). *Führer*, after all, means "leader, head," which suggests that emulation of a (male) leader, or author, is essential to all Fascist systems. Whereas Benjamin focuses primarily on technological reproduction as a way of gradually distancing the "creator" of an artifact, and thereby potentially eroding the esteem traditionally accorded to authority, Joyce examines the same issues in terms of biological and spiritual reproduction as represented by the institutions of family and church. Like Benjamin, he shifts his attention from the creator to the created; but whereas Benjamin analyzes the potential of created objects, Joyce focuses on objectified words, and whereas Benjamin sees egalitarian potential in the sameness of artistic reproductions, Joyce finds hope in linguistic diversity.

He Who Himself begot middler the Holy Ghost and Himself sent Himself, Agenbuyer, between Himself and others, Who, put upon by His fiends, stripped and whipped, was nailed like bat to barndoor, starved on crosstree, Who let Him bury, stood up, harrowed hell, fared into heaven and there these nineteen hundred years sitteth on the right hand of His Own Self but yet shall come in the latter day to doom the quick and dead when all the quick shall be dead already. (*U* 9.493–9)

This parody of Christian belief acts as a Mulligan-esque "entr'acte" to Stephen's theory of *Hamlet*, which according to Stephen's theory tells a different version of the same story.

In the light of Stephen's insights into the redundancy of the father/son relationship as represented by God and Christ, *Hamlet* may be seen to dramatize the destructive implications of that relationship. By splicing Stephen's theory of *Hamlet* with a parody of the Apostle's Creed, Joyce suggests that *Hamlet* can be read as a critique of "Christian" imperatives to give ultimate authority to the ghost of fatherhood, and to allow a substanceless father to enlist the aid of his son and namesake to destroy the father's enemy – who is also his brother. *Hamlet* dramatizes the catastrophic results of accepting paternal authority – however reluctantly – to the exclusion of all other claims: at the behest of his dead father, the son is eventually alienated from all other human ties – lover, mother, uncle, friends – and all are destroyed in a climactic massacre. That final massacre, as Stephen might read it, suggests that traditional, patriarchal patterns of alliance and conflict are not only destructive of others, but apocalyptically self-destructive as well.

Like the Judeo-Christian God, any authority is, by the law of self-perpetuation, his own father. So construed, fatherhood is not contingent upon the mating of equals, but is instead a kind of self-dissemination. An author is a "father" only in the sense of "sower" or "planter." His crops, as Joyce stresses in *Finnegans Wake*, also constitute his corpse, since "sons" will unite to displace the father: "on the bunk of our breadwinning lies the cropse of our seedfather" (*FW* 55). Unlike, for example, Eliot's *The Waste Land*, *Finnegans Wake* appreciates the comedy and pathos of this repetitive male cycle, juxtaposing it with the equivalent "female" narrative of condensation and dispersal. (*The Waste Land*, by contrast, plays heavily, even leadenly against such onanistic imperatives, which direct each man to replant or bury both seed and harvest to ensure the continuation of male privilege. For Eliot, "burying" for men is the dispersive equivalent of "marrying" for women, as *The Waste Land* suggests through the implicit parallelism of "The Burial of the Dead" with its rituals of self-suppression, and "A Game of Chess," which locks its marital opponents in an inevitable checkmate.)

As father, author, and intellectual, Joyce was able to respond sympathetically as well as critically to the patriarchal desire to control all cultural transmissions. He saw that the desire for control masked an anxious intimation of powerlessness, whether in establishing fatherhood or in reproducing straightforward authorial intent via the wayward medium of language. This is Stephen's point in "Scylla and Charybdis," when he argues that

> Fatherhood, in the sense of conscious begetting, is unknown to man. It is a mystical estate, an apostolic succession, from only begetter to only begotten. On that mystery and not on the madonna which the cunning Italian intellect flung to the mob of Europe the church is founded and founded irremovably because founded, like the world, macro and microcosm, upon the void. Upon incertitude, upon unlikelihood. *Amor matris*, subjective and objective genitive, may be the only true thing in life. Paternity may be a legal fiction. (*U* 9.837–44)

Stephen's argument reverses the implications that patriarchal organizations such as the church have made so familiar – the view that women are imperfect imitations of men, that their appeal is largely illusory – by suggesting that the *male* ethos is based on a more unnatural illusion, that it is sufficient unto itself. What is most damaging about this "male" ethos, however, is its claim to truth, to absoluteness, to exclusivity of value. Power is passed "from only begetter to only begotten," without the love of opposition represented by biological reproduction. In this obsolete rather than supreme fiction, no "cold copulars" embrace to bring forth "particulars of rapture."

An authority that privileges men and mentality cannot change because it is designed to combat the uncertainty of a tenuous estate – fatherhood – an estate that can only be built on a woman's word. The duplicity of sexuality and language inspired a desire for a more univocal, authoritative utterance, and the Word of a male God was conceived to surpass the word of a woman by creating, not just a child, but a universe in such a way that his authority, or fatherhood, could not be challenged, because his Son is his alone. The urge to assert the power of men and mentality over women and sexuality may be understandable, but the unacceptable byproduct of male self-defense, Joyce suggests, is the institutionalization of oppression and violence.

Explicitly in *Finnegans Wake* – to the extent that anything can be explicit in *Finnegans Wake* – and implicitly in the works that precede it, Joyce attributes the phenomenon of oppression to the denial of human doubleness, a denial licensed by partiality towards any half of a human whole. From such a perspective, factions are necessarily "fractions" of a divided figure (see *FW* 281.1 for one of the many examples of this). The privileging of one extreme and the marginalization of its counterpart emerge as the basis of all destructive conflict: in the language of the *Wake*, "violence to life, limb and chattels, often as not, has been the expression, direct or through an agent male, of womanhid offended" (*FW* 68.36–69.2). To favor man over woman – or woman over man – is comparable in its futility to a preference for space over time: it leaves us with half a world. As a narrator asks of Issy, mediatrix of human existence, "What if she love Sieger [clock; Caesar] less though she leave Ruhm [space; Rome] moan [more]? That's how our oxyggent [occident] has gotten ahold of half their world . . . Enten eller, either or. And! Nay, rather!" (*FW* 281.22–29). Joyce parodies Kierkegaard's celebration of choosing between extremes (either/or), suggesting that a more wholesome course is to choose *both* ("And!") and neither ("Nay, rather!").

The comic "heroes" of *Ulysses* and *Finnegans Wake* all share a commitment to double vision, ranging from Bloom's "ambidexterity" and the sexual and religious ambivalence it betokens to the visions of Einstein and Yeats at the borders of the *Wake*. "Doubbllinnbbayyates" (*FW* 303.7–8) and the double gyres that structure *A Vision* are as relevant to the children's studies in "Night Lessons" as the theories of Einstein, who changed the course of modern physics by demonstrating the unanticipated doubleness of physical reality, and in particular the complex interdependence of space and time, mass and energy (see "Eyeinstye," *FW* 305.6; "Ulm," *FW* 293.14).

From *Dubliners* through *Finnegans Wake*, Joyce illustrates the inevitability of doubling: denial of doubleness affects only our awareness of the extent to which we mirror our opponents, as the boy unwittingly comes to reflect the priest in "The Sisters," or Farrington inadvertently becomes the counterpart of Mr. Alleyne, or Gabriel Conroy the "living" equivalent of a dead man whose memory is very much alive. At the end of the tenth section of *Finnegans Wake*, as the text counts to ten in Irish, the Shaun commentator experiments with eleven alternative terms for doubleness in the left margin: "*Pantocracy. Bimutualism. Interchangeability. Naturality. Superfetation. Stabimobilism. Periodicity. Consummation. Interpenetrativeness. Predicament. Balance of the factual by the theoric Boox and Coox, Amallagamated*" (*FW* 308. 5–19). However we may choose to define the doubleness of relation that Joyce maps out in all of his works, it is most frequently and most simply indicated by the name of the city where Joyce's major works are set: Dublin. In *A Portrait of the Artist as a Young Man*, Dublin represents the one paradoxical condition of his existence that Joyce's sensitive aspiring artist cannot appreciate.

PART II

DOUBLE AUTHORITY

Logos and logic, crystal hypothesis,
Incipit and a form to speak the word
And every latent double in the word,
Beau linguist.

Wallace Stevens,
"Notes toward a Supreme Fiction"

2

A PORTRAIT OF THE ARTIST AS A
YOUNG MAN

IN *DUBLINERS*, the characters are haunted by dead or deadly
counterparts they cannot bring themselves to acknowledge; but
in *A Portrait of the Artist as a Young Man*, the theme of hidden
contradiction produces not a ghost story but a comedy. Stephen
Dedalus is represented as a sensitive reader of cultural signs, trying
to forge an identity for himself consistent with his patrimony. What
he finds is that his fathers have bequeathed him not one, but two
mutually incompatible models of responding to their authority,
and as the book progresses, we watch Stephen alternating helplessly
between obedience and rebellion, idealism and hedonism, with little
awareness of how such alternatives might be bridged. Stephen continues to shuttle back and forth between the two programmed
responses to the authority of his fathers because he never questions
the major premise and implication of authority: its privilege. His
aim is to establish for himself an authority comparable to the authority he admires and resists, to see himself raised above his peers,
and to resist any awareness of the universality – the commonness
– of his feelings. Stephen's respect for authority remains constant
throughout *Portrait*, although the figures embodying that authority
change. In the beginning, the authoritative point of reference for
all his thoughts and actions is Christ; next, he takes his penis as a
figurative authority for rebellious uprising, following the example
of Lucifer; in the end, his authority is the idea of becoming an

author, and his subject neither salvation nor the body, but salvation *and* the body, represented through words. Although his chosen image of authority changes, Stephen's commitment to authoritarian privilege never diminishes.

In one respect, Stephen's method of reading is predictable: he never abandons a belief in "the myth of a mastermind." In two other respects, however, his method of reading is unusually flexible: (1) he pays homage to a diverse array of authorities in the course of his youth, presumably making it more difficult for him to defend the primacy of any one authority when he matures, and (2) he evinces a subconscious sensitivity to the "unauthorized," figurative dimension of language, a sensitivity that anticipates Molly's. When, for example, the priest at the end of the third chapter tells him, "As long as you commit that sin, my poor child, you will never be worth one farthing to God" (*P* 145), his conscious interpretation of the sentence acknowledges the priest's benevolent intention: Stephen knows that the priest is urging him to reform so that his soul may regain its value in God's eyes. Unconsciously, however, he registers the economic nature of the metaphor very sharply, as we can see three pages later, when he pictures his devotion as a heavenly "sale": "he seemed to feel his soul in devotion pressing like fingers the keyboard of a great cash register and to see the amount of his purchase start forth immediately in heaven, not as a number but as a frail column of incense or as a slender flower" (*P* 148). Stephen has intuited the underlying materialism of what he believes to be a purely spiritual order, and he expresses his unauthorized knowledge through figures, figures that illustrate his determination to insure that he will be worth much more than one farthing to God. Like Issy in *Finnegans Wake*, who will "confess it by her figure and . . . deny it to your face"(*FW* 271.14–15), Stephen "knows" two faces of verbal meaning at any one time, one conventional and intentional, the other sensual and figurative. Stephen's approach to language is as material as his approach to materiality is logocentric, but he lacks conscious awareness of the doubleness of his response. As a result, his two kinds of knowledge are frequently in conflict, whereas later, in *Ulysses*, Leopold Bloom will learn to embrace comparable contradictions.

Portrait, like *Ulysses*, *Finnegans Wake*, and even *Dubliners*, explores two different facets of authority, and the area between them. The authority Stephen consciously acknowledges is the authority of will, of intentionality. Such an authority is powerful, but, as we have seen, undermined by an inevitable contradiction between theory and practice. In Stephen's case, the contradictions that his language reveals are conflicts between will and desire, between his intended meaning and the meaning that his metaphors imply. Joyce prompts us to hear, in the underlying figures that shape language less obtrusively than do conventionally determined meanings and logic, the clusters of puns that trace the lineaments of ungratified desire, or what James Merrill once called "the hidden wish of words."[1]

It is the conflict between the authorities Stephen consciously embraces and those that he unconsciously, but demonstrably, hears and responds to that makes *Portrait* difficult to read.[2] It is because

1   In a review of *Braving the Elements*, Merrill writes that the pun "is suffered, by and large, with groans of aversion, as though one had done an unseemly thing in adult society, like slipping a hand up the hostess's dress. Indeed, the punster has touched, and knows it if only for being so promptly shamed, upon a secret, fecund place in language herself. The pun's *objet trouvé* aspect cheapens it further – why? A Freudian slip is taken seriously: it betrays its maker's hidden wish. The pun (or the rhyme, for that matter) "merely" betrays the hidden wish of words." "Object Lessons" [review] in *The New York Review of Books*, 19 (Nov. 30, 1972), pp. 31–34. Cited by Judith Moffett, *James Merrill: An Introduction to the Poetry* (New York: Columbia, 1984), p. 118.

2   The first spurt of sustained critical interest in *A Portrait* was a belated one: it wasn't until the fifties and early sixties that the critical dialectic grew to its polemical crescendo, taking Stephen as its issue. Those who read Stephen as "Stephen Hero" faced off against Hugh Kenner, Stephen's wittiest detractor. Constituting, as it did, a critical Scylla and Charybdis, *Portrait* attracted an impressive array of minds to map its dangers, including Wayne Booth, Caroline Gordon, Robert Scholes, Maurice Beebe, and S. L. Goldberg. Then, in 1966, Arnold Goldman articulated an acute synthesis in his often neglected study, *The Joyce Paradox*. His solution is, essentially, not a solution at all but a sharp definition of the problem that gives it both a name (paradox) and a philosophical legitimacy (via Sartre, Ibsen, and Kierkegaard). The doubleness of the concept of doubling locked the readers of *Portrait* in a classical double-bind, until the name "paradox" gave us a means of distancing ourselves from a reading experience that, in its wild fluctuations between appreciation and contempt, reproduced Stephen's

Stephen reacts to conflicting authorities that our response to him may (and should) be ambivalent: his acute sensitivity to the latent metaphoricity of language evokes sympathy from similarly "artistic" readers, but his willful insensitivity to the discrepancy between his intuitive knowledge and his rational determinations prompts sharply analytical readers to regard him ironically. Stephen's growing power to articulate and encompass his experience is similarly double-edged. As *Portrait* progresses, Stephen learns to double and redouble his story, which is itself a doubling of "history," producing a gradual enrichment of text and context. At first we may be tempted to see Stephen as an ever-widening frame who manages to recapitulate, in his mind and verse, the stylistic evolution of the nineteenth century from Byron through Pater. By the last chapter, however, it has become apparent that Stephen's very ability to appropriate various styles constitutes an artistic failure: his poetic productions are doubly derivative of his reading and of his adolescent emotions. The process of doubling – sexually and textually – is at once a principle of evolutionary development and a redundancy that limits change as surely as it enables it; as a result, Stephen can both develop and remain the same. It is at this point, when we see that Stephen himself has been "framed," that we are in a position to appreciate the way Joyce's language has succeeded in overspilling the boundaries of Stephen's consciousness. The power of Joyce's language to frame Stephen illuminates the power of Stephen's own language to surpass as well as contain his thought. Stephen's discoveries can never be more than recoveries as long as he overlooks

own experience. The relief of that name served to stave off a continuing awareness of the multifaceted ways that *Portrait* analyzes the schizophrenia of naming, an insight that Dorothy van Ghent began to explore as early as 1953 in *The English Novel: Form and Function* (New York: Holt, 1953, pp. 263–76).

For an account of the controversy between sympathetic and ironic readings of Stephen, see Thomas Staley, "James Joyce," in *Anglo-Irish Literature: A Review of Research*, ed. Richard J. Finneran (New York: Modern Language Assn., 1976), pp. 402–10; Staley, *Recent Research on Anglo-Irish Writers: A Supplement to Anglo-Irish Literature: A Review of Research*, ed. Finneran (New York: MLA, 1983), pp. 195–6; and James J. Sosnowski, "Reading Acts and Reading Warrants: Some Implications for Readers Responding to Joyce's Portrait of Stephen," *JJQ* 16 (1978–9): 43–64.

his own desire for authority, refusing to see that the basis of authoritarian power is not the person wielding it, but the mental habits of those who respond to it, habits that direct us to choose one of two opposed alternatives.

AUTHORITY AS DOUBLE-BIND

Joyce poses the problem of the double-bind in both the first and last chapters of *Portrait*, bracketing the book with the dilemma it is meant to reproduce and leave behind. The first major event to leave its mark on Stephen's consciousness is the experience of being bullied – first by Wells, then by Father Dolan. When Wells shoulders him into the square ditch, Stephen retaliates physiologically, by getting sick, and imaginatively, by intertwining his story with history, projecting a vision of himself as Little and Parnell, dead: "And Wells would be sorry then for what he had done" (*P* 24). Stephen actively implements the same strategy when he is later bullied by Father Dolan: he takes as his precedent "somebody in history," "some great person whose head was in the books of history," and in particular, the great men mentioned in Peter Parley's tales about Greece and Rome whose names resembled his own (*P* 53, 55). His trust in names ultimately seems justified when the rector fulfills the promise of his title by rectifying Stephen's wrong.

The glory of Stephen's double triumph, imaginative and active – a triumph that transforms him in his own eyes into "Stephen Hero" – tends to overshadow the fact that Wells bullies him twice, verbally as well as physically, and that Stephen fails to overcome or even understand the more subtle taunting that imitates his own habits of mind. When Wells asks Stephen whether or not he kisses his mother before he goes to bed, he implicitly limits the range of responses to two mutually exclusive possibilities, so that whether Stephen answers yes or no, he is still bound by the configuration of the question. The questioner retains his authority and reaffirms his superiority as long as the respondent accepts the terms of the question, a situation that bewilders Stephen, when Wells and his friends laugh at him:

> Stephen tried to laugh with them. He felt his whole body hot and confused in a moment. What was the right answer to the question? He had given two and still Wells laughed. But Wells

must know the right answer for he was in the third of grammar. (*P* 14)

What Stephen fails to see is that Wells' question encapsulates the dilemma of distance that has baffled, not only Stephen, but many of his readers as well. The only way to escape ridicule is to reject, not the gesture of kissing and the love that gesture represents, but the simplistic model of relationship as something that is either neurotically close or unnaturally distant. Stephen never succeeds in escaping the domination of that question: his responses to his mother at the beginning and end of the book – naive identification and insensitive independence – are his two answers to Wells writ large.

When Cranly asks Stephen a version of Wells' question near the end of the book – "Do you love your mother?" – Stephen answers, "I don't know what your words mean" (*P* 240). By the end of the book, Stephen has learned to escape laughter but cannot escape the rhetorical tines of a two-pronged question. Ten days later, Cranly, who alone among Stephen's friends seems sympathetically implicated in the pathos of the dilemma, propounds the problem in an altered form to Dixon and Emma's brother, as Stephen records in his diary:

A mother let her child fall into the Nile. Still harping on the mother. A crocodile seized the child. Mother asked it back. Crocodile said all right if she told him what he was going to do with the child, eat it or not eat it. (*P* 250).

The tone of easy familiarity that Stephen assumes in retelling the story is misleading in one sense, but absolutely appropriate in another: the story of the mother and the crocodile exemplifies in an almost scholastic form the comic hopelessness of unnaturally limited alternatives, a trap that Stephen, despite his knowledgeable air, has never been able to elude. Like the mother who can't save her child by giving the crocodile either of the answers he suggests, Stephen stands to lose no matter how he responds to the riddle of relationship as traditionally formulated. He has tried both answers (with Wells) and no answer (with Cranly), but neither his eagerness to give the appropriate answer nor his refusal to respond at all constitutes an effective challenge to the question.

Readers of *Portrait* who accept the model of relationship imposed by the questions of Wells, Cranly, and the crocodile are themselves caught in a cognitive trap that resembles Stephen's. The reader who chooses to sympathize with Stephen without balancing such sympathy with a more detached analysis of Stephen's shortcomings may see his own image when Stephen chooses to identify himself with a literary or historical "hero" such as Parnell, Byron, or Daedalus. As Stephen shows, such proclivities, while evidencing imagination and feeling, leave those who indulge them vulnerable to ridicule. If, on the other hand, the reader goes to the other extreme and reads everything ironically, Stephen again gives back the reader's own image. An ironic reading must inevitably condemn Stephen for not knowing "what the heart is and what it feels" (P 252) as he jauntily escapes to Paris, but a reader who eschews sympathy altogether becomes guilty of the same intellectual jauntiness he criticizes in Stephen: the ironist is implicated in the very ironies he perceives.

Stephen continues to regard his attachment and vulnerability to others as a problem that must be affirmed or denied, but elsewhere in the first chapter Joyce presents him with an alternative approach to the dilemma of relationship: he could restructure the question. When Stephen is in the infirmary suffering the consequences of Wells' bullying, Athy gives him a breezy reading lesson that takes his name as its text. Having told Stephen that Athy is the name of a town, he asks him a riddle: "Why is the county Kildare like the leg of a fellow's breeches?" When Stephen gives up, Athy answers the riddle – "Because there is a thigh in it" (P 25). He then challenges Stephen to ask the riddle another way, but when Stephen declares himself unable to re-riddle the question, Athy refuses to help him. The reader, like Stephen, is being asked to reformulate old riddles ("That's an old riddle, he said" [P 25]), to structure them in new ways. In the infirmary, Athy presents to Stephen a way to get well (and to get Wells), but Stephen is still entranced with the old riddle of heroism and betrayal, as his subsequent vision of Parnell's death shows. When readers in the sixties debated the question of our esthetic distance from Stephen, they reenacted Stephen's own dilemma about authority. Whether defending or attacking Stephen's character, the reader is trapped by a single question, and for that reason vulnerable to the laughter of more experienced schoolfellows. As we now know, both responses and neither response are appropriate. The "old" riddle of relationship must be analyzed and reformulated.

Athy's riddle has a significant structural defect; it is "gnomic" in a way that excludes and empowers speaker and listener. Although the riddle forges a relation between a town and a part of the leg, it fails to indicate explicitly that it is Athy's own name that makes such a pattern of relationship significant. The structure of the question makes it possible for the listener to separate the riddle from the context that makes it personally meaningful – its relation to the person recounting it, as well as its relevance to the person listening to it ("You have a queer name, Dedalus, and I have a queer name too, Athy" [*P* 25]). The riddle allows us to bypass teller and auditor as named entities importantly implicated in the network of language, and to focus instead on more coincidental and remote symmetries of sound. Finally, the riddle challenges us to link two different contexts that enclose a common sound – trousers containing a thigh, and a county that includes the town of Athy – and thus celebrates the power of auditory correspondence by presenting perceived incongruities as a problem that language solves. The exercise of solving the riddle forces us to reverse the usual flow of thought from names to the objects they designate, moving instead from objects to a common name. As a result, we are reminded of the power of names not only to represent but to integrate objective experience.

Athy's riddle is difficult to reformulate because it mimics the operations we collectively tend to perform in the act of reading. We learn to abstract the author from the puzzle, honoring him or her as the operator of language and not as someone upon whom language operates, an exemption that we can then extend to ourselves as readers. The separation of authors and readers from language facilitates a denial of the doubleness of existence; we can appear to possess or "have" control only by "halving" it, splitting it into two mutually exclusive alternatives. Joyce uses the taunts of Wells and the crocodile to ironically undercut the belief that choice is control. The only possibility of autonomy lies in a conscientious objection to halving reality. "Doubling" emerges as a more pleasurable alternative to possession through division; moreover, doubling has the added advantage of being a double referent: it denominates a process, but it also, like "Athy," echoes the name of an Irish town that silently authorizes and historicizes the author's riddles.

The other way to ask Athy's riddle is buried in the darkness of *Finnegans Wake*: it is Shem's "first riddle of the universe." Shem asks, "when is a man not a man?" "All were wrong, so Shem himself, the doctator, took the cake, the correct solution being – all give it up? – ; when he is a – yours till the rending of the rocks, – Sham" (*FW* 170.5; 170.21–24). Athy might have answered, "when he is a thigh"; or a more general respondent, "when he is a name" ("Shem" means "name" in Hebrew). A name is a sham, and "sham" is here a variation of the teller's name, a teller inevitably implicated in the riddle of naming he contemplates.[3] The relationship between man and name that Shem posits, like the relationship between Magritte's picture of a pipe and its title, "Ceci n'est pas un pipe," is an unsettlingly double one, an uncomfortable correspondence that is also and always an incongruity. Shem's riddle, itself tellingly similar to and different from Athy's, affirms a tension that Athy's dispels, the tension of difference-in-similarity indispensable to true relationship.

In order to ask Athy's riddle "the other way," Stephen would have to revise his assumptions about language, seeing it as something that overflows the boundaries of any one of its formulations, its authority more capacious and capricious than that of the person or structure that gives it a momentary shape, but meaningless without a shape to exceed. Moreover, he would have to be more consciously aware of the way that a text must interact with a variable context to produce meaning. He would have to recognize language as the sham double that makes reflection possible. *Ulysses* forces its readers toward such realizations: its willful opacity compels the reader to look *at* language, as well as trying to peer through it, and its disorienting panoply of changing styles forces us, finally, to regard and use language as the ever-varying constant that allows us to plot and evaluate temporal and spatial change. In *Portrait*, however, language plays its double role of hero and enemy more subtly: it acts as a variable standard of reference for the perceptions

3 Although it does not discuss this particular instance, John Paul Riquelme's *Teller and Tale in Joyce's Fiction* gives the fullest account of this relationship as it shapes Joyce's works.

of author, character, and reader without compelling any recognition that it *is* the dominant system of reference.

The language that comprises *Portrait* can serve as a double for author, character, and a variety of readers precisely because it is a system that grows out of and replicates doubleness; both the supplements and the contrasts that make articulation possible are defined in relation to some other, presumably normative concept that they either repeat or deny. Not only does the linguistic system itself grow from a double root, but it also fulfills its function of representation by supplementing and opposing the physical world that it both reflects and fails to comprehend. Even as a double, language reflects two ways: it can draw together and reflect the image of an individual type, and it can reflect its world prismatically, focusing and splaying the images and narratives bound up in it by time and usage. Stephen is aware of the different reflective capacities of language, although he prefers its ability to reflect an individual private world to its panoramic particularization of the public one, asking,

> Did he then love the rhythmic rise and fall of words better than their associations of legend and colour? Or was it that, being as weak of sight as he was shy of mind, he drew less pleasure from the reflection of the glowing sensible world through the prism of a language manycoloured and richly storied than from the contemplation of an inner world of individual emotions mirrored perfectly in a lucid supple periodic prose? (*P* 166–7)

Stephen's preference is clearly symptomatic of his overall limitations: he favors a personal over a shared reality. Our challenge is to avoid replicating his error in our practice of reading without denying the reciprocity of our relationship to him, to participate actively in the doubling – and Dublin – that Stephen longs to escape, in order to avoid an unintentional duplication of his experience as his lifeless and unselfconscious shadow.

REVERSIBLE CONTRARIES

When the respondent in "Ithaca" describes Bloom's recumbent position as that of "the childman weary, the manchild in the womb" (*U* 17.2317–18), he reduces the difference between child and man to a difference of accent, challenging the simplicity of the verbal distinction between them. In *Portrait*, too, the abstract purity of the opposition between youth and age is exposed as a convenience through the ease of its reversal: the verbal motif that accompanies Stephen throughout is the refrain of weariness, a poetic languidness that stands in cold contrast to the childlike enthusiasm of his father and his father's friends. Johnny Cashman, who "must be nearing the century," declares himself "just twentyseven years of age," whereupon Simon Dedalus admits to feeling no more than eighteen himself – unlike Stephen, whose "mind seemed older than theirs: it shone coldly on their strifes and happiness and regrets like a moon upon a younger earth" (*P* 95).

As opposite stages of life run together within the fiction, so do the opposite positions of artist and reader with respect to the fiction. Artist and reader exchange roles and ultimately emerge, not only as doubles of each other, but as processes that are equally contradictory. For years, readers have argued over whether Stephen actually becomes an artist or writer in *Portrait*, focusing attention on the two instances where his verbal productions are presented directly to us so that we may evaluate them: the esthetic theories that he propounds to Lynch in the last chapter and the villanelle that he composes in the section immediately following (*P* 204–16; 217–24). Ironically, however, the determination of whether or not Stephen has a right to the title of artist tends to be made independently of an equally important determination that is intimately related to the first: what kind of a *reader* do Stephen's productions reveal him to be? Stephen's ability to imagine is intertwined with his ability to apprehend, just as our ability to apprehend *Portrait* is dependent on our imaginative power to recreate it. As a result, the villanelle Stephen composes should not be evaluated apart from its relationship, not only to Stephen's reading experience, but to our own experience of reading the preceding portion of the book; similarly, the esthetic theories become most pretentious when divorced from Joyce's writing. Both the villanelle and the esthetic theories gain their fullest meaning in the interface between reading and writing.

If we abjure the illusion that we can evaluate Stephen finally or objectively, and avoid the opposite temptation to conclude that we cannot evaluate him meaningfully at all, the dialectic of response throws up a third, more synthetic possibility, that Stephen serves as a changing point of reference that allows us to plot the variable relationship between the author and the reader, the living and the dead, with greater precision. Our challenge is then to position, somewhere between Joyce's and our own, Stephen's growing ability to balance imaginative engagement and critical detachment, and his increasing facility in interweaving and disentangling his story and history. Stephen's value is precisely that he, unlike Joyce, is not a "finished artist," despite his drunken assertion to the contrary in "Circe" (*U* 15.2508). He represents, not the artist, but the dialogical process of verbal recreation that we tend to split into reading and writing.[4]

When writer and reader are exposed as imaginatively intermingled in a shared text that has the power to reflect both, the illusion of authorial privilege is shattered. Language emerges as the shared domain of reader, author, and character, the place where all "multiplicity is focused."[5] It becomes more difficult for the author and reader to disguise the relationship between their own identities and the answers to the riddles they contemplate, as Athy did by memorably emphasizing the link between a town and a part of the body, rather than the link between the names of both and his own. Language, so conceived, acts as an interface which, like a portrait, gives back a compound image that both resembles and fails to resemble the perceiver. Joyce's *Portrait* has this capacity: it changes as the artist changes, but it also changes as its reader changes, acting as a stylistic equivalent to what Wilde used as subject rather than medium, the picture of Dorian Gray.

In *The Picture of Dorian Gray*, Basil Hallward tells Harry that "every portrait that is painted with feeling is a portrait of the artist, not that of the sitter." Basil knows that the beauty and corruption in his picture of Dorian is his own – that in painting it, he has exposed himself. What Basil has no way of knowing is that his portrait is also a portrait of the man observing it, Lord Henry; that it is their dual participation in Dorian's life that the portrait will monstrously come to reflect. The first five words of Joyce's title, when considered in relation to their context in *The Picture of Dorian*

4 Derrida's attack on the desire to freeze and thereby contain meaning in "The End of the Book and the Beginning of Writing," *Of Grammatology*, pp. 2–26, is relevant here.

5 Barthes argues that the reader is where all multiplicity is focused (*Image–Music–Text*, p. 148).

Gray, suggest that Joyce's portrait, like Basil's, is a composite portrait of artist, character, and observer with an uncanny power to adapt its features to reflect our own. The distinction between writing and reading is, for someone engaged in either, a misleading one, since artists are always readers, and readers are always artists with the power to paint verbal portraits anew through the inevitable selectivity of observation and memory.

If the ability to write is bound up so tightly with the ability to read, then Stephen's modes of reading should be examined as carefully as his mode of writing, and compared both to Joyce's own reading, which is his frame for the book, and to the reading methods that have served as our frame.[6] Stephen's theory of reading must be considered in relation to his reading practice, but his theory and practice should then be compared to that of the book's author and readers. Such an approach produces a more complex practical awareness of the book's reflexivity, its emphasis on the parallels between Stephen's attempts to read his world and our attempts to read Stephen. To the extent that our activity reproduces Stephen's, the text contextualizes us; if we accurately identify a representation of our mode of reading within the novel, we can then supplement that methodology with alternatives that are also represented within the fiction. By applying strategies represented in the novel to our own way of reading the novel, we allow the text to teach us more sophisticated ways of framing it and in that way regain momentary interpretive control over the "portrait" that had framed us, and will do so again – in different ways – upon subsequent readings. If we then repeat the process, it is with the awareness that we are using the interplay between text and context to multiply the number of available interpretive frames. Event and context, reader and character, story and history repeatedly exchange positions as a condition of their mutual development. The condition that makes development possible but never finite is the imbalance between the employment of a word and the multiple possibilities for meaning that such employment excludes, between an individual story and history.

6 Riquelme, Sosnowski, and Brook Thomas ("Not a Reading *of*, but the Act of Reading *Ulysses*," *JJQ* 16: 81–93) have all called for a more reader-oriented study of *A Portrait*, but so far their impact has been more theoretical than practical.

THE RHYTHM OF APPREHENSION

The tension between a realized network of meaning and potential networks of meaning, between the precision of definition and its inadequacy, is the central conflict in *A Portrait of the Artist as a Young Man*, a conflict that is dramatized in both social and linguistic terms. In the first chapter Stephen's attempt to realize a relation to his name, to his schoolfellows, to his country, and to history itself is intermingled with his desire to define the meanings of words and phrases that puzzle him: God, politics, "tower of ivory." Comparably, his growing isolation in the second chapter presents itself as an evaporation of the meanings he has succeeded in attaching to language, and he watches words and names lapse back into a meaningless sensuality that reflects his own: when he tries to recall some of the vivid moments of his childhood, he remembers only names, dissociated from the images and events that gave them significance – Dante, Parnell, Clane, Clongowes (*P* 93). The ability to read, to attach significance – quite literally – to signs, deserts him: "He could scarcely interpret the letters of the signboards of the shops" (*P* 92). When language loses meaning, the speaking subject also dissolves, and the capability of speech is assumed by the sensual organs that convey it, the tongue and the lips.[7] When Stephen encounters the prostitute at the end of the second chapter, "his lips parted though they would not speak," and when Stephen surrenders to her, "body and mind," he is "conscious of nothing in the world but the dark pressure of her softly parting lips. They pressed upon his brain as upon his lips as though they were the vehicle of a vague speech," but what issues from between them is not speech but the sensual reality of her tongue, its pressure "softer than sound" (*P* 101).

Stephen's perception of language continues to fluctuate with the rhythm of his experience: words die and come to life, form interlocking fabrics that dissolve and reweave themselves in different configurations as he alternates between triumph and unrest. The

---

7 See Derek Attridge's excellent account of this phenomenon in the "Sirens" episode of *Ulysses*: "Joyce's Lipspeech: Syntax and the Subject in 'Sirens,' " in *James Joyce: The Centennial Symposium*, ed. Beja et al., pp. 59–66.

sense of exile he experiences in response to the sensual urges of adolescence is also an exile from the pleasures of language; his perception of himself as "a beast that licks his chaps after meat" is illustrated by the slothful movement of letters through his consciousness: "The letters of the name of Dublin lay heavily upon his mind, pushing one another surlily hither and thither with slow boorish insistence" (*P* 111). Father Arnall recollects language into vivid meaning at the beginning of the third chapter, but by the time Stephen receives his invitation to enter the priesthood in chapter four, that meaning has become leaden and obsolete. As the director speaks, Stephen relives an intuition that he was "slowly passing out of an accustomed world" and was "hearing its language for the last time" (*P* 156). His freedom from "the order" is confirmed by "a din of meaningless words" that "drove his reasoned thoughts hither and thither confusedly" (*P* 161). That din resolves into "a confused music . . . as of memories and names" (*P* 167) as he gathers language together into a new tissue of meanings on North Bull Island, an idealization of flight that he partly unravels and partly affirms in the diary entries that anticipate his flight to Paris.

In the last chapter, Joyce fastens Stephen's experience of language to his experience of Dublin. Early in the chapter, Stephen describes his walks through Dublin as mental journeys through literature in which familiar urban locations dissolve into equally familiar characters and words:

> The rainladen trees of the avenue evoked in him, as always, memories of the girls and women in the plays of Gerhart Hauptmann; and the memory of their pale sorrows and the fragrance falling from the wet branches mingled in a mood of quiet joy. His morning walk across the city had begun, and he foreknew that as he passed the sloblands of Fairview he would think of the cloistral silverveined prose of Newman, that as he walked along the North Strand Road, glancing idly at the windows of the provision shops, he would recall the dark humour of Guido Cavalcanti and smile, that as he went by Baird's stonecutting works in Talbot Place the spirit of Ibsen would blow through him like a keen wind, a spirit of wayward boyish beauty, and that passing a grimy marine-

dealer's shop beyond the Liffey he would repeat the song by
Ben Jonson which begins:
   I was not wearier where I lay. (P 176)

The memory of Cranly's listlessness erodes such stylistic fragments
shored against Dublin's ruin, and Stephen finds himself suddenly
alienated from words that bind and mock him:

> he found himself glancing from one casual word to another
> on his right or left in stolid wonder that they had been so
> silently emptied of instantaneous sense until every mean shop
> legend bound his mind like the words of a spell and his soul
> shrivelled up, sighing with age as he walked on in a lane
> among heaps of dead language. His own consciousness of
> language was ebbing from his brain and trickling into the
> very words themselves which set to band and disband them-
> selves in wayward rhythms. (P 178–9)

The apparent capriciousness of language as it gathers up and then
empties itself of meaning illustrates, in practical terms, the "rhythm
of beauty" that Stephen attempts to explain theoretically to Lynch
later in the fifth chapter (P 206). Such a rhythm, according to
Stephen, has the power to prolong and finally dissolve a state of
mind that he describes as "esthetic stasis." Moreover, the rhythm
of beauty is also the rhythm of truth, since in Stephen's view "the
true and the beautiful are akin" in formal terms. If beauty appeases
the imagination through "the most satisfying relations of the sensible," truth gratifies the intellect through "the most satisfying
relations of the intelligible," producing, like beauty, a "stasis of
the mind" (P 208). What Stephen calls "stasis" is simply the momentary appreciation of these satisfying relations, relations that are
dissolved by the very rhythm of apprehension that prolongs them.
"Stasis," then, is a moment of integration that temporarily satisfies
the intellect and/or the imagination, an achieved construct that must
repeatedly be dissolved and reconstituted as the relationship between individual events and their narrative contexts change.
   What Stephen experiences as the achievement and dissolution of
relation, and what he describes more analytically as the rhythms
of beauty and truth, is a structural rhythm that individuals may
participate in but not initiate or control. However, Stephen finishes

"what (he) was saying about beauty" (*P* 211) by analyzing the stages of apprehension, an understanding of which allows us to initiate and accelerate the rhythms of imaginative and intellectual comprehension. Three words from Aquinas provide the text for Stephen's commentary – *integritas, consonantia,* and *claritas* – but the arrangement of these prerequisites for beauty into a dialectic of apprehension that can be learned and applied is Stephen's. Stephen's formula for apprehending the uniqueness of any perceived object is simply to separate it from its immediate context and then to analyze its structure and significance. The synthesis of this process of separation and integration is the "enchantment" or stasis that is born of the momentary balance of two forces – forces such as illumination and darkness, which reach equilibrium in the image of a "fading coal" that Shelley used to describe the mind in creation (*P* 213).

How is the stasis of a mind that has apprehended beauty or truth different from the paralysis that Joyce anatomizes in *Dubliners*? Stephen employs "stasis" in a way that connotes rest or equilibrium, but stasis is also "stagnation"; in *Dubliners*, the most operative meaning of "paralysis" is "loss of the ability to move; a state of powerlessness or incapacity to act," yet "paralysis" comes from the Greek *paralyein*, meaning to loosen. Both "paralysis" and "stasis" are paradoxically double words, and Joyce uses them, in *Dubliners* and *Portrait*, to balance one another. Stasis – which replaces the more reverent term "epiphany" that Joyce used to mark the moment of revelation in *Stephen Hero* – is the counterpart and opposite of paralysis, producing a similar effect but of different duration, its accent more liberating than deadening. Joyce presents esthetic stasis as a momentary apprehension and acceptance of contradiction rather than a battle against it, a battle that eventually reveals its opponent to be the ineluctably divided self.

Stephen uses the term "apprehension" to designate the appreciation of the structural relations that define any whole. Stephen's theory is, in short, a theory of reading, and if we consciously apply it to our reading of *Portrait*, it allows us to evaluate Stephen's own reading in a more detached way. If, for example, we detach ourselves from Stephen when he is puzzling out the meaning of a word or phrase and perform the same activity independently as well as vicariously, we can arrest and contemplate the point where Stephen's strengths meet his limitations, generating a "balanced" view that should in turn produce an ambivalent response. In the first chapter Stephen is repeatedly troubled by a phrase from the Litany of the Virgin Mary, "Tower of Ivory." He connects it in his mind with Eileen because she is a Protestant and "protestants used to make fun of the litany of the Blessed Virgin. *Tower of Ivory*, they used to say, *House of Gold!* How could a woman be a tower of ivory or a house of gold? Who was right then?" (*P* 35) Stephen solves the problem by linking Eileen with the Virgin: he calls up an image of Eileen's hands, "long and white and thin and cold and soft" and thinks, "That was ivory: a cold white thing. That was the meaning of *Tower of Ivory*" (*P* 36).

Stephen's "definition" of *Tower of Ivory* is ingeniously economical: he furnishes his conception of the Holy Virgin with attributes of the virgin who lives on his street. However, if we take it out of its immediate context (appreciating its *integritas*), "apprehend it as complex, multiple, divisible, separable, made up of its parts, the results of its parts and their sum, harmonious" (*P* 212; Stephen identifies the structural complexity of an individual unit as its *consonantia*), and then "make the only synthesis which is logically and esthetically permissible" (*P* 213), we can see that "Tower of Ivory" is also "ivory tower," an encoded commentary on Stephen's habits of mind. For all of his ingeniousness, Stephen lives in a many-storied ivory tower. He has written himself into a fairy tale that begins, "Once upon a time and a very good time it was," a tale that takes place in Clongowes castle, site of heroic deeds that he hopes to imitate, a tale passed down to him by his father, a gentleman who, he fondly believes, may one day be a magistrate.

IN THE BEGINNING WAS THE WORD, AND THE WORD WAS [CHRIST]

Story antedates subject, as the opening of *A Portrait of the Artist* illustrates. The book begins with a story, but not until the third sentence do we learn that "he" is the subject of that story. The story is told before its subject is identified, before the life-story of the subject has even begun. Like a reader whose knowledge of language precedes specific knowledge of an individual text, Stephen's experience of language anticipates and shapes his experience of the world; but knowledge of the world and the text forces both the reader and Stephen to redefine the meaning of language as it was first conceived. Our experience of Stephen's esthetic theory allows us to redefine and recontextualize Stephen's experience at Clongowes as his storied rendition of a lived experience that is itself an unconscious response to the stories of childhood, and in particular, to the fairy tale.

The first chapter traces the impress of the fairy tale on Stephen's mind, a narrative akin to that of the gospels. The last of the four New Testament gospels explicitly affirms the primacy of word over world: St. John proclaims, "In the beginning was the Word," a word that precedes its own definition: "and the Word was God." The movement from word to reality to a more complex understanding of the word is the movement of the Christian Bible from Word to Incarnation ("And the Word was made flesh") to the crucifixion that makes ultimate Revelation possible. So perceived, the gospel, like the fairy tale, is a fable of identity motivated and shaped by a desire for self-definition partly realized through the definition of human doubles – words.

As an account of the crucifixion and resurrection of the Word, the gospel can be read as one of the most powerful narrative illustrations of the rhythm of truth that Stephen analyzes more abstractly in the last chapter: the human referent must be lost in the flesh in order to be regained through the word, a process that must be periodically repeated if our dual consciousness of word and flesh, and their reciprocity, is to be kept alive. In the first chapter Stephen establishes, almost unconsciously, a meaning for his name through identifying himself with Christ and Christ's doubles in the twin realms of Church and State: St. Stephen, on the one hand, and Parnell along with the Greek and Roman national heroes recalled by Stephen's Latinate surname, on the other. However, the principle of connection that binds the various narratives is not allegorical, which would place history in the service of this story, but verbal, which equalizes the relationships among narratives and allows them to illuminate each other.[8]

As Joyce demonstrated in *Dubliners*, opposed points of view can be made to intersect most economically through the double meanings of an accented word or phrase, such as "gnomon." In *Portrait*,

8 The assumption that Joyce's allusions have an allegorical significance is responsible for many of the more rigid and less credible interpretations of both *Portrait* and *Ulysses*. Some of the allegorical grids have been classical, but most have been Christian.

Stephen's guidelines for apprehending "the *whatness* of a thing" help us to isolate and reconnect those words to achieve a more multidimensional perspective. If we apply Stephen's formula to "Tower of Ivory," its reconstitution as "ivory tower," when supported by the fairy-tale structure of the chapter, presents us with an instantaneous double image of the beauty and limitation of a sensitive child's vision. When, in the midst of the discussion of the mysterious sin committed by Simon Moonan, Tusker Boyle, and the others, Stephen comforts himself by remembering his triumph of definition, reflecting with satisfaction, "By thinking of things you could understand them" (*P* 43), his connection should prompt the reader to rethink and reevaluate the relationship between the situations through the key words that unlock their double meaning.

Stephen's memory of Eileen's ivory hands is sparked by his recollection of "Lady" Boyle paring his nails. The associative link is hands, which brings together two mysteries: the puzzle of virginity and the enigma of sexual transgression and punishment. If we apply Stephen's formula for insightful apprehension to his description of the hands of Mr. Gleeson and Lady Boyle, the inner narrative that manipulates Stephen, turning him into his schoolfellows' savior, becomes clear. The word "nails," detached from the referent that its immediate context dictates, attaches itself to different hands, and to an older narrative that serves not as an allegorical equivalent to but as a critical commentary upon this one. The focus of Stephen's concern has shifted from the Virgin to the Son, from the puzzle of purity to that of sin and symbolic atonement. Sharp nails can excruciate as well as extend and beautify a hand, and Stephen's unconscious understanding of this is reflected in his concentration on Mr. Gleeson's hands as an image of the paradox of gentleness and pain, implicated in the sin as well as in its punishment:

> He had rolled up his sleeves to show how Mr Gleeson would roll up his sleeves. But Mr Gleeson had round shiny cuffs and clean white wrists and fattish white hands and the nails of them were long and pointed. Perhaps he pared them too like Lady Boyle. But they were terribly long and pointed nails. So long and cruel they were though the white fattish hands were not cruel but gentle. And though he trembled with cold and fright to think of the cruel long nails and of the high whistling sound of the cane and of the chill you felt at the

end of your shirt when you undressed yourself yet he felt a feeling of queer quiet pleasure inside him to think of the white fattish hands, clean and strong and gentle. And he thought of what Cecil Thunder had said; that Mr Gleeson would not flog Corrigan hard. And Fleming had said he would not because it was best of his play not to. But that was not why. (P 45)

When Stephen is cast in the role of scapegoat, punished, as Fleming anticipated, "for what other fellows did" (P 43), when his own hands are made to burn, tremble, and crumple "like a leaf in the fire" (P 50) for the sin of Tusker Boyle's long white hands and Mr. Gleeson's fattish ones, he takes it upon himself to complete the narrative by interceding with the Father, the "rector" whose name promises rectification of wrongs, on behalf of himself and his schoolfellows. In the process, he constructs a glorious and recognizable meaning for his own name, translating it, in his own mind, into "Stephen Hero."

In the first chapter of *Portrait*, the reader, like Stephen, is confronted with problems of definition: specifically, she or he is asked to define Stephen's relationship to a world of words by contrasting the fantasies that he uses to define mysterious words, phrases, and songs with the more complex meanings and associations that Stephen does not yet understand. Such definitions show not only what Stephen has read – the Bible and fairy tales – but *how* he reads them, vicariously and not critically. He positions himself within them, and never outside them, a strategy that makes heroes, but not authors or critical readers. What he does manage to do is to assimilate, in his own life story, heroic figures that history has set in opposition to one another: Christ and the Romans, Christ and Parnell. He has constructed "the most satisfying relations of the intelligible" – what is intelligible to him as a hopeful, obedient, and naive child – and in the process has defined for himself a cluster of puzzlingly attractive words. To the extent that we can appreciate those definitions, our reading is sympathetic, whereas more ironic possibilities emerge when we focus on the larger contexts of Stephen's definitions, the contexts that he ignores. As Stephen will later understand in theory, the only balanced reading is a double one that can appreciate, in rhythmic alternation, both the triumph and the inadequacy of definition.

NIGHT WORSHIP: HEAVENLY BODIES

In chapter one, Stephen gradually defines a heroic identity for himself by constantly interrogating individual words, and by unconsciously exploring his relationship to the Word. By juxtaposing Stephen's unconscious identification with Christ with an account of Stephen's repeated attempts to understand the meaning of language, Joyce emphasizes the extent to which the New Testament presents itself as an allegory of communication, as a history of a creative Word moving toward a Revelation expressed as a final sentence, or judgment. The larger contours of the New Testament are, according to such a view, reproduced in miniature in the life of one man, conceived as a divine word penetrating the tympanum of a woman's ear, his corpus/corpse a literal embodiment of human communication, represented by the eucharistic bread and wine. Such an allegory represents and promulgates an idealistic view of reading as a transcendent communion made possible through communication, which is always, by definition, a sacramental act. The story of Christ suggests that the sensual incarnation of the abstract Word is significant primarily because it makes ultimate transcendence possible, a transcendence effected through atonement and symbolic communication. Christian scripture celebrates the power of language to abstract itself – eventually – from its sensual referents, its mesh of defining circumstances, and to reunite itself with the will of its creator. A Christian ideology, as its constitutive language suggests, celebrates oneness: atonement is a way of being "at one" with the will of another, an experience that, in Christian scripture, defines communication.[9]

Stephen's initial response to the problems posed by language and identity is primed by a literal, if unconscious, reading of the gospels as a parable of how communication works. Identity must be defined through language, and language incarnated in experience so that it may be abstracted and reassimilated. Stephen's struggle to equate language and sensual experience – to understand "tower of ivory"

---

9 At the end of *Portrait*, Stephen can understand love and communication only in these terms, as a humiliating at-one-ment. When Cranly asks him if he has ever loved anyone or anything, Stephen replies that he has tried to love God, which he defines as uniting his will "with the will of God instant by instant" (*P* 240).

as Eileen's hands, "suck" as the sound of draining water (*P* 11), Leicester Abbey as the lights of Clongowes castle (*P* 10) – is an effort to give flesh to words, to effect their incarnation. These words have life but no meaning for Stephen, like the vivid words that pass between Dante and Mr. Casey over Christmas dinner. Stephen responds physically and almost reflexively to the passionate words – the glow of anger on Mr. Casey's face rises in his own as "the spoken words thrilled him" (*P* 38) – but he knows no larger context to play the words against, so he can neither assimilate perspectives nor produce a meaning that can help him bridge the distance between himself and the scene he is witnessing. It isn't until Stephen inadvertently atones for the sins of Tusker Boyle and Simon Moonan that he discovers a way of being "at one" with the worlds from which he had been alienated through his relative youth and ignorance: with the community at Clongowes, and with his divided family. His punishment allows him to seal the rift separating him from his immediate environment, as well as the rift that divided his family, by playing the role of savior, a role that reconciles the narratives of Parnell and Christ, allowing him to live out and join the meanings of two abstract words that had puzzled him – God and politics.

Christian scripture, when considered as a commentary upon language, takes as its ideal the transcendent power of imaginative integration. But, as Joyce suggests in the second and fourth chapters, the language of scripture can be interpreted imagistically as well as literally, as an exploration not of the word, but of the body. This more romantic interpretation reads Christ and Lucifer as representations of heavenly bodies, Lucifer as falling star and Christ as rising sun, as well as rising Son (see "Was Jesus a Sun Myth?" in "Circe," *U* 15.1579). Stephen's formula for apprehension, when applied to key words in Christian scripture, shows how coherently its language supports such an interpretation, unveiling "East-er" as the time (place) where the Son (sun) rises in order to compensate for the fall of Eve (eve) – the coming of "Eve ill," evil. So interpreted, Christian narratives, like pagan ones, are anthropomorphic accounts of heavenly bodies that differ from their Greek counterparts in focusing not on constellations and their genesis, but on the dramatic opposition between day and night, the perpetual revolution in the heavens.

If, as a parable of reading, scripture idealizes the value of communion through a transcendence of meaning, it reverses that emphasis when read poetically, in terms of the images that the sounds of its words imply. Whereas the philosophical idealist represents the ideal as a heavenly abstraction, the sensual idealist pays romantic homage to heavenly bodies, the moon or the stars, thereby idealizing *distance* rather than at-one-ment. If Christ sheds his mortal body to live eternally as an abstract and transcendent Word, Lucifer takes two forms, both of which are physical. In his prelapsarian state, he takes the form of a heavenly body, the morning star, a traditional symbol of pride of the intellect, having the power to enlighten ("Lucifer" means "light-bringer") but doomed to fall. In his fallen state, he takes the form of a snake, a representation of the sexual part of a male body that like the intellect is marked by rise and fall. Lucifer, in his duality and in the relative weakness of the light he brings, is inferior to a greater heavenly body, the Son (sun), who must fall in order to re-arise into heaven during the mourning. The counterpart of Lucifer–Satan in his opposition to the Son is woman, who also takes two forms – Mary and Eve, virgin and temptress. Mary, like the unfallen Lucifer, is represented by the morning star, harbinger of the sun; not only does she take the form of the same heavenly body as Lucifer, but her mortal body is made heavenly as well: she is impregnated when God's Word passes the membrane of her ear, not by the rupturing of a "lower" membrane. The fallen Eve, Satan's lure and victim, sins by listening, not to God's word, but to the blandishments of the body and promises of divine knowledge offered suggestively to her by a snake. The stories of Lucifer–Satan and his female counterparts facilitate not an imaginative transcendence of the body, but a particularization of the symmetry of mental and sexual processes, fraught with a warning to privilege thought and communication over sexuality.

In *Portrait*, Stephen learns to see the transcendent desires of childhood as unrealistic and escapist by replaying his story, in chapter two, in the "anatomical" theater of troubled adolescence. The readings that frame Stephen shift accordingly: the classical heroes of Peter Parley's Tales (*P* 53) are replaced by their romantic counterparts, particularly Byron and Shelley; the fairy tale yields to tales of adventure; Christ as portrayed in the gospel is displaced by a Miltonic Satan, romantically interpreted. Stephen's heroes are no longer saviors, but heretics; his drive is not toward atonement, but toward separation and exile – what, from an orthodox point of view, is called "sin." Exiled from the fairy tale, he discovers adventure, a narrative different in mood and in the *nature* of its resolution, but identical in its movement from isolation to reconciliation. Stephen exiles himself from the spiritual world he had built in chapter one through the painstaking accretion of sensual definitions, and gravitates instead toward a physical one, where communion is private and sensual rather than public and symbolic, and the desire to consume the body is subsumed by the desire to experience its sensual particulars. Whereas the first chapter celebrated a triumph of social and historical at-one-ment, the second represents the pleasures of critical deconstruction, the process by which human and written characters shed their more symbolic significations and display their hidden sensuality.

In chapter two, Stephen's growing sense of alienation is most frequently expressed in his own mind as a process of fading. What is fading away in the second chapter is the network of self-defining associations that Stephen had constructed in the first. His removal from Clongowes and the physical dislocation of his family from Blackrock to Dublin has the effect of eroding all of the heroic fantasies that he had shored around himself in childhood. As in the first chapter, Stephen longs to shed "weakness and timidity and inexperience" (*P* 65), but initially, in his proud and rebellious phase, what he actually shuns is the consciousness of his own body, an awareness that his idealistic yearnings are shadowed by sexual drives. Stephen's fantasies are repeatedly interrupted by reminders of the ineluctable physicality of existence, reminders from which he recoils in horror. When he is watching the firelight, listening to an old woman's pathetic reports about "Ellen," he focuses his attention on "the words," "following the ways of adventure that lay open in the coals," until the physical counterpart of the name the old woman evokes appears incarnate in the doorway (*P* 68). Ellen materializes as a grotesque reminder of the feeble animality of the body; Stephen sees her as "skull," a feeble, whining, monkey-like creature whose silly laughter exposes the silliness of his own idealizations. Similarly, the word "foetus" that Stephen discovers carved into a desk at the anatomy theatre in Cork mocks him with its semantic specificity, its horrifying power to bring the dead and the unborn to life and to challenge, with its uncompromising realism, the more attenuated sensuality of romantic desire.

Stephen's desire to fade out of existence manifests itself verbally as the desire to divest word and narrative of any personal or worldly meaning. When he writes his Byronic poem to E— C— he strips the account of their shared tram ride of all of its noncelestial characteristics: all the "elements which he deemed common and insignificant fell out of the scene. There remained no trace of the tram itself nor of the trammen nor of the horses: nor did he and she appear vividly. The verses told only of the night and the balmy breeze and the maiden lustre of the moon." (*P* 70) As Stephen's carefully constructed myth of himself lapses, his definitions of words and names undergo a similar divestment. The first chapter illustrated ways in which words accrued meaning, and as Stephen learned to define words and phrases sensually, the reader was prodded to resituate those phrases in other well-known narrative contexts. In the second chapter, Stephen concentrates on the art of dissociating words from contexts to create a soothing, rhythmic music, as he does when he "prays" on the night mail to Cork:

> His prayer, addressed neither to God nor saint, began with a shiver, as the chilly morning breeze crept through the chink of the carriage door to his feet, and ended in a trail of foolish words which he made to fit the insistent rhythm of the train; and silently, at intervals of four seconds, the telegraphpoles held the galloping notes of the music between punctual bars. This furious music allayed his dread and, leaning against the windowledge, he let his eyelids close again. (*P* 87)

The sensual sounds of words also soothe him when gathered into the less furious music of poetry or song: Shelley's fragment on the moon (*P* 96), or the "come-all-you" that his father sings about exile and the fading of love (*P* 88).

Stephen's physiological changes have exiled him from the theatre of his mind, forcing him to look for a new part to play in a different theatre, an anatomical one that will allow him first to displace and eventually to act out his physical desires. Stephen's weary sense of fading and being stripped, along with the language that reflects him, prepare him for the experience of physical contact, anticipating his observation of the prostitute as "she undid her gown" (*P* 100). The desire for familial reconciliation that drew him to the "family romances" of Christian scripture and fairy tale has been ousted by the desire for sexual union that draws him from family romance to romanticism, from the general and mythic to the particular and physical, from a respect for the power of symbolic communication and revelation to an appreciation of the sibilant and sensual activity of the tongue. Memories of his family and his childhood fade in preparation for his initiation into "another world" (*P* 100), a "fallen," "evening" world of darkness and abandonment, in which other, softer ties replace familial ones, and other lips press their story upon his brain.

Stephen's yearnings for a higher existence, his lyrical preoccupation with "the maiden lustre of the moon" (*P* 71), "wandering companionless" (*P* 96), are bound to his fierce physical desires, which he describes as "the tides within him" (*P* 98). The moon governs these tides, as it governs those of the sea; his identification with a heavenly body both masks and represents a new awareness of his physical body: both bodies induct him, subtly, into the rituals of night worship, although he fails to appreciate their interdependence. Not until the opening of the third chapter does he begin to betray an unconscious awareness that heavenly and earthly bodies may be equated, and that the prototype for such an equation is Christ's counterpart, Lucifer.

At the beginning of the third chapter, Stephen solves two equations, interpreting the widening and folding together of the calculations in two opposite ways, which are implicitly bound together by the operation that produces both. He sees the tail of the first equation as an image of "the vast cycle of starry life," with a tail "eyed and starred like a peacock's" and eyes opening and closing like stars (*P* 103). Only the word "peacock," with its comic overtones of male sexual pride, ruffles the lyricism of Stephen's image, an image of the heavenly expanse of his own mind. In apparent contrast, the second equation presents him with an image of "his own soul going forth to experience, unfolding itself sin by sin, spreading abroad the balefire of its burning stars and folding back upon itself, fading slowly." The heavenly eyes have become lustful and fiery sins, but Stephen sees no equation between the two equations. Even when he contemplates his "pride in his own sin" (*P* 104), he fails to connect that pride to the figure embodying it in Christian lore, who is both the "light-bringer" – the morning star

that represents intellectual pride (see Yeats' essay on Shelley)[10] –
and a synecdoche of male sexual pride in his role as serpent.

Lucifer, as the sermon will remind Stephen, is a star turned snake,
a "son of the morning" who "took the shape of a serpent" (*P* 118).
In these two forms, he represents intellectual and physical asser-
tiveness, the double pride that doubles Christ's humiliation. As
Stephen fails to appreciate the relationship between intellectual and
physical desire, he also fails to understand the similarity between
Lucifer and the Virgin; but he notes with puzzlement that his sins
have brought him closer to her:

> If ever his soul, reentering her dwelling shyly after the frenzy
> of his body's lust had spent itself, was turned towards her
> whose emblem is the morning star, *bright and musical, telling
> of heaven and infusing peace*, it was when her names were mur-
> mured softly by lips whereon there still lingered foul and
> shameful words, the savour itself of a lewd kiss.
>   That was strange. He tried to think how it could be but
> the dusk, deepening in the schoolroom, covered over his
> thoughts. (*P* 105)

Not until he composes the villanelle of the temptress does Stephen
imaginatively intertwine the Virgin with the temptress, and, less
prominently, Lucifer with Christ as complementary representations
of the same interaction. Stephen addresses his poem, and the question it repeatedly poses, to woman, "*Lure of the fallen seraphim,*"
who also inspires an upswelling of religious devotion – the "*smoke
of praise*" arising out of the flame she made of man's heart, accompanied by a "*eucharistic hymn*" (*P* 223–4).

Giacomo Joyce, which Joyce was working on as he revised *Stephen
Hero* into *Portrait*, helps to show how Joyce puzzled out an unexpected link between Lucifer's sexuality and intellect and that of the
Virgin. In *Giacomo Joyce*, Joyce portrays his virginal pupil *as* Lucifer,
proudly distant and coldly lascivious, who ultimately attacks him
with basilisk eyes and snaky body; and he casts himself as Lucifer's
victimized counterparts, Eve and Christ. In the dream sequence of

10 *Essays and Introductions* (New York: Macmillan, 1961), 88–89. First
    published in *Ideas of Good and Evil*, which Joyce owned in Trieste; see
    Ellmann, *The Consciousness of Joyce*.

Giacomo Joyce, as in the third chapter of *Portrait*, Joyce attempts to represent the sexual impulse by relating it to both of the images associated with Lucifer: snake and star. Near the end of the sketch-book, he dreams that she comes to him in a Parisian room to tempt him as a voice of "wisdom" ("This voice I never heard"). She tells him, "I am not convinced that such activities of the mind or body can be called unhealthy," and her "starborn" flesh coils towards him, kissing him with "soft sucking lips" that burn him, and he cries, "A starry snake has kissed me: a cold nightsnake. I am lost!" (*GJ* 15) Joyce's dream portrayal of his pupil is initially puzzling partly because the logic of linking a star to a snake is unexpected, submerged, and insufficiently supported by the context. The mythic stature of "Giacomo" and his pupil is unconvincing, even absurd: "Giacomo" looks histrionic in the guise of Christ and silly in the role of Eve, and his virginal pupil is, both anatomically and temperamentally, an equally unlikely Lucifer. In *Portrait*, however, Joyce resolves these problems by making Stephen play both Christ and Lucifer in alternation, defining each role as a paradox. Christ rights through being wronged, an ethical paradox that takes a more sensual form through Lucifer, who is both the highest and the lowest perceivable object, an idealist and a hedonist – in short, a romantic.

In the third chapter of *Portrait*, Stephen is most aware of himself as a snake, whose mind winds itself in and out of curious questions of "spiritual and bodily sloth" (*P* 106), whose soul sickens "at the thought of a torpid snaky life feeding itself out of the tender marrow of his life and fattening upon the slime of lust" (*P* 140), whose archetype is his penis, "the most subtle beast of the field" that "feels and understands and desires" (*P* 139). If Stephen sees his body as serpentine, he sees his soul as Luciferian, "stars being born and being quenched" (*P* 103). At the beginning of the chapter, the stars begin to crumble "and a cloud of fine stardust" falls through space (*P* 103), a simultaneous idealization and literalization of a Luciferian fall. Stephen's identification with Lucifer, in its paradoxical dou-bleness, teaches us how to interpret his female soul's virginal sub-mission to her Creator in chapter four. Stephen thinks that he is experiencing a "spiritual communion" that the ritual of communion does not inspire in him, but his surrender to his creator is a recon-textualized version of his surrender to the prostitute in chapter two. As the prostitute had caressed his body, "slowly, slowly, slowly"

(*P* 101), an inaudible voice now seems to caress his soul, "telling her names and glories" (*P* 152). Clasped in the arms of the whore, "feeling the warm calm rise and fall of her breast," Stephen surrendered himself to her, "body and mind" (*P* 101). Now, he is the virginal and female soul surrendering herself to a male creator, murmuring, "*Inter ubera mea commorabitur*" ("He shall lie between my breasts"). As Stephen admits, "The idea of surrender had a perilous attraction for his mind" (*P* 152). Both of Stephen's surrenders were inspired by books: the surrender of his body was anticipated in *The Count of Monte Cristo*; the surrender of his soul is facilitated by his use of a "neglected book written by Saint Alphonsus Liguori," its prayers "interwoven with the imagery of the canticles" (*P* 152). Stephen cannot purge language of its sensuality any more than he can mortify his senses, because goodness, like sin, is defined by the relationship between word and flesh.

Viewed in one way, Stephen's experiences in the first and second chapters are as different as day and night; viewed in another way, they illustrate complementary phases of the same experience. In the first chapter he is alienated from family and peers through youth and ignorance; in the second chapter he wills such a separation, finally objectifying his sense of difference through sin. In both cases, he is punished for his detachment: in the first chapter, he is pandied for breaking his glasses, for his helpless inability to see what is nearest him; in the second chapter he is twice chastised for a more calculated and critical detachment – for his written affirmation of the soul's inalterable distance from the Creator, which Mr. Tate condemns as "heresy" (*P* 79), and for the detachment from conventional morality reflected in his preference for Byron over Tennyson. As in the first chapter, he is again cast in the role of scapegoat: he is whipped with Heron's cane, pummelled with a knotty cabbage stump, and pushed into barbed wire for his defense of Byron's "heresies." Both at Clongowes and at Belvedere, in both his Christian and his Luciferian incarnations, Stephen is brought to book for differing from his fellows. At Clongowes, Stephen uses his chastisement to bridge that difference, whereas at Belvedere his treatment at the hands of his friends confirms the apprehension of difference that Stephen has learned to savor: "He chronicled with patience what he saw, detaching himself from it and testing its mortifying flavour in secret" (*P* 67). However, even his critical detachment leads him back to the world he had scorned, not through social communion or verbal communication, but through the private pleasures of physical contact.

Sin brings its own sense of at-one-ment, a physical oneness that Christianity defines as the opposite of spiritual atonement. With the help of a double, in this case Yeats, Joyce defined sin as a separation that is paradoxically inseparable from atonement, arguing, in his essay on Wilde, that "the truth inherent in the soul of Catholicism" is the understanding, which Wilde had, "that man cannot reach the divine heart except through that sense of separation and loss called sin."[11] The "sin" of sexuality and the "virtue" of atonement are evaluative interpretations of the same paradox, the paradox of identity and difference. Christ's atonement is portrayed as a reconciliation with the heavens, but it is also an excruciating separation from the earth; comparably, sexual sin may sunder an individual from the community, but it also constitutes the most intimate form of contact. Lucifer's "fall" from the heavens is also a "rise" – a rising against God that takes as its alternative form a rising of the flesh.

If a "fall," interpreted one way, constitutes a rise when interpreted another, then the very separability of opposites when divorced from the contexts that authorize them must be called into question. Joyce's methodologies not only emphasize the importance of contexts, but they also generate new interpretations for the narrative contexts they recall. Both Lucifer and Christ participate, in complementary ways, in a single rhythm, the rhythm of separation and integration that multiplies and individuates language and experience. Scripture – and language – can only be understood as a double experience, as allegory and poetry, meaning and sense. The last half of *Portrait* illustrates Stephen's unusual sensitivity to both kinds of experience, and his comic blindness to their interrelationship. If we read, not only with Stephen, but against him, reading imagistically when he reads literally, and literally when he reads imagistically, playing his story off against the history that informs and shapes it, then the full humor of that interdependence can emerge.

11 *CW* 205; see Yeats' "Tables of the Law," in *Mythologies*, which according to Ellmann and Mason, Joyce knew by heart.

RETREAT

The atonement that climaxes the third chapter of *Portrait* is also, as the event that prompts it suggests, a retreat. The Church uses the strategy of "retreat" to simulate the "withdrawal," or separation, that can inspire a desire for its counterpart, atonement. This is how the rector, another righter of wrongs, defines it (*P* 109), but Stephen's formula for apprehension, which is basically a strategy for gaining a more distanced perspective on language and narrative, allows us to appreciate the relevance of its other meanings – a recession, a retrogression, a place of safety or refuge (*OED*). This is the effect of the retreat on Stephen: he regresses to a childlike piety and simplicity, reestablishing his imaginative association with obedient goodness and purity. Stephen's retreat to the world of childhood innocence is precipitated by the unexpected resurgence of the past: he notices his old master, Father Arnall, seated at the left of the altar, and the narrator explains, "The figure of his old master, so strangely rearisen, brought back to Stephen's mind his life at Clongowes" (*P* 108). "His soul, as these memories came back to him, became again a child's soul" (*P* 109). He reenacts, in response to the words of the sermon, the highlights of his experience at Clongowes: instead of a burning hand, he is given a "burning ear" (*P* 115), a fire that spreads through his body and brain (*P* 125). As at Clongowes, he longs to "be at one with others and with God" (*P* 143), a longing that leads him toward the renewed experience of communication and communion that the eucharist, through the language that clothes it, represents for him (*P* 146).

The irony of the hellfire sermon is that its suasive power is, in its own terms, demonic: the sin of Adam and Eve was to listen to "the poison of his [Satan's] eloquence" (*P* 118). As a serpent, Satan has a "poison tongue" that can draw his listeners into the *mouth* of hell (*P* 118) with its *tongues* of flames (*P* 125). The conflict between good and evil is a war of words; sin, like atonement, is a matter of communication. Hell itself is a verbal torture, an endless repetition of the same name – "Hell! Hell! Hell! Hell! Hell!" (*P* 125) – or an eternity of repetitive rhymes, as envisioned by one of the Jesuit fathers:

> It seemed to him that he stood in the midst of a great hall, dark and silent save for the ticking of a great clock. The ticking

went on unceasingly; and it seemed to this saint that the sound of the ticking was the ceaseless repetition of the words: ever, never; ever, never... O what a dreadful punishment! (*P* 132–3)

Ironically, repentance provides no escape from the hell of repetition, but represents it in another form:

> – *O my God!* –
> – *O my God!* –
> – *I am heartily sorry* –
> – *I am heartily sorry* –
> – *for having offended Thee* –
> – *for having offended Thee* – (*P* 135)

Christ's separation from authority through incarnation mirrors Lucifer's separation from authority through insurrection, as his refusal to plead with his Roman captors mirrors and reverses Lucifer's suasive triumph over Adam and Eve. Joyce's treatment of Stephen in the contexts of both narratives suggests that the conflicts of "scripture" are representations of different attitudes toward language, attitudes that have also defined the alternating tendencies of literary history – the classical and the Romantic tempers, which Joyce associates with Christ and Lucifer, respectively. Joyce's presentation of these tendencies as fundamentally identical, their apparent differences merely differences of accent, disrupts the simplicity of the more familiar account of their antithetical relationship. In *Portrait*, Joyce portrays classicism, usually characterized as a predominantly rational attitude, as a triumph of imaginative integration, and romanticism, frequently portrayed as irrational, as a triumph of critical deconstruction.[12] The emphasis of classicism is upon truth, but the road to its apprehension is imaginative, not critical, and the emphasis of romanticism is on beauty, apprehended through uncompromising criticism. Both individually and together, classicism and romanticism reproduce the rhythms of beauty and truth, which in structural terms are identical.

12 Joyce's distinction between the classical and romantic tempers is first presented in his 1902 essay on "James Clarence Mangan" (*CW* 73–83) and is re-presented in *Stephen Hero*, pp. 78–9.

TEMPERING CLASSICISM

I have suggested that "classicism," as Joyce implicitly represents it
in the first chapter of *Portrait*, is allied to Christianity, and that
together they privilege a "heroism" of transcendence through self-
denial, in contrast to "romanticism," which Joyce represents in the
second chapter as a preoccupation with the "highest" (intellectual,
heavenly) and "lowest" (sexual, bestial) parts of the body. Joyce
presents romanticism and classicism as opposite in emphasis, but
comparable in structure, a position significantly different than the
one he had staked out in the college essay on "James Clarence
Mangan" delivered in 1902 (*CW* 73–83). In that paper, Joyce declares the classical temper clearly superior to the one he labels romantic, suggesting that even in their lowest forms, the materialism
latent in the one is preferable to the incoherence approached by the
other. His early attempt to characterize each school is, however,
both confused and confusing. He argues that

> The romantic school is often and grievously *mis*interpreted,
> not more by others than by its own, for that impatient temper
> which, as it could see no fit abode here for its ideals, chose
> to behold them under insensible figures, comes to disregard
> certain limitations, and, because these figures are blown high
> and low by the mind that conceived them, comes at times to
> regard them as feeble shadows moving aimlessly about the
> light, obscuring it. (*CW* 74, my emphasis)

The problem with Joyce's formulation lies in the suggestion that
the view of romanticism he goes on to outline is a *mis*interpretation,
although he eliminates this implication in *Stephen Hero*.[13] However,
certain aspects of his view of romanticism remain constant from
1902 through 1914; the associations of romanticism with darkness
and with the impulse to behold its ideals under "high and low"

---

13 In *Stephen Hero*, Joyce clarifies his intended meaning by changing the
    punctuation and phrasing, arguing that "the romantic temper, so often
    and grievously misinterpreted and not more by others than by its
    own, *is* an insecure, unsatisfied, impatient temper which sees no fit
    abode here for its ideals and chooses therefore to behold them under
    insensible figures" (*SH* 78).

figures blown apart by restless desire are still apparent in *Portrait* in the figures of heavenly bodies and sexual organs that preoccupy Stephen in the second and third chapters. What is missing in *Portrait* is Joyce's earlier conviction that the romantic temper is a lesser one ("the highest praise must be withheld from the romantic school" [*CW* 74]). In *Portrait*, Stephen's "romantic" phase is the mirror image of his "classical" triumphs. As a romantic, moreover, Stephen becomes mindful of the beauty of mortal conditions, an apprehension that is unavailable to him as a child longing for an heroic and imperishable triumph.

Joyce began his career by favoring classicism over romanticism because he saw in it a respect for the limitations of mortal existence; but in *Portrait*, he treats classicism and romanticism as equally rich in productive contradictions. If romanticism may be signaled by a desire for flight, by a dissatisfied and ambitious overreaching, as Joyce implies in his Mangan essay, evidence of such overreaching is as plentiful in classical myth as it is in its "romantic" counterparts: Icarus is, by such a definition, a "romantic" whose overweening ambition prompts him to challenge the sun, which in turn causes his fall. Classicism and romanticism, defined as mutually exclusive tendencies, intermingle in the fortunes of Daedalus, but the romantic poets that Stephen emulates in the second stage of his development are seldom viewed as similarly mixed exemplars. Unlike Daedalus, Byron and Shelley tend to be read as Stephen reads them, as yearning poets who long to escape the coils of mortal existence, their dissatisfaction unalloyed by humor or a serious critical engagement with social injustice.[14] Readers familiar with the Romantic poets will appreciate the absurdity of such a treatment; in recent years, in particular, it has become easier to see that Joyce's assessment of the complexity of romanticism differs quite radically from Stephen's (anticipating recent critical reevaluations of the period). As Joyce presents it, romanticism is driven by twin imperatives to reform as well as to transcend the injustices of an unlovely humanity. As a result, it behooves us to remember that Byron and Shelley are critics as well as poets, and that their more critical works

14 One notable exception is Hermione de Almeida's *Byron and Joyce through Homer: Don Juan and Ulysses*, which argues that the romantic period is more "classical" than it is reputed to be. See, in particular, chapter one, "Odysseus and the Realm of Gold," pp. 5–22.

offer a relevant analysis of the inadequacies of lyricism, one that Stephen fails to apply to his own situation.

In *Portrait*, Stephen responds sensually to the musical qualities of Romantic poetry, but he is also drawn to Byron and Shelley as imagined paradigms of his own altered self-image as outcast, heretical immoralist, and lover. Ironically, however, Byron's work, regarded as a whole, supplies an implicit critique of Stephen's adolescent one-sidedness. What Stephen lacks is Byron's self-awareness – his talent for stylistic self-consciousness, or critical parody, and his willingness to admit that he plays two roles, that of a comic Don Juan as well as that of a world-weary Childe Harold. Stephen's appreciation of Shelley is similarly short-sighted: he singles out for admiration a fragment of Shelley's address to the moon, interpreted as an address to himself, "drifting amid life like the barren shell of the moon" (*P* 96). Stephen finds in Shelley lyrical correlatives for his sense of weary detachment,[15] but in a more subtle way, Joyce evokes Shelley's thought as a more complex frame of reference for Stephen's experience. Although Stephen responds to the beauty of Shelley's portrayal of isolation, he neglects Shelley's insistence on the importance of community in "A Defence of Poetry," and the more imagistic analysis of the problems of communication present in *Prometheus Unbound*. If, rather than echoing the question that Shelley's fragment poses, positioning himself within the poem as a satellite – itself a reflection – he had instead listened to it and its implications, he might have recognized both his own interpretive narcissism and the alternative to it that Shelley celebrates in the "Defence":

> The great secret of morals is Love; or a going out of our own nature, and an identification of ourselves with the beautiful which exists in thought, action, or person, not our own. A man, to be greatly good, must imagine intensively and comprehensively; he must put himself in the place of another and of many others; the pains and pleasures of his species must become his own. ("A Defense of Poetry")

---

15   In *Waiting for Godot*, Beckett has Didi and Gogo evoke the same passage that Stephen quotes in *Portrait*, Shelley's fragment "To the Moon," thereby doubling the irony of allusion.

The paradoxical richness of Shelley's thought helps to define the tension between Stephen's perception of himself and Joyce's more complex portrait of him. When, after his "retreat" into the obedient order of childhood piety, Stephen discovers a romanticism motivated by intellectual as well as physical beauty, he fancies himself not only as Daedalus in flight (*P* 169), but as Prometheus unbound, whom Shelley offers (in the "Preface" to *Prometheus Unbound*) as a more poetical version of Satan. In Shelley's version, Prometheus gives speech as well as fire to humanity (II.iv, 72), yet unlike Aeschylus' Prometheus he refuses, with Luciferian pride, to serve the god whose reign he decries as tyrannical (I, 376–80, 400). Instead, he retreats into the enclosed world of the human mind, a sensual and intellectual utopia free from the ravages of time and change. When Prometheus is unbound, he tells Asia of a "cave" where they shall go, which, as Shelley suggests in his preface, represents a state of mind.[16] Prometheus' cave, as an idealized type of "the dim caves of human thought" that house the spirits summoned by the Earth (I, 659), is also, like Coleridge's Kubla Khan or Yeats' Byzantium, the abode of art, "Where we will sit and talk of time and change, / As the world ebbs and flows, ourselves unchanged" (III.iii, 23–4). However, Shelley presents art not as a copy of nature, but as a reassimilation of the natural, the "Strange combinations" made "out of common things" (III.iii, 32).

Joyce's reading of the cave's significance is, as is so frequently the case in his reading of Romantic poetry, mediated by Yeats, who represents it as derived from Platonic and Neoplatonic thought. In "The Philosophy of Shelley's Poetry" (1900),[17] Yeats argues that Shelley's description of Prometheus' cave carries echoes of both Plato's cave and of Porphyry's description of Homer's cave in Ithaca. Yeats presents the cave as one of Shelley's ruling images, an image of the enclosed and isolated poetic life, noting:

Again and again one finds some passing allusion to the cave of man's mind, or to the caves of his youth, or to the cave

---

16 "The imagery which I have employed will be found, in many instances, to have been drawn from the operations of the human mind."
17 *Ideas of Good and Evil* (1905), from Joyce's Trieste library; see Ellmann, *The Consciousness of Joyce*. Included in W. B. Yeats, *Essays and Introductions* (New York: Macmillan-Collier), pp. 65–95.

of mysteries we enter at death, for to Shelley as to Porphyry it is more than an image of life in the world. It may mean any enclosed life, as when it is the dwelling-place of Asia and Prometheus, or when it is "the still cave of poetry," and it may have all meanings at once.[18]

Shelley represents the poetic mind as an enclosed space, bounding a natural yet perfect world that contains what he identifies in his preface as "beautiful idealisms of moral excellence." At the beginning of the second chapter of *Portrait*, Joyce, like Shelley, uses a cave as an image of Stephen's mind, but the particular cave that entrances Stephen, although Shelleyan in nature and function, is the creation of another romantic, Dumas. Stephen rebuilds the "wonderful island cave" of *The Count of Monte Cristo* on the parlor table with "transfers and paper flowers and coloured tissue paper and strips of the silver and golden paper in which chocolate is wrapped" (*P* 62), but by the end of the third chapter, the cave of his mind has lost its romantic tinsel and emerges as a hell of sensual forms, populated by lecherous goats and fouled by defecation. After the hellfire sermon, when Stephen ascends to his room to be alone with his soul, his feverish imagination transforms his room into the "dark shell of a cave" haunted by voices and visions. As Stephen looks into his room "as at the entrance to some dark cave" (*P* 136), he sees murmuring faces, hears murmurous voices, and has his dream–epiphany of a goatish hell. Stephen gains a momentary insight into the hidden counterpart of the idealized caves of Dumas and Shelley, and it is partly this vision of the lecherous underbelly of romanticism that drives him to repent, and to retreat. Implicitly, Joyce – like Shelley before him – has challenged and exposed the one-sidedness of Prometheus's, and Stephen's, view of intellection and the physicality that embodies it.

The logical culmination of Stephen's renewed commitment to Christianity is his induction into the Order, but when the director invites him to declare his vocation, Stephen's mind is again likened to a cave. Here, Stephen's mind is reflecting not the idealized retreats and hidden hells of a romantic sensibility, but the comparable enclosure of a more "ordered" one. Joyce employs the same image to depict the limitations of a classical or religious sensibility that

18   *Essays and Introductions*, p. 86.

he used to expose the ideals of a romantic one, although Stephen fails to appreciate the extent to which his mind reflects the cloister he thinks he rejects (see *P* 192). As Stephen talks with the director, "the caves of his mind" are besieged with numerous apparitions the meaning of which he fails to grasp. He cannot see the priest's face, but only its shadow, "its image or spectre only passing rapidly across his mind" (*P* 155). The shadow of the priest brings up the shadows of his early Jesuit masters, and Stephen is troubled by the sensation that there is something that he cannot see behind the images in his mind: "Masked memories passed quickly before him: he recognized scenes and persons yet he was conscious that he had failed to perceive some vital circumstance in them" (*P* 157). Stephen's vision of the priesthood melds into a vision of his own mind, and the imagery that characterizes both is decidedly Platonic. He, like the priests he ostensibly rejects, is one of the prisoners in the cave of body and world that Plato presents as an image of worldly existence in the *Republic*. Chained there from childhood, the prisoners can see only apparitions flitting before them:

> . . . prisoners so confined would have seen nothing of them-
> selves or of one another, except the shadows thrown by the
> fire-light on the wall of the Cave facing them, would they? . . .
> Now, if they could talk to one another, would they not
> suppose that their words referred only to those passing shad-
> ows which they saw? . . .
> And suppose their prison had an echo from the wall facing
> them? When one of the people crossing behind them spoke,
> they could only suppose that the sound came from the shadow
> passing before their eyes . . .
> In every way, then, such prisoners would recognize as real-
> ity nothing but the shadows of those artificial objects.[19]

Unlike Prometheus' cave, which encloses only the most beautiful physical forms, the mental cave that defines the religious sensibility contains, like Plato's, not physical beings but their shadows. Both caves, the Platonic and the Neoplatonic, deny the doubleness of the human mind, perceiving it as a single term in the opposition

19 *The Republic*, trans. and ed. Francis MacDonald Cornford (New York: Oxford, 1941), pp. 228–9.

between the ideal and the real. A younger Joyce had once castigated Shelley for a one-sided idealism comparable to that of Griffith, Ibsen, Skeffington, Bernard Vaughn, St. Aloysius, and Renan, declaring in a letter to Stanislaus that his novel (*Stephen Hero*) would represent and expose their pretensions along with his own: "I am nauseated by their lying drivel about pure men and pure women and spiritual love and love for ever: blatant lying in the face of truth" (*SL* 129). However, Joyce's response to Shelley fluctuated: he also announced that in his history of literature he gave "the highest palms to Shakespeare, Wordsworth, and Shelley" (*SL* 32), and while he was in Rome he made a point of tracking down the house where Shelley wrote *The Cenci* and *Prometheus Unbound* (*SL* 90) and even Shelley's "granddaughter or grand-niece" (whose name, as he noted, happened to be Nora), to whom he gave ten pounds (*SL* 131).

The contradictory nature of Joyce's early response to Shelley helps to fortify the distinction between author and persona in *Portrait*. Stephen is attracted by the aspects of Shelley that Yeats praised: his apparent otherworldliness, together with his plangent idealization of reflections, both mental and lunar. However, Joyce mines *Prometheus Unbound* for the more complex and internally inconsistent insights that are unavailable to Stephen: Shelley's understanding of the interrelationship of classicism and romanticism, and his appreciation of the way that language molds and even creates the shape of the realities we experience.

In the "Preface" to *Prometheus Unbound*, Shelley declares his intention to imitate the "arbitrary discretion" of the Greeks in their selection and treatment of subject matter, and at the same time to take issue with Aeschylus' treatment of Jupiter in *Prometheus Bound*. Shelley's appropriative and yet critical attitude toward his classical model is exactly the double attitude that Joyce adopts toward Shelley. Moreover, Shelley's characterization of Prometheus is as indebted to Milton's Satan as to Aeschylus' Prometheus, and his depiction of Prometheus' cave springs from a marriage of Plato and Porphyry. Joyce, following Shelley's lead, leads his predecessors into the ark of fiction in pairs: Shelley with Byron, Christ with Lucifer, Aristotle with Aquinas, Homer with Shakespeare, Pater with Penelope, himself with Yeats.

Shelley's classicism permeates his romanticism in a particularly fruitful way for anyone interested in the name "Dedalus." His imagery suggests that Daedalus' labyrinth exists inside the cave of the mind in the form of language and thought. When the spirits "Whose homes are the dim caves of human thought" (I, 559) flee, their words continue to reverberate: "Which through the deep and labyrinthine soul, / Like echoes through long caverns, wind and roll" (I, 805–6). Shelley makes the classical allusion more overt in the last act, when the Earth declaims that

> Language is a perpetual Orphic song,
> Which rules with Daedal harmony a throng
> Of thoughts and forms, which else senseless and
>   shapeless were. (IV, 415–17)

Language creates both apprehension and beauty. It has a twin capacity to imprison, in its intellectual complexity, the bestial side of human experience, and to summon it back with its sensual song; it combines the inventiveness of Daedalus, beset by the Minotaur he helped to create, with the charms of Orpheus, surrounded by the beasts his song entrances.

Shelley's cave is Platonic to the extent that it seems to owe its existence to words, shadows of the sensual forms they represent, and Neoplatonic to the extent that words are themselves objects that can be experienced only through the senses. Stephen, like Shelley, sees language on the wall of his mental cave, but the character of the language that he sees is always shifting: it is alternately a vision of abstracted forms, a world of Platonic "copies," and a world of sensual experiences that challenges the authority of abstract thought. Stephen experiences the doubleness of language, but lacks, in his immaturity, any awareness of or control over that doubleness, since, as Joyce suggests in *Ulysses*, recognition is the province not of Daedalus, the inventor, but of Ariadne, the critic, who by threading the labyrinth of language rediscovers the perfidy of the word.

Joyce discredits an optimism that could imagine Prometheus unbound, presenting blindness as its counterpart and punishment (see Dante's threat, that if Stephen does not apologize, "the eagles will come and pull out his eyes"[P 8]). Stephen, like Prometheus, is blind to the complicity of order and disorder, freedom and imprisonment, imitation and recreation, in a way that Shelley, paradoxically, and Joyce, more consistently, are not. Joyce went beyond Yeats' reading of Shelley, deconstructing Shelley's stated intentions in order to reconstruct a paradoxical complexity that makes romanticism the structural counterpart of a disturbing and equally complex classicism. Joyce's sensual mode of reading allowed him to recover the "Roman" aspects of "romanticism," as his use of Ovid's retelling of Greek myth allowed him to romanize and "romanticize" Greece.

When Stephen tries, in Platonic terms, to model himself on an ideal, his language reasserts his – and its – ineluctable materiality; when he revels in his own sensuality, the structure of his experiences and his accounts of them betray his indebtedness to more general "types." When, in the fourth chapter, Stephen is attempting to transform himself into a hero of the early Church, beginning each day "with an heroic offering of its every moment," imagining himself "kneeling at mass in the catacombs" (*P* 147) and believing that he can mortify his senses (*P* 150–51), the sensuality of his own response to language betrays him. Sensitive to the hidden rose in "rosary," he relates without conscious irony that "The rosaries too which he said constantly – for he carried his beads loose in his trousers' pockets that he might tell them as he walked the streets – transformed themselves into coronals of flowers of such vague unearthly texture that they seemed to him as hueless and odourless as they were nameless" (*P*148). The flowers present themselves as "nameless" because their names – roses – would force Stephen to admit that a sensual metaphor is directing his response to even a "sacred" word.

When Stephen attempts to turn words, and himself, into reflective shadows of an ideal meaning, the sensuality of the body and of the word asserts itself, exposing the comic naiveté of Stephen's project. In counterpoint, it is when Stephen would affect an appreciation of purely carnal or sensual knowledge that his expressions become most typically soulful: chaste and chastened outlines of the lineaments of gratified desire. His account of the prostitute's caresses is as transparently reverent as his ecstasy in the presence of the bird-girl. Stephen's desire for flight – realized in his imagination, reflected in his high-flown prose, and projected onto the vision of a wading girl – is an attempt to deny the limitations of the body that the "pitiable nakedness" of his adolescent friends so clearly represents. Stephen, "remembering in what dread he stood of the mystery of his own body" (*P* 168), casts himself as a triumphant Daedalus, "and the body he knew was purified in a breath and delivered of incertitude and made radiant and commingled with the element of the spirit" (P 169). Listening to "a voice from beyond the world," he shuts out the voices from the world that call him a garlanded ox: "Bous Stephanoumenos! Bous Stephaneforos!" (P 168) Dreaming of Daedalus, the "hawklike man flying sunward above the sea," Stephen ignores the voices from the sea that remind us of Icarus' fall: "O cripes, I'm drownded!. . . Stephaneforos!" (P 169). He fancies himself a classical hero and a risen Christ, whose "soul had arisen from the grave of boyhood, spurning her grave-clothes" (P 170), when in reality he has only separated himself once more from the "dull gross voice of the world of duties and despair" (P 169).

In his epiphany of the bird-girl, Stephen has found another deity ("Heavenly God!" [P 171]), has "felt the strange light of some new world" (P 172), and has surrendered himself to the embrace of yet another breast, that of the earth. He thinks that he has discovered a new vocation, when he has simply combined the calls of the older ones. His "discovery" is an imaginative retreat into religious ecstasy, but it is also a sensual surrender to the romantic blandishments of language. He sees himself as Daedalus, but with "his cheeks aflame and his throat throbbing with song" (P 170) he is also Shelley's skylark, a "blithe Spirit" and an "unbodied joy whose race is just begun." Addressed to him, Shelley's lines frame his unworldly ecstasy with good-humored irony:

> Hail to thee, blithe Spirit!
> Bird thou never wert,
> That from Heaven, or near it,
> Pourest thy full heart
> In profuse strains of unpremeditated art.

Stephen's song, like that of the skylark, derives its beauty from "ignorance of pain"; like the unseen bird, he expresses the "shrill delight" of a "scorner of the ground." After his flight of fancy, which is "heavenly" in both a Christian and a romantic sense, he surrenders himself to the earth, conscious of the movement of heavenly bodies and the approach of darkness:

> He felt above him the vast indifferent dome and the calm processes of the heavenly bodies; and the earth beneath him,

the earth that had borne him, had taken him to her breast.
(*P* 172)

By the end of the fourth chapter, Stephen has drawn together his classical and his romantic yearnings, but only in the world of his own mind. What is most palpably lacking is an understanding of his human community – an awareness of Dublin.

DUBLIN, IRE: TEXT AND CONTEXT

The delusion that inspires Stephen more often than any other is the delusion that he can transcend the meanness of his environment. The euphoria that accompanies his anticipations of transcendence is expressed in many ways – in the literal uplift that raises him above his fellows at the end of the first chapter, as he is carried along in "a cradle of their locked hands" (*P* 58); in his expectation that he will be transfigured when he encounters his Mercedes, that "weakness and timidity and inexperience would fall from him in that magic moment" (*P* 65); in the ascent of prayers from his purified heart (*P* 145); in the idealized flights that conclude both the fourth and the fifth chapters. The most celebrated passage in *A Portrait of the Artist* is one in which Stephen directly expresses his determination to transcend the claims of his environment:

> When the soul of a man is born in this country there are nets flung at it to hold it back from flight. You talk to me of nationality, language, religion. I shall try to fly by those nets.
> (*P* 203)

It is Stephen's desire for transcendence that makes him heroic in *both* a classical and a romantic sense, yet the continuity of life and narrative impedes any real transcendence, which would be possible only through death. Any reader of *Portrait* whose reading is impelled by a transcendent ideal, by a desire to escape the "nets" of language, religion, and nationality and in so doing ascend into an esthetic ether, will experience the resistance the book offers to such flightiness. The only lecture Stephen attends in the last chapter is on the subject of electrical resistance, which should alert us to the importance of resistance as a paradigm for Joyce's narrative technique; yet the precise nature of the resistance the book offers, as well as the significance of that resistance, are among its least understood aspects.

In *A Portrait of the Artist,* as in *Dubliners, Ulysses* and *Finnegans Wake,* the last chapter recomplicates the context in which the book has been read up to that point. Chapter five makes it clear that Stephen's struggle is the struggle between an individual and his context, a struggle that also defines the process of reading. The end of the chapter, in particular, is not only a diary of a young man preparing for flight, his entries alternately callow and full of hope – dismissive of the past, contemptuous of the present, and in love with the "wild spring" of the future – but also a compressed casebook of the problems posed by language, nationality, and religion, bringing them into shared focus as representative problems of context: the pressure of a collective, past-laden present on the future-oriented individual. Stephen's "nets" are the nets of context (from *contextus,* woven together), nets that can and must be unwoven and rewoven, but can never be left behind, as the comic ironies of the first four chapters demonstrate.

A character can alter his or her context, but context also determines character. Like Gerty MacDowell in "Nausicaa," who not only authors a fiction of soulful encounter but is authored in turn by fictions such as *The Lamplighter* that unconsciously determine the style and structure of her own inner narratives, Stephen is authored by religion (Christ and Lucifer), language (classicism and romanticism, with their emphases on truth versus beauty), and nationality (the native foreignness of Dublin). The last chapter focuses on Dublin as a double city in a divided country, its divisions subsuming and authorizing the divisions inherent in religion, language, and in Stephen himself. The literary presence that broods over the end of *Portrait* is, appropriately, that of the early Yeats, the outsider who both gave modern Ireland her romantic voice and who portrayed her contradictions honestly, a literary nonpareil who in 1899 was both celebrated and decried.

Joyce represents Stephen as an Irishman who, like Yeats, has heard the call of Fergus to abandon responsibility in order to follow poetic beauty, and this is the attitude toward his environment that has captured the attention of most readers. However, Stephen's means of escaping "the sloblands of Fairview" through a mental contemplation of "the cloistral silverveined prose of Newman" (*P* 176), memorable as it is, represents only half of his attitude toward

Dublin. He uses his reading to retreat from Dublin, but he also reads Dublin and its contradictions with painful acuity. He reads the narrowness of judgment and slackness of expression celebrated in its monuments: when passing the grey block of Trinity college, he feels it as an immobilizing weight. It "pulled his mind downward; and while he was striving this way and that to free his feet from the fetters of the reformed conscience," he comes upon its lightweight counterpart, "the droll statue of the national poet of Ireland" (*P* 180). If Ireland's conscience is rigid and weighty, its poetry is slack and lightweight: "sloth of the body and of the soul crept over it like unseen vermin." Similar contradictions characterize not only the city, but its more patriotic inhabitants as well: Davin, for example, sees no conflict between petitioning for universal peace and owning a Fenian drill-book (*P* 201–202). Stephen remembers his jaded isolation at the opening of the national theater, as he watched his fellow students protest the honesty of *The Countess Cathleen* – "We never sold our faith!" (*P* 226) – yet he still searches for the "soul of the gallant venal city which his elders had told him of," a soul that had "shrunk with time to a faint mortal odour rising from the earth" (*P* 184).

When Dixon, Cranly, and Stephen are leaving the library, they meet another image of romantic Ireland: the dwarfish "captain" with "stubblegrown monkeyish face" whose only love is Sir Walter Scott and who springs, according to local legend, from an ancestry both noble and incestuous (*P* 227–8). Stephen associates this image of Ireland's decayed gentility with Davin, whose "rude Firbolg mind" attracts and repels his own mind in a similar way, "drawing it by a quiet inbred courtesy of attention or by a quaint turn of old English speech or by the force of its delight in rude bodily skill," and repelling it "swiftly and suddenly by a grossness of intelligence or by a bluntness of feeling or by a dull stare of terror in the eyes, the terror of soul of a starving Irish village in which the curfew was still a nightly fear" (*P* 180–1).

Davin asks Stephen, "What with your name and your ideas . . . Are you Irish at all?" (*P* 202), but what he doesn't see is that Stephen is attracted, not to the superstition, insularity, and corruption that he sees represented in Mulrennan, Burnchapel Whaley, and his fellow students, but to a version of Yeats' Ireland, represented by a contradictory woman. Stephen pictures Ireland as the woman in Davin's story, "a type of her race and his own, a batlike soul waking to the consciousness of itself in darkness and secrecy and loneliness and, through the eyes and voice and gesture of a woman without guile, calling the stranger to her bed" (*P* 183). The woman who calls a stranger to her bed, like the country who welcomes invaders, provides Stephen with an unsettlingly double image of his country: on the one hand, he sees her as a "batlike soul," groping blindly in darkness toward a knowledge of itself through a knowledge of strangeness (see *P* 238), and on the other, as a positive image of inviting contradiction. Emma embodies such contradiction for him, as Maud Gonne embodied a sterner contradiction for Yeats; he suspects that "the secret of her race lay behind those dark eyes" (*P* 221). She is the flower girl selling her wares, both guileless and hoydenish (*P* 183); she is Rosie O'Grady as Stephen imagines her, "woman as she appears in the liturgy of the church" (*P* 244); she is the rose which for Yeats was both mystical and sexual, a religious, literary, and national symbol. Stephen's attitude toward her is most Yeatsian when he composes the villanelle for her, a poem inspired by "the rose that was her wilful heart" (*P* 218),[20] but even then Stephen's debt is not simply to an individual, but to the contexts that define both himself and Yeats, since his poem intertwines Yeats' imagery with the Christian and romantic imagery that influenced him so strongly in his youth. Stephen's rose is not only that of Yeats, but of Dante and Samuel Butler as well, his weariness an echo of 1890s weariness that runs through all the passages from Shelley, Jonson, and Newman that have furnished his thoughts from adolescence onward.[21]

Stephen, like Yeats in *The Countess Cathleen,* has seen the Ireland that would sell her soul, and he has tried, similarly, to envision a justification for that impulse, but despite the critical acumen that allows him to anatomize Dublin with painful precision, he opts to transcend its contradictions through flight. However, the jaunty optimism with which the book ends parades itself as uncharacteristically poor reading, which in turn highlights the sharpness of Stephen's reading earlier in the chapter. In the last chapter, Stephen

---

20 Stephen's multiple plays on heart, beat, and rose as flower and rise are indebted to *The Rose* and *The Wind Among the Reeds.*
21 *"Art thou pale for weariness"* (*P* 96); *"that pain and weariness . . . which has been the experience of her children in every time"* (*P* 164); *"I was not wearier where I lay"* (*P* 176).

shows himself to be both an exceptionally precise reader and a limited one, but both his strengths and his limitations map out avenues through which the reader can enter Joyce's *Portrait* and his Dublin. Stephen's insistence on precise definition pleads its own value when contrasted to the dean of studies' sloppy attitude toward language; the scholastic thoroughness of a reading that seeks to reformulate as well as to echo time-worn phrases contrasts sharply with Donovan's smug approbation of Goethe and Lessing on "the classical school and the romantic school and all that" (*P* 211). Unlike the undisciplined Temple – the Rousseau of University College – Stephen trains himself to hear "the unspoken speech behind the words" (*P* 242), which is how he comes to realize that Cranly "felt then the sufferings of women, the weaknesses of their bodies and souls: and would shield them with a strong and resolute arm and bow his mind to them" (*P* 245). Moreover, Stephen schools himself to suspend judgment in the knowledge that every "shaft" comes "back to its bowstring," chiding himself for his impatience with MacAlister by asking himself, "Can you say with certitude by whom the soul of your race was bartered and its elect betrayed – by the questioner or by the mocker?" (*P* 193–4)

As a reader, Stephen is potentially rigorous and honest, but his reading, like his experience, is not extensive; as he notes in his diary, "Have read little and understood less" (*P* 248). He still shows little awareness of the dialectical relationship between his story and history, the double interplay of text and context. His diary is significant partly because it is a record of Stephen's interpretations, a record that he himself makes. That record serves as a compendium of various interpretive possibilities that the rest of the book enables us to evaluate. Contextualized, Stephen's "readings" all emerge as different ways of contextualizing perception, as relevant to our way of reading him as they are to his way of reading his peers.[22]

Stephen's diary begins with a grossly reductive reading of Cranly that is all the more repulsive in contrast to the eloquent scene that precedes and inspires it. For a moment, Stephen understands Cran-

22 My analysis of the diary section concentrates mainly on what it implies about the reading process, both ours and Stephen's. For the best account of the diary as an appropriately ambivalent ending to the entire book, see Michael Levenson's excellent essay, "Stephen's Diary in Joyce's *Portrait* – The Shape of Life," ELH 52 (1985): 1017–35.

ly's sympathy for women as a product of his loneliness and fear, but he distances himself from that realization by using a particular exegetical strategy: he uses only one fact to "explain" Cranly's difference in perspective – the age of his mother. Stephen frames Cranly through his imaginative reconstruction of the circumstances of Cranly's life, dismissing his "despair of soul" as that of a "child of exhausted loins" (P 248). Stephen's first "reading" is almost a parody of the biographical fallacy, an exposé of the distortion caused by oversimplifying the contexts of interpretation.

The next morning Stephen elaborates on his reading of Cranly by identifying him with a single biblical analogue – John the Baptist. Not only is his reading allegorically reductive, but it is clearly self-serving as well: he subordinates Cranly to himself by casting Cranly as his precursor, which makes Stephen Christ. Again, Stephen's ploy exposes, through caricature, the distortion caused by reading through only one frame of reference, a distortion often motivated by the desire to see in someone else's situation a prophecy of one's own. The one-sidedness of Stephen's interpretation of Cranly acts as a warning against methodologies that link a character with a single precursor, whether that precursor be Christ, Satan, Daedalus, or Icarus. By implication, the contexts of interpretation must be as complex and variable as Dublin itself.

When Stephen quotes a portion of Blake's "William Bond" as an expression of his fear that Emma might die, his error is again to ignore the context of the excerpt. Stephen makes fun of the pathos of the poem – "Alas, poor William" – and in so doing violates the spirit of the poem as a whole, which imprecates its readers to "Seek Love in the Pity of other's Woe." Insensitivity to context does not increase sensitivity to the individual; on the contrary, it stifles it. It is only when Stephen glimpses the inadequacy of his prior readings, the reductiveness of his interpretive tendencies, that he begins to appreciate and even to enjoy his experience of others. When he records his meeting with Emma in Grafton Street, he caricatures his own posturings, and for a moment he approaches genuine liking for her and a consciousness of his own limitations: "Yes, I liked her today. A little or much? Don't know. I liked her and it seems a new feeling to me. Then, in that case, all the rest, all that I thought I thought and all that I felt I felt, all the rest before now, in fact . . . O, give it up, old chap! Sleep it off!" (P 252).

What Stephen lacks is not an awareness of his own contradictory nature, but an acceptance of it. This is apparent throughout the last chapter, where Stephen's omissions help to create the very context by which he can be evaluated. What he omits in his theoretical discussion with Lynch is consistent with what is lacking in each of the other climactic scenes of the last chapter: he tells Lynch that "When we come to the phenomena of artistic conception, artistic gestation and artistic reproduction I require a new terminology and a new personal experience," and Lynch replies, "But you will tell me about the new personal experience and new terminology some other day" (*P* 209–10). Similarly, in the scene with Cranly, Stephen is unable to answer when Cranly asks him if he has ever loved anyone (*P* 240); during his composition of the villanelle, Stephen's onanism suggests that his artistic creations are as fruitless as is his solitary, physical ejaculation. Artistic conception, gestation, and reproduction result from a union of opposites in the act of love, a doubling that, together with Dublin, Stephen elects to escape. What he fails to understand is the double nature of authority, an awareness that would make him an "artist" as well as a portrayed subject, an acceptance of the fact that, in the words of Jeremy Lane, there is "no final authorisation, no simple authority, no single author; but a relative authorisation, the sanction of relation whose dual principle seeds plurality, admitting and containing its contrary."[23]

To paraphrase Wordsworth's famous statement, an author differs from other characters in degree, but not in kind. What differentiates authors – and readers – of a fiction from the characters within a fiction is, potentially, a more disturbing awareness of the nets that no individual can elude, and that all must attempt to elude, a sensitivity to the complex interdependence of all human and verbal contexts, and an acceptance of the multiplicity and sameness of all characters participating in an interactive system. With such an awareness, an "author" can recreate and interpret such systems through imaginative doubling, whereas without such an awareness the "character" will reenact prior narratives in unintentional and unproductive – repetitive – ways. However, this distinction between "author" and "character" is itself, like all oppositions, an

---

23 "His master's voice? The questioning of authority in literature," in *The Modern English Novel: The Reader, the Writer and the Work,* ed. Gabriel Josipovici (New York: Harper and Row, 1976), p. 126.

heuristic one, since it is impossible to be permanently inside or outside a system so long as that system and our awareness of it are subject to change. Every author is necessarily a character, or subject, and every character an author – and authority – in a dialogical process that produces no final synthesis: Joyce is, alternately, both within and outside the book, as are other authors, such as Shelley and Byron, and all of its readers, including ourselves. In this respect, as in several others, the language of the book defines a community not unlike the community Stephen is attempting to escape at the end, as he goes "to encounter for the millionth time the reality of experience" (*P* 252–3). Ironically, the book ends with Stephen asking his father, and author, to direct him by his precedent: "Old father, old artificer, stand me now and ever in good stead" (*P* 253). Stephen is recording his hope that his father will continue to do what he was doing for Stephen when the book opened, authoring and authorizing the story of Stephen's youth.

3

REFLECTION AND OBSCURITY IN
ULYSSES

THE DEFINITION of Stephen's contradictory nature by means of literary and religious analogues – classicism and romanticism, Christ and Lucifer – is appropriate for a character whose main preoccupation is words. When Joyce shifts his focus from the high-flown prose of Stephen's mind to the more prosaic Bloom, he continues to probe the identity of extremes, but he does so not only by evoking classical and romantic myth, but also by analyzing the two household objects that have long symbolized alternative ways of seeing what couldn't otherwise be seen: the mirror and the lamp. Joyce's treatment of the mirror and the lamp in the "Circe" episode of *Ulysses* suggests that they, like the classicism and romanticism they have been said to represent,[1] are structural counterparts to one another: each is designed to extend the faculty of vision by separating and reuniting a set of extremes – the subject and object of perception, divided and reintegrated

---

1   The most comprehensive modern example of linking classicism with the mirror (because of its emphasis on realistic mimesis) and romanticism with the lamp (because of its emphasis on emanations from within) is M. H. Abrams' well known study, *The Mirror and the Lamp: Romantic Theory and the Critical Tradition* (Oxford: Oxford University Press, 1953).

through a mirror, and darkness and light, which are equally essential to the functioning of a lamp.

When seen as twin images of interdependent extremes, the mirror and the lamp, together with the conceptions of classical realism and romanticism that they represent, display their fundamental similarity, and their differences emerge as differences of emphasis. In his treatment of the mirror, Joyce refuses to privilege the perceiver over the reversed self-image he perceives, thereby restoring reciprocity as a condition of reflection; in his treatment of the lamp, he redirects attention to the double agency of lamp and shade in producing the desired diffusion of light. Although the mirror has been used to illustrate the primacy of external reality over its reflections, and the lamp to legitimate the opposite view that vital truth emanates from within, Joyce commonsensically suggests that the utility of both mirror and lamp is a function of the doubleness of each. His attention to shades, as images of the necessary limits of body and imagination, is an implicit challenge to a view of romanticism as purely transcendent, just as his insistence on the imaginative need for a reflected image helps to mitigate the skepticism characteristic of realism. Just as in *Portrait* Joyce deauthorized the privilege of Word over flesh simply by emphasizing the constant rhythm of fall and rise, integration and separation, that characterizes both, so in *Ulysses* he deauthorizes the privilege of perceiver over perceived and of light over darkness, reminding us in the process that an unreflected individual is necessarily unreflective, and that an unshadowed light is blinding.

Mirror and lamp both illustrate the mutual dependence of opposites, but the character of the interaction also differs in a way that clarifies the main difference between Stephen, who wages drunken war upon a lamp, and Bloom, who is associated primarily with mirrors. In a lamp, light and shade seem more sharply opposed than similar; they carry out their compound function by working against one another. In a mirror, perceiver and perceived seem more like than unlike; the differences are in the reversed orientation of the image and its lack of actual depth. This is also the difference between Stephen's reaction to a contradictory authority and Bloom's: in Stephen, two opposing modes of thought – one authoritative, the other figurative – fight for mastery, a conflict that produces some unusually illuminating theories. In contrast, Bloom, at least by the end of "Circe," sees opposed reflections as essential to a conscious or unconscious appreciation of the fullness of the contradictory reality they heuristically partition, an insight that allows him to return home to his "opposite," and to himself.

THE MIRROR

Ulysses employs reflective devices at every level. Not only does the book itself reflect, in different ways, *The Odyssey* and *Hamlet,* but Stephen, Bloom, and Molly all mirror various aspects of one another, as do individual chapters and even sections.[2] Such instances of reciprocal relation help to construct a value that the book sometimes parodies, but never denies: the value of reflection, the reflexivity of relation. Reflection is valuable primarily as a means of dislocating our perspective, momentarily repositioning it in opposition to ourselves. This is the objective Bloom contemplates in "Nausicaa": "See ourselves as others see us. So long as women don't mock what matter? That's the way to find out" (*U* 13.1058–9).

The climax of *Dubliners* is a series of reflections that give Gabriel Conroy a chilling perspective on past and present. The self-images that he comes to recognize are cold and dead, but by positioning himself in opposition to them – which he has to do in order to discover his own reflection in them – he gives evidence of a latent vitality. In *Portrait,* the only image Stephen encounters that even remotely reflects the conflicts that divide him is Dublin, and when we last see him, it is Dublin that he is attempting to flee. Stephen meets his image unexpectedly, and with little or no conscious awareness that he has done so, in Leopold Bloom. Bloom, in turn, confronts not one but two images of himself, in Stephen and in Molly. It is less surprising that he would seek his image in Stephen, whom he admires, than that he would discover and accept an equal

2 The last three chapters offer a reversed reflection of the first three, as Joyce's schema makes apparent (see Ellmann, *Ulysses on the Liffey*); chapters four through six mirror one through three in a slightly different way, through simultaneity; the beginning of "Wandering Rocks" (Father Conmee, as a representative of the Church) reflects its end (the Viceroy, representative of the State); and "Circe" gives back a detailed and reversed reflection of the first fourteen episodes, to give just a few examples.

likeness in Molly, whom he – on this day, at least – resents. The "Circe" episode propels Bloom toward a half-conscious recognition of the defensive motives that prompt him to pursue Stephen and distance himself from Molly, when both serve as objectified reflections of different parts of himself. They both authorize, in opposite ways, the fullness of his being, and he discovers himself in the act of trying to choose *between* them. In the end, he accepts the fact that, in Wallace Stevens' words,

> He had to choose. But it was not a choice
> Between excluding things. It was not a choice
>
> Between, but of. He chose to include the things
> That in each other are included, the whole,
> The complicate, the amassing harmony.
>   ("Notes toward a Supreme Fiction")

It is reflection that makes his modified (and somewhat mollified) decision possible.

"Circe" itself is the most extended and complicated mirror in *Ulysses*. In "Circe," Joyce instructs his phantom players to hold a real mirror up to Bloom and Stephen, a stylistic mirror up to the first part of *Ulysses,* and a symbolic mirror up to nature, art, and the reader. Throughout "Circe," the material object and its illusory image are presented as interdependent, and interchangeable, as Joyce shows by using stylistic techniques that imitate the properties of a mirror. In one of the "Circe" notesheets, Joyce observed that a mirror reflects what is behind the spectator,[3] a property that he reproduces stylistically by turning the episode into a jumbled reprise of what the reader has left behind – events and episodes from the first fourteen chapters of the book.[4] Moreover, "Circe" is full of verbal and onomastic reversals that represent the reversal of reflection: reversals of roles, sexes, names, phrases, slogans, and religious practices. "Circe" even inverts in a general way the progression of

---

3 See Herring, ed., *Joyce's "Ulysses" Notesheets in the British Museum,* "Circe" notesheet 10, p. 320: "see behind in mirror."

4 Two of the notesheets for the episode are careful compendia of the characters who have appeared so far in the book. See Herring, ed., *Notesheets,* "Circe" notesheets 20 and 21, pp. 362–7.

the day, ending, as the book began, with Stephen asleep.[5] Joyce presents the difference between perceiver and image not as a hierarchy of value, but as the neutral median of a single human reality. The saved and the damned sing the same message, forward and backward respectively. The parity of opposite values is even displayed through Bloom's ambidexterity, with its "sinful" suggestion that the two halves of the body, although "mirror images" of each other, are essentially equal.

Joyce's insistence on the parity between material objects and their reflected images, between external reality and the internal reflections that make self-consciousness possible, tends to disorient – sometimes profoundly – many readers of "Circe." That disorientation, when we experience it, should warn us that we are finding it difficult to process a systematic treatment of material and imaginative reality as equal, which in turn suggests that we automatically privilege one (material reality) over its counterpart (internal and external reflections). We tend to be more comfortable with representations that present images as mere copies of material reality, lacking the depth and autonomy of the "original." Such a model of relative value can then be applied to sexual, artistic, and moral oppositions – to justify a view of women as inferior to men, art to life, "vice" to "virtue." The counterparts and opposites of culturally designated authorities are thus, by definition, simulacra, unchanging and unchangeable, denied autonomy and speech, relegated to obscurity behind the reflections of light.[6] However, the legend of Narcissus (encapsulated for Bloom in the statue of Narcissus he contemplates

---

5   Black Liz, the laying hen from "Cyclops" (*U* 12.846–9), appears as a rooster in "Circe" (*U* 15.3707–11); the hackney car driver Barton James from "Sirens" (*U* 11.878–9) is listed as James Barton (*U* 15.3727); Mulligan, instead of intoning "*Introibo ad altare Dei*" (*U* 1.5), announces "*Introibo ad altare diaboli*" (*U* 15.4699); and the war on the last day is a conflict between factions with reversed names: "John O'Leary against Lear O'Johnny, Lord Edward Fitzgerald against Lord Gerald Fitzedward, The O'Donoghue of the Glens against The Glens of The O'Donoghue" (*U* 15.4685–8). This list could be greatly expanded.

6   See the analysis of the way women have been imprisoned "beyond the looking glass" in Sandra Gilbert and Susan Gubar, *The Madwoman in the Attic: The Woman Writer and the Nineteenth-Century Literary Imagination*, pp. 3–45.

in "Ithaca") warns that the love of a reflection paradoxically deprives the narcissist of the experience of a human counterpart; in Bloom's words, Narcissus is "sound without echo, desired desire" (*U* 17.2034). The alternative to the inequities of a silvered reflection is the possibility of a human one, like the one the narrator of "Ithaca" pictures for us in the penumbra of Bloom's garden: "Both then were silent? Silent, each contemplating the other in both mirrors of the reciprocal flesh of theirhisnothis fellowfaces" (*U* 17.1182–4).

A mirror can be used to represent and legitimate the inequality of doubles, but it can also represent the process of doubling and reuniting the self essential to cognitive and biological evolution. If the relationship between object and image is seen as an illustration of the heuristic splitting of the self necessary for self-consciousness, doubleness then illustrates the necessity of human relationship. The interdependence of doubleness and identity becomes more apparent if we consider not the *effect* of a mirror, its ability to produce reflection, but its composition, the *process* by which recognizable reflection is produced. A mirror is created by highlighting the *surface* of some transparent medium, whether glass or water, silvering it with metal or light. A mirror, then, can be seen as something that facilitates a recognition of the identity of opposites as well as their difference through a medium that is both transparent and opaque. In this respect, it "mirrors" the duality of language, with its power to serve as a transparent showcase for intended meaning, apparently effacing itself as a medium, and its concomitant ability to block the transmission of conscious meaning, asserting its own opaque materiality as a system that relates only to itself. Like a mirror, language offers both a means of self-recognition and a way of avoiding such recognition. Seen as a construct that is inherently double, it can alert us to contradictions in the perceiver; but seen as a method of establishing meanings that are absolute and unchanging, it may arrest the process of knowledge. Naming can and must temporarily freeze the movement of life, subsuming the love of pattern in what Meyer Abrams once called a "hardening of the categories," but it can also represent a temporary stage in the continuous process of self-articulation made possible by verbal doubling.

"Circe" is Joyce's most direct and complex representation of the interchangeability of sensual object and silvered reflection, and of the necessity of such interchange for a responsible awareness of the relationship between the self and its many reflected images. "Circe" shows how the tendency to disconnect a reflected image from its object allows the perceiver to disclaim responsibility for either. Bloom, by splitting his conception of Molly into idealized nymph and nymphomaniacal whore, has protected himself from the realization that he, too, can be divided along similar lines, caricatured as pig and prig. Circe holds a mirror up to Bloom to show him his identity with the woman he has regarded as a traitor, and he sees how his conception of her constitutes a like betrayal. In this respect, "Circe" resembles Joyce's only other "play," *Exiles,* which similarly moves us toward a recognition that opposition is always a mirage: when Richard accuses Robert of betrayal, he hears Robert leveling the same charge at him. The play ends in a psychological echo chamber, with each character by turns accusing and being accused of treachery, leading the audience to realize that the experience of treachery is always mutual. No one betrays without feeling betrayed, a realization that shatters Richard Rowan's assurance and threatens the self-righteousness of his opposition to the people he loves. By the end of the play, we have seen the illusion of opposition disperse itself into the reality of isolation, creating a "community" of exiles.

The firm conviction that treachery, almost by definition, is something perpetrated by a friend or rival but never by oneself, is a comfortable means of disclaiming responsibility for the mutuality of relation. In the earliest extant draft of "Circe," Joyce presents evasion of responsibility as one of Stephen's main targets: Stephen attacks the British soldiers for their refusal to accept individual responsibility for their actions. He repeats Haines' earlier thoughtless remark, "It seems history is to blame . . . not you"(*U* 1.649), and winds up his speech with a direct sarcastic accusation against both the soldiers and the state that brainwashes them:

> You are at present my uninvited guests in this the common-woe of Ireland. You may not be aware of it but you were sent to burgle on the premises. That is the wisdom of the State. Guilt is not brought home to the individual. In a firing party each man believes his neighbor killed the victim.[7]

7 Draft V.A. 19. See Phillip Herring, ed., *Joyce's Notes and Early Drafts for Ulysses: Selections from the Buffalo Collection,* pp. 236–7.

"Circe," as Joyce first conceived it, was apparently meant to function as a "trap" for the unwary citizen who disclaims responsibility for the rottenness of the state, like the "Mousetrap" in *Hamlet,* which Hamlet sets so deliberately for Claudius.

In Shakespeare's play Hamlet stages an illusion – a play – to give Claudius, when confronted with his own image, the opportunity to "proclaim his malefactions" and recognize his responsibility for the canker that is rotting the entire state. Like the play that Hamlet puts on for Claudius, "Circe" – even in its final form – has a moral purpose as well as an artistic one: it is aimed at the pretenses that serve both its readers and its characters as defenses. Bloom, unlike Claudius, does proclaim his malefactions before he leaves Nighttown, confessing that he has been "a perfect pig" and begging "Moll's" forgiveness (*U* 15.3397, 15.3151), but some characters, like Richie Goulding, prefer to adopt Claudius' role, calling for an end to the painful performance. (See his echo of Claudius' "Give me some light" as "Brights! Lights!" [*U* 15.516].) The reader's possible responses to "Circe" are represented in the play itself: he or she can choose either to see a personal reflection in Circe's mirror or merely to call stridently for the "play" to end. In *Ulysses*, every reader is a Claudius, given the opportunity to accept or reject one of the likenesses that "Circe" gives back.

Throughout *Ulysses*, Joyce carries on an intermittent dialogue with Shakespeare which takes as one of its recurring themes the nature of art as defined by Hamlet. In Hamlet's famous advice to the players, he advocates a mimetic view of art as a faithful mirror: art should hold "the mirror up to nature; to show virtue her own feature, scorn her own image, and the very age and body of the time his form and pressure" (III.ii). If Hamlet's assertion is taken to mean that art, like a mirror, should attempt to give individuals and even communities a detached view of their moral and physical make-up, his statement is inoffensive enough; but as the players would be the first to realize, such advice is vague – it can't be acted upon unless there is agreement about how a mirror gives back an image. Traditionally, of course, the mirror has been used as an image of *mimesis,* art as characterized in Aristotle's *Poetics* and in the tenth book of Plato's *Republic.* Joyce, however, seems to suggest that it is irresponsible to compare art to a mirror without defining more carefully what we mean by the metaphor. A mirror can represent a flawed, narcissistic, and slavish means of representation as easily as it can represent a means of self-recognition. The first mirror to appear in *Ulysses* is the cracked mirror held up by Buck Mulligan, which Stephen bitterly characterizes as "a symbol of Irish art. The cracked lookingglass of a servant" (*U* 1.146).

The limitations of Irish art as Stephen sees them are overcome by the more flexible methods of reflection Joyce employs in "Circe," methods that he illustrates through his treatment of actual mirrors. The first mirror that Bloom passes when he enters Night-town represents an attempt to remedy the "distortion" of a less distorted and more slavish mirror by multiplying the image and altering it in opposite ways. The three surfaces of this tripartite mirror are concave, level, and convex, and each surface is supplemented by a portrait of a historical figure, so that the various images constitute a "composite" portrait:

> *From Gillen's hairdresser's window a composite portrait shows him gallant Nelson's image. A concave mirror at the side presents to him lovelorn longlost lugubru Booloohoom. Grave Gladstone sees him level, Bloom for Bloom. He passes, struck by the stare of truculent Wellington, but in the convex mirror grin unstuck the bonham eyes and fatchuck cheekchops of jollypoldy the rixdix doldy.*
> (*U* 15.143–9)

The concave and convex mirrors give back, respectively, the Bloom of "Sirens" and the Bloom of "Circe" in the language and imagery appropriate to each episode, anticipating the imminent bifurcation of Bloom into Henry Flower and Virag, and they also identify historical analogues to the different Blooms that could be multiplied still further. The tripartite structure of the composite portrait even mimics the structure of *Ulysses* itself, implicitly linking Stephen to the poetic Bloom of "Sirens," and Molly to the animalistic Bloom of "Circe."

The mirror not only reflects a diverse cluster of Blooms, but it suggests that they comprise a single portrait. A sentimental Bloom, without bestial urges or practical levelheadedness, would be as mournfully lethal as Henry Flower, whose poetic idealization of women is portrayed as his habit of caressing a severed female head (*U* 15.2620). (See also Flower's pipe, the bowl of which is "fash-ioned as a female head" [*U* 15.2481–2].) In contrast, the animalistic Virag, when projected into a body uninhabited by Bloom or

Flower, treats his head as a dispensable accessory, unscrewing it and holding it under his arm (*U* 15.2636). Flower addresses himself only to the head of woman, and Virag doesn't need his head at all. As the mirrors suggest, Bloom has the potential to be any or all of these men; like HCE, "There [are] three men in him" (*FW* 113.14).

If the tripartite mirror of Nighttown, inserted into an episode which is itself an inverted reflection of the book up to this point, demonstrates the inadequacy of a single undistorted reflection to represent the variousness of identity, the next Circean mirror compensates for the inability of an ordinary mirror to reflect the unity of *different* spectators. Lynch recalls the context of Joyce's criticism of mimesis by announcing, "The mirror up to nature" (*U* 15.3820). When Stephen and Bloom look together into the mirror, they are confronted with a single image, the *"face of William Shakespeare, beardless, . . . rigid in facial paralysis, crowned by the reflection of the reindeer antlered hatrack in the hall"* (*U* 15.3821–4). The reflection speaks to Bloom, taunting him with the suggestion that Shakespeare's beardless and cuckolded image is Bloom's own, and obscurely reminding him that the destructive implications of Bloom's domestic situation are played out in *Othello*: "(*to Bloom*) Thou thoughtest as how thou wastest invisible. Gaze. (*he crows with a black capon's laugh*) Iagogo! How my Oldfellow chokit his Thursdaymornun. Iagogogo!" (*U* 15.3826–9)

The blending of Stephen and Bloom in Shakespeare is reflected not only through the mirror image, but through the allusion to *Othello*. *Othello* dramatizes the destructiveness of sexual jealousy, warning Bloom of the necessity to accept his parity with other men. The implied alternative to the violence engendered by fear and jealousy is a double awareness of the identity of different men and of the different identities that comprise a single man, an apprehension of individuality that is incompatible with jealousy and violence.

The last time that Bloom contemplates his own image is in "Ithaca," where the narrator explicitly articulates and sums up the kind of reflection that we should now be seeing, an image of a man definable *both* in relation to himself and in relation to others:

What composite asymmetrical image in the mirror then attracted his attention?

The image of a solitary (ipsorelative) mutable (aliorelative)
man. (*U* 17.1348–50)

The image of a man is inherently double when defined in terms of
relationship; he is ipsorelative and aliorelative. But his relation to
others isn't simply a relationship to human contemporaries; it is
also a relationship to a community of imagined and recorded
figures.

What final visual impression was communicated to him by
the mirror?

The optical reflection of several inverted volumes improperly
arranged and not in the order of their common letters with
scintillating titles on the two bookshelves opposite. (*U*
17.1357–60)

Bloom shares the mirror with his library, reminding us that he is
a composite of type, as well as a collection of types, a disorderly
assembly of written, recorded, and imagined characters.

Joyce's various treatments of mirroring in *Ulysses* are all subtle
reminders that mirrors do not simply *copy* originals unchanged.
The classical ideal of *mimesis* is not a love of imitation, but an
appreciation of doubleness, since mirrors produce not copies, but
doubles that help the perceiver define the extremes of his or her
own individuality. Similarly, Joyce treats the romantic image of
the artist as a lamp not, as it is sometimes used, as an indication
that truth is an emanation from within, but as another concrete
illustration of the fact that enlightenment can only be produced
through the juxtaposition of opposites. A lamp is not, by definition,
an uncontained flame, but the partial confinement of a light within
a shade. Romanticism, like "classic" mimesis, can be reinterpreted
as a complex and subtle affirmation of human duality.

THE LAMP

The conflict between light and shade is one of the earliest and
most recognizable conflicts in *Ulysses*. Initially dramatized by the
contrast between the black-clothed Stephen and the "sunny" Buck,
whose "gowned form" gives off a "yellow glow" (*U* 1.314–5), it

emerges again in "Nestor" to highlight the opposition between Deasy and the Jews he fears:

– They sinned against the light, Mr Deasy said gravely. And you can see the darkness in their eyes. And that is why they are wanderers on the earth to this day. (*U* 2.361–3)

The narrator parodies Deasy's obsessions with a materialistic enlightenment by painting him in harsh sunlight, "the garish sunshine bleaching the honey of his illdyed head" (*U* 2.197–8), and the final image of him, chortling over the imagined triumph of Ireland over the Jews, hardens sunlight into the gold he loves: "On his wise shoulders through the checkerwork of leaves the sun flung spangles, dancing coins" (*U* 2.448–9).

Stephen, by contrast, aligns himself with those who take a dark view of humanity, with the Jewish and Arabic philosophers that the fathers of the Church worked to refute: "Averroes and Moses Maimonides, dark men in mien and movement, flashing in their mocking mirrors the obscure soul of the world, a darkness shining in brightness which brightness could not comprehend" (*U* 2.158–60; see John 1:5). When Deasy charges the Jews with sinning against the light, Stephen responds, "Who has not?"; and in "Proteus," he broadcasts "Somewhere to someone in [his] flutiest voice": "You find my words dark. Darkness is in our souls do you not think?" (*U* 3.415–16, 3.420–1).

In *Ulysses,* darkness, as a concept definable only through its negativity, signifies the cultural impotence of Stephen and Bloom, their status as outcasts from the literary and social establishments. They represent, in dress and in person, the "limit of the diaphane" that Stephen puzzles over in "Proteus" (*U* 3.7), in sharp contrast to the lighter aspect and attitude of Buck, Deasy, Haines, and Boylan. As *Ulysses* proceeds and the daylight is swallowed up in darkness, however, the ability of Stephen and especially Bloom to absorb and comprehend the lighter characters becomes increasingly apparent. Seen this way, *Ulysses* resembles a kind of inverted morality play in which the ethical advantages of negative capability are dramatized with the aid of nightfall, a drama that reaches its climax when Stephen shatters a light with his ashplant, crying "Nothung" as if, like Siegfried, apocalyptically calling forth a twilight of the gods.

In testimony to the power of darkness, *Ulysses* suggests that the human race resembles a horse race, and in particular the Gold Cup, Joyce's representation of a "black" human comedy in which undervalued darkness and waste ultimately win out over favored gold. When a dark horse, "Throwaway," unexpectedly wins by long odds over a general favorite, "Sceptre," whose name suggests sovereignty (both king and coin), the moral payoff undoubtedly goes to Bloom. The race playfully represents and celebrates the defeat of racist attitudes, but there is also a darker side to Joyce's analysis of racism. Through glancing allusions to Swift's Houyhnhnms, Joyce implies that an equation of humans with horses is both unnaturally rational and naturally irrational, thereby complicating the easy allegory of defeated authority, and suggesting that prejudice is more insidious than a rational view of the human "race" would lead us to believe. The more irrational evidence represented by the *chiaroscuro* of the characters' minds suggests that both Bloom and Stephen wage a private war against darkness that betrays their unconscious complicity in a system that, on another level, they consciously deplore.

Subconsciously, both Stephen and Bloom fear the very darkness that they appear externally to represent, a darkness that for them takes female form. Stephen is shadowed by the phantom of his dead mother, and Bloom by a Molly devoid of reproductive promise, as Joyce shows through the responses of both to the same "matutinal cloud (perceived by both from two different points of observation, Sandycove and Dublin) at first no bigger than a woman's hand" (U 17.40–2; Stephen perceives the cloud in 1.248, Bloom in 4.218). In the context of this more subversive reading, Stephen's triumph at the end of "Circe" is to smash not the light but the shade, as Bloom demonstrates when he relumes Bella's chandelier: "*Puling, the gasjet lights up a crushed mauve purple shade*" (U 15.4284–5). Bloom's psychological triumph is, correspondingly, to see Molly denoted at the end of the day, no longer by a cloud, but "by a visible splendid sign, a lamp" (U 17.1178).

The central tension in *Ulysses* might be described as the discrepancy between these two versions of its movement, between the valorization of darkness that constitutes its outer drama and the secret desire for enlightenment that motivates the inner thoughts and feelings of both Bloom and Stephen. The relationship of inner to outer drama, so conceived, is that of light to shade, turning

Ulysses into the structural equivalent of a lamp – as, seen in terms of its spatial and temporal reversals, it also resembles a mirror. A lamp, understood as the collaboration of inner light and outer shade, is an emblem of truth, but if the interdependence of light and shade is denied or repressed, the scales of justice are sprung. Unperceived, the conflict between public and private, announced and subconscious values constitutes a fundamental dishonesty, the dishonesty of rationalization. Joyce exposes Deasy and the Citizen by emphasizing such discrepancies: the contrast between Deasy's Tory politics with its rhetoric of union and his private exclusionary practices, and the disjunction, both comic and ugly, between the Citizen's hatred of England as the oppressor of the Irish nation and his own readiness to persecute Bloom as a representative of the even more disenfranchised Hebrew nation. Although most readers register the irony of the way that the Citizen's love of freedom serves him as a license for denying the freedom of others, relatively few are prepared to acknowledge that Stephen and Bloom are bound by analogous contradictions.

Although doubly disenfranchised by their marginal status in a dependent country, Bloom and Stephen still deny autonomy – which is to say complexity – to women, whom they alternately fetishize and fear. For both, women privately represent the silvered but alienated image or the constant shadow of their being, the limit of their otherwise agile understanding. Stephen, in a haze of spirits, never quite acknowledges that limit, which extends to include Bloom's Jewishness, as he unwittingly makes clear by chanting the anti-Semitic and misogynistic ballad of Little Harry Hughes in "Ithaca" (*U* 17.801–28). Bloom, however, does come to apprehend the injustice as well as the justice of his attitudes toward Molly, with appropriately mixed feelings. His perceptions are not rendered analytically, however, but imagistically, through an altered awareness of the interrelationship of light and shade.

What I am calling the outer drama of *Ulysses*, its gradual valorization of darkness as it is represented by Stephen and Bloom, is too clear to be controversial; but what has remained controversial through its relatively poor definition is the counterpart to that outer drama, the characters' inner drama that comes to life most fully in "Circe." Criticism of "Circe" reveals more about the assumptions that have shaped our interpretations of *Ulysses* than the criticism of any other episode, since with few exceptions, it attempts to view the chapter as the dream-climax of the book's "outer drama," rather than as a deeply disturbing counter-narrative.[8] One of the main functions of "Circe" is to suggest, through the complex language and imagery of dream, the extent to which Stephen and Bloom replay in their own subconscious minds the same primitive drama that they see at work in society as a whole – a denial of the duality of human identity and relationship in the name of enlightenment.

"Circe" is not only an uncompromising reflection of the book and its characters; it is also an extravagant imagistic revelation of the lights that mislead and blind them. Moreover, it shows that the lights the characters follow and the shadows cast by those lights are identical, underscoring the psychic identity of desire and fear. Stephen's fear of death and his desire for spiritual authority are the same urge, bound up in an image of his mother that serves as guiding light as well as haunting shade. Whereas Stephen concentrates on the internality of light, Bloom is drawn to its externality, its traditional associations with rational enlightenment, as well as to its hidden power to figure social reform, physical contact, and biological continuity through the irrational transformations of his subconscious mind. The lights that draw him in "Circe" are the "soapsun," what Virag identifies as a female "nightsun," and his own dead son. Moreover, the images associated with all his "suns" reveal that his hopes for political and reproductive potency are all contingent on his relationship with Molly – the soapsun, after all, arises out of the soap he brought when ordering her lotion in "Lotus Eaters." Molly, in "Circe," appears not as an image of shadowy sterility but of overpowering sexuality and abundant flesh – Bella/o, her power over men figured in the power of her chandelier over blind moths – and it becomes apparent that the image of her as blinding light is identical to her matutinal representation as a wasted and shadowy land. In their daytime minds, Stephen sees his mother as an image of the fatal flesh and Bloom sees Molly as an idealized nymph; it is only in "Circe" that those views emerge as rationalizations for prejudices that are exactly the opposite, making it apparent that Stephen has an overly spiritualized view of women and Bloom an overly carnal one. It is only through ap-

---

8 Riquelme's treatment of "Circe" in *Teller and Tale* is one of the exceptions.

prehending and thereby fusing these unacknowledged double visions that a more enabling perception of female – and human – wholeness emerges.[9]

"THEY ACTED ACCORDING TO THEIR LIGHTS"

In "Wandering Rocks," Father Conmee forces himself to be charitable toward "invincible ignorance" by thinking, "They acted according to their lights" (*U* 10.71–2). If acting ignorantly can be described as acting according to one's lights, then those lights must effect a kind of blindness; moreover, Conmee shares that blindness, since his ability to tolerate ignorance is born of his own ignorance of those he is forcing himself to tolerate. Joyce's relentless exposure of the easefully oblivious Conmee showcases a double irony: the irony of acting according to one's lights, a euphemism for acting ignorantly, and of using the unfocused notion of individual lights as a vague defense for one's own ignorance.

9 It is interesting to notice the extent to which the problem that Joyce dramatizes in "Circe" has prevented readers from seeing what is being dramatized. Although it would be inconceivable to see Joyce portrayed as anti-Semitic, he is still frequently represented as sexist, despite the clear suggestion in "Nestor" that racism and sexism are, in his mind, different expressions of the same phenomenon. What seems to have happened is that feminists such as Sandra Gilbert have acutely recognized the sexism of Bloom and Stephen ("Costumes of the Mind: Transvestism as Metaphor in Modern Literature," in *Writing and Sexual Difference,* ed. Elizabeth Abel, pp. 193–201) and have attributed similar attitudes to Joyce. Other critics, some of them feminist, reject such a view but have difficulty responding to the charge that Molly, as the book's only speaking woman, is hardly a balanced or desirable representative of the female gender. (See Bonnie Scott, *Joyce and Feminism,* chapter eight, for a recent account of the critical controversy over Molly.) These different readings can only be mediated through finely tuned distinctions between outer and inner realities as Joyce represents them, since *Ulysses* does not offer an external response to prejudice, but investigates the grounds that make prejudice, or one-sidedness, possible. Joyce demonstrates in *Ulysses* through the blindness of Stephen and Bloom what Richard Rowan understands more abstractly in *Exiles,* that sexism is the subtlest and most revealing form of prejudice.

Joyce first explored the misleading potential of the idea of individual lights in *Stephen Hero,* where Stephen uses the metaphor
of different kinds of light to represent different ways of interpreting
reality. He likens "traditional" ways of approaching the world to
magic lanterns that distort what they would reveal, arguing that
the only reliable source of illumination is the natural light of day:

> The modern spirit is vivisective. Vivisection itself is the most
> modern process one can conceive. The ancient spirit accepted
> phenomena with a bad grace. The ancient method investigated
> law with the lantern of justice, morality with the lantern of
> revelation, art with the lantern of tradition. But all of these
> lanterns have magical properties: they transform and disfig-
> ure. The modern method examines its territory by the light
> of day. (*SH* 186)

Stephen's distinction between natural daylight and the decep-
tiveness of "magic lanterns" sets the stage for an analysis of the
lighting of "Circe." Here, as in *Stephen Hero,* the only true light
is the light of day, but one of the first things we learn upon entering
Nighttown is that the "great light," the sun, is "Ghaghahest" – in
the West (*U* 15.22–4). The "illumination" that lights the district is
magical, deceptive; the red and green will-o'-the-wisps at the beginning (*U* 15.2–3) warn us that we are entering a region of delusive
hopes, mare's nests, and phantoms, where the tracks of locomotion
are set with "ignis fatui," or foolish fires, to lead travelers astray.

The many-colored lights of the episode, like the changing lights
of Bella's pianola, are both vivid and confusing, partly because they
don't illuminate the external action so much as the ideals of the
individuals who follow them. The two British soldiers, for example, are introduced as red lights in a red-light district, "*their
tunics bloodbright in a lampglow, black sockets of caps on their blond
cropped polls*" (*U* 15.60–2). As red lights plugged into socket caps
they are comparable to the lights on the tram tracks, signaling
danger, their "bloodbright" coats serving as a reminder that their
profession is to shed blood. Secondly, they humanly reconstitute
the "red lights" of whoredom in their readiness to sell not only
their own lives but those of the Irish for material gain.

Green as well as red signals flash along the skeleton tracks at the
beginning of "Circe," and when John Eglinton "*produces a greencapped dark lantern*" and claims to be out for plain truth, it is a signal

that the guiding light of Irish, as well as British, nationalism is about to be scrutinized (*U* 15.2257). His light is the "greencapped desklamp" of the library room in "Scylla and Charybdis" (*U* 9.29), warning us that we are about to be plunged into the green sea of "formless spiritual essences" (*U* 9.49). AE, the luminary of murky, theosophical and Platonic lore, appears as Mananaan MacLir, the Irish god of the sea, making unintelligible proclamations and displaying the eagerness of the Irish nationalist to play messianic victim. Echoing Christ, AE proclaims, "I am the light of the homestead," but immediately, "*A skeleton judashand strangles the light*" and "*The green light wanes to mauve*" (*U* 15.2277–8), the color associated with death throughout *Ulysses*. Irish nationalism is another false light, easily extinguished.

Bloom and Stephen, too, are blinded by the lights that guide them. In "Circe," Bloom, who typifies the modern, scientific, investigative spirit, repeatedly looks for the sun, source of the "light of day" that Joyce associated with the modern spirit in *Stephen Hero*.[10] Instead of the "great light" of day, however, Bloom is blinded by a "nightsun," which is literally the chandelier in Bella's brothel, and figuratively the whore herself. Virag, Bloom's earthy double, is the primary explicator of the way that lust makes men "insectuous," blinded by their "light[s] of love" (*U* 15.760). He presents the moth circling the chandelier in Bella's parlor as a "nightbird" blinded by a "nightsun" ("That is his appropriate sun,"[*U* 15.2426]). A few moments later, he becomes the moth, staring at the lamp and flapping against the shade, which he calls "Pretty pretty pretty pretty pretty pretty petticoats" (*U* 15.2477). The equation between lightshade and petticoat reveals that the identity of the "great light" of Nighttown that blinds men is the double power of female sexuality produced through body and clothing. The lamp is the fire of female loins, the shade the clothing that contains it, and men are the moths who eat through cloth and burn themselves on contact. As Virag explains, "night insects" only *appear* to follow the light: in reality, they are blinded by it, and he fears that they "shall be most badly burned" by the lamp that is their "nightsun," their desire to possess or to become women (*U* 15.2421–6, 15.2463), as Bloom has already been quite literally

10 In "Ithaca," Bloom is described as a "suncompelled" wanderer (*U* 17.2017).

burned for the sexual sins of his past (*U* 15.1926–56). Joyce suggests, in a treatment of insectuousness that he would go on to develop more outrageously in *Finnegans Wake,* that insects represent one of the many forms that all men assume, which makes their readiness to condemn one another's blindnesses that much more ironic. Bloom, for example, is handed over to the Fire Brigade to be burnt by a "brother" night insect: "Brother Buzz."

The nightsun that blinds Bloom is an image of what Bloom most fears: an unfaithful woman. By night, as by day, he is mesmerized by a "light of love," a "flash woman," a "nightsun," but Joyce also uses the image of the sun to illuminate Bloom's most cherished dreams: his desire for home rule, for social reform, and for a male child. Bloom keeps looking for the sun throughout the darkest hour of the night. One of his first actions in Nighttown is to wonder if a distant light is the *"Aurora borealis"* (*U* 15.170), and later the stage directions present us with one, in the form of a torchlight procession (*U* 15.1373). An "aurora borealis" is a false dawn, an optical illusion, and in that sense it represents a delusive hope, but it also means literally "northern dawn." The literal meaning of the phrase links the *aurora borealis* to the emblem of Home Rule, which also pictures a "northern dawn," the sun rising in the northwest (*U* 8.473–4). A sunburst in the northwest is, according to the stage directions, *"Bloom's weather"* (*U* 15.1469). Bloom's loyalty to Britain suggests that he doesn't want Home Rule for Ireland as much as he wants to rule his own home, but the subtle web of connections between the *aurora borealis,* the emblem of Home Rule, and a false dawn suggests that the desire for Home Rule, whether for Ireland or for Bloom, is a delusory hope.

The second "sun" to rise upon Bloom's horizon is his clean lemon soap. The soapsun rises cheerfully and antiseptically, singing,

> We're a capital couple are Bloom and I.
> He brightens the earth. I polish the sky. (*U* 15.338–9)

This vision highlights our awareness that another of Bloom's delusive "hopes" is to clean up the world, but one major problem is that reforms require money, as we see when the freckled face of Sweny, the druggist, appears in the disk of the soapsun demanding the payment of "three and a penny, please" (*U* 15.343). The face of Sweny in the soapsun recalls, with a comic twist, the vision of dawn that concludes Flaubert's *Tentation,* in which the face of Christ shines in the disc of the sun. For an English speaker, Flaubert's vision of the Son in the sun might naturally prompt the question posed in the title of one of the World's Twelve Worst Books, distributed by Bloom's bodyguard to the citizens of the New Bloomusalem: *"Was Jesus a Sun Myth?"* (*U* 15.1579). With the homophonic logic of dream, the pun on "son" and "sun" reappears throughout "Circe" as an index to another of Bloom's brightest hopes: his desire for a son, emblem of the home rule that he doubly lacks. "Circe," like Flaubert's *Tentation,* ends with just such a vision of the son, with Stephen as the dead Rudy, a vision that may well be just another "false dawn."

If Bloom is searching for external, physical light that takes a variety of concrete personal and social forms, Stephen is looking for a different kind of light: the internal, spiritual illumination of truth – constructed rather than found, and represented by the lamp. Joyce's metaphorical use of the lamp in "Circe" is anticipated by Stephen's famous discussion of the lamp as an aid to truth in *A Portrait of the Artist.* Stephen attempts to explain his method of analyzing esthetics to the dean of studies metaphorically, saying that he works by the light of two great church fathers, Aristotle and Aquinas, and adding,

> I need them only for my own use and guidance until I have done something for myself by their light. If the lamp smokes or smells I shall try to trim it. If it does not give light enough I shall sell it and buy another. (*P* 187)

The irony of the scene is engendered by the dean's insensitivity to metaphor. He begins talking about real lamps, his face "like an unlit lamp or a reflector hung in a false focus" (*P* 187), and when Stephen tries to explain that he is using the word as it is used in literary tradition and not as it is used in the marketplace, the dean again mistakes the tenor of his meaning. In "Circe," we are no longer granted the privileged position of *witnessing* misunderstanding, but are instead allowed to practice it, with only the episode from *Portrait* as warning that Stephen's continuing interest in lamps should not be construed only in literal terms.

In "Circe," more apparently than in the rest of the book, Stephen is looking for a spiritual father to replace both his lost God and the intellectual lights of Aristotle and Aquinas. Bloom wants to rule his home, but Stephen wants to free himself from the home that continues to rule him. Whereas Bloom places his faith in social reform, fancying himself as union leader, king, and emperor, Stephen longs to "save" people spiritually, as he reveals not only through his priestly garb and behavior but through his triumphant intonation of the conclusion to the Antiphon used during the Paschal season: "*Salvi facti sunt*" (*U* 15.98; "and they are made whole" – saved). If Bloom's fears are grounded in uncertainty, the uncertainty of sexual fidelity, Stephen's all center around certainty: the certainty of death and the need for salvation thereby engendered.

As Joyce dramatized Bloom's unwillingness to recognize his own image in his projections of Molly by confronting him with *two* mirrors representing, in turn, the multiplicity and sameness of his identity, he dramatizes Stephen's struggle against the "shade" of death by directing him to shatter not one but *two* lamps: one that he encounters near the beginning of the episode, and another that he attacks near the end. Together, the two incidents demonstrate the interdependence of love of light and fear of shade, of desire for salvation and fear of death. "Circe" shows where Stephen was when the lights went out: "In the dark" (see *U* 17.2067–70). More importantly, it shows that the darkness with which Stephen is struggling is his own shadow, that he has turned his mother's image into an alienated version of himself, "ended not endless." His sexism, like Bloom's, is a crippling mode of self-pretense.

For Stephen, as for Bloom, the lamp shares some of the characteristics of a human being. Whereas Bloom and Virag see the lamp as a symbol of Circe herself – its shade her skirts, its flame the fire of her loins – Stephen sees the flame as an image of the human spirit, with the shade as the mortal flesh enclosing it. This becomes apparent in his first encounter with a lamp. He is playing the role of priest, saving souls, and just as he triumphantly proclaims that they are saved, "*He flourishes his ashplant, shivering the lamp image, shattering light over the world*" (*U* 15.99–100).

Literally, what Stephen has done is to smash the glass that protects the jet of the gas lamp. The stage direction emphasizes that it is the *image* of the lamp that he shatters, or its reflection on the glass. When the glass, which is presumably smoky, is removed, a flood of light illuminates the area more brightly. Stephen is posing as a saver of souls, freeing them from the shackles of the flesh.

Stephen's drunken gesture humorously dramatizes his desire to shed artistic, "spiritual" illumination over the world, and at the same time expresses his urge to shatter, or defy, the limitations of the body; he longs to free the spirit of humankind from the chains of desire and death. His attempt to liberate the spirit in a brothel district is quite literally an "expense of spirit in a waste of shame," with all the astonishing egotism of such an attempt. His desire to "save" souls, to shatter light over the world, is identical to the desire he expressed in *Portrait* when thinking of the "patricians of Ireland housed in calm": "How could he hit their conscience or how cast his shadow over the imaginations of their daughters, before their squires begat upon them, that they might breed a race less ignoble than their own?" (*P* 238) Stephen's desire to shed light, like his desire to cast a shadow, is doomed by its exclusive self-referentiality.

Stephen is searching for spiritual illumination, but every lamp has its "shade," and Stephen's spirit is accordingly darkened by a shade without and a shade within. The "shade without" is the body, and it is this shade that he symbolically defies the first time that he shivers a lamp image; the "shade within" is the shade of Stephen's mother, the shade he is attempting to vanquish when he shatters the lamp in Bella's parlor near the end of the chapter. When standing *outside* the brothel, he dramatizes his attempt to free the spirit from the "external" shade of the body by shattering the smoky glass shade of a lamp. Whereas before he saw "through a glass darkly," he now sees the flame "face to face" (I Cor. 13:12).[11] Stephen's internal tormentor is the shade of his dead mother, who appears as the incarnation of Death, breathing, "All must go through it, Stephen. More women than men in the world. You too. Time will come" (*U* 15.4182–4). Later, Stephen announces to Private Carr, "Damn death. Long live life!" (*U* 15.4474) He dramatizes his defiance of the shade within once again by shattering the shade of a lamp *inside* the brothel, and he thinks for one apocalyptic moment

---

11   Paul plays upon the image of God as a flame behind a glass and man as a lesser version of the same divine "lamp" throughout Corinthians; see, for example, II Cor. 3:18. At the Last Judgment, the flame of the spirit will be "liberated" from the confining glass, which explains why Stephen imagines the final flame of the Apocalypse when he shatters the glass chimney of the chandelier in Bella's brothel.

that he has not only crushed the shade that imprisons his spirit, but that he has put an end to death for all time. He sees the brief flare of the lamp as time's final livid flame, and he imagines that he has finally escaped, not only from his private nightmare, but from the nightmare of human history.

Although the stage directions suggest that Stephen has put out the light for all time, Bloom reignites the gas and discovers that Stephen only smashed the chimney and crushed the mauve shade. But even the color of the tissue paper that shades the chandelier helps to emphasize the connection between the shades that Stephen has tried to crush and his terrified defiance of death. The shade was originally red, a reasonable choice for a red-light district,[12] but Joyce changed it to mauve, the color of Rudy's dead face.[13]

Despite their sensitivity to the injustice of stereotyped thinking, a thinking that focuses on single effects and not on the double or stereoscopic instruments that produce them, Bloom and Stephen caricature the women closest to them just as they themselves are caricatured. Women not only reflect their own image, but they remind us of their complicity in creating such images, a complicity that every human being casting a shadow must share. A shadow, as a human double, is the equivalent of a mirror image, representing the darkness as opposed to the accuracy of reflection, but emphasizing, at the same time, the inevitability of doubling the human form. But, Joyce suggests, the limitation of the shadow is the same as that of the mirror image: it is necessarily bound to the self that produced it, incapable of expressing relationship to others. As Stephen thinks in "Proteus,"

> His shadow lay over the rocks as he bent, ending. Why not endless till the farthest star? Darkly they are there behind this light, darkness shining in the brightness, delta of Cassiopeia, worlds... I throw this ended shadow from me, manshape ineluctable, call it back. Endless, would it be mine, form of my form? (U 3.408–14)

12 Herring, *Joyce's Notes and Early Drafts,* p. 223; draft V.A. 19.
13 When the tiny coffin flashes by the funeral procession in "Hades," Bloom imagines that the dead child within has a mauve face like Rudy's (U 6.326), and when the figure of Rudy appears at the end of "Circe," *"He has a delicate mauve face"* (U 15.4965).

The ended shadow, self-reflective only, gives rise in Stephen's mind to the words he has just written: "Who ever anywhere will read these written words?" (*U* 3.414–15) Communication, like sympathetic human contact, is only possible through an apprehension of shared darkness, a darkness that is endless, as well as ended; communal, as well as individual.

Stephen, as the character most given to contemplating his own shadow, gives little indication that fate has given him an altershadow in Bloom. In "Ithaca," however, Bloom apprehends Molly, who had heretofore served as his unacknowledged shadow, in a subtly different way. When they, "first the host, then the guest, emerged silently, doubly dark, from obscurity by a passage from the rere of the house into the penumbra of the garden" (*U* 17.1036–38), they are confronted with a spectacle of stars, the "darkness" that is always shining behind the brightness of day, which they discuss until a "visible luminous sign attracted Bloom's, who attracted Stephen's, gaze" (*U* 17.1171–2). That sign is produced by "a paraffin oil lamp with oblique shade projected on a screen of roller blind supplied by Frank O'Hara," and it denotes Molly, whose mystery Bloom "elucidates" through words (*U* 17.1171–81). Watched over by the image of light on blind, Bloom and Stephen silently, mutually, regard a reflection that is alien, "each contemplating the other in both mirrors of the reciprocal flesh of theirhisnothis fellowfaces" (*U* 17.1183–4). Comically, they urinate together "in penumbra," "their gazes, first Bloom's, then Stephen's, elevated to the projected luminous and semiluminous shadow" (*U* 17.1186–90). From the egress of Bloom and Stephen to the final period of "Ithaca," Joyce depicts a series of apprehensions that are truly double – similar yet different – from the doubled light and shade that represents a newly complex woman, to "the double reverberation of retreating feet on the heavenborn earth, the double vibration of a jew's harp in the resonant lane" (*U* 17.1243–4). Bloom, "with deep inspiration" (*U* 17.1270), resists his inclination to await the dawn, and reenters the darkened house.

At the end of *Ulysses,* despite the many dissatisfactions that linger in the characters' consciousnesses, light and shade, object and reflected image commingle in repeated images of double relationship. Even as Molly interrogates Bloom, the narrator draws our attention away from the narrated discourse to something that "moved visibly above the listener's and the narrator's invisible thoughts": "The

upcast reflection of a lamp and shade, an inconstant series of con-
centric circles of varying gradations of light and shadow" (*U*
17.2298–301), and Bloom's odyssey ends with a dark circle on a
light page. Consciously, little has been resolved, but the relationship
of dominant images has shifted slightly, away from narcissistic
projection and rejection, and toward a recognition of D(o)ublin.

FROM IMAGE TO CLOTH, FROM SUN TO EVE

Ulysses returns repeatedly, even obsessively, to the processes of
reflection and illumination, to mirrors and to lamps, accenting the
contradictory nature of each. Even when reinterpreted as double
figures, however, the two images share a limitation that *Ulysses*
helps to expose: both express a conception of the self that is individual rather than social. Neither the mirror nor the lamp can
adequately represent the multiple interrelationships and disjunctions
of created *systems,* whether linguistic or political. If the history of
Romanticism, together with the modern criticism that has extended
it, could, as Abrams has argued, "in some part be told as the search
for alternative parallels . . . which would avoid some of the trou-
blesome implications of the mirror, and better comprehend those
aspects and relations of an aesthetic object which this archetype
leaves marginal or omits,"[14] then the history of modernism and
the post-modernist criticism and theory that has emerged in its
wake might be told in terms of related metaphors of mind. Re-
written from the vantage point of *Ulysses*, Abrams' statement
would read slightly differently:

> The history of modern criticism may in some part be told as
> the search for alternative metaphors which would avoid some
> of the troublesome implications of the mirror *and the lamp,*
> and better comprehend those aspects and relations of *aesthetic,*
> *psychological, and political systems* which these archetypes leave
> marginal or omit.

Joyce suggests in *Ulysses* that both the mirror and the lamp are
incapable of reflecting or illuminating the aliorelative, mutable na-

14 Abrams, *The Mirror and the Lamp*, p. 35.

ture of human and written characters, and for that reason he supplements them with images of intricate interconnection, images that have continued to inform post-modernist literature, criticism, and theory.

A figure that expresses the systemic nature of language more readily than the mirror is the image of the labyrinth (navigable only with the help of thread), and finally its more flexible equivalent, the web. The labyrinth, like the image of a web that complements it in classical literature, is both a triumph of ingenious design and a prison, in which artist and Minotaur mirror one another, an insight Joyce shared with Picasso.[15] The counterpart of Daedalus the artist is Ariadne, the critic, who teaches Theseus how to thread the maze. When, after completing *A Portrait of the Artist as a Young Man,* Joyce left behind the mythological figure of Daedalus, it was to replace architect with storyteller, the creator of a literary maze with a classical Houdini as skillful at escape as at plotting: Ulysses. Whereas Daedalus' inventions entail the sacrifice of a woman and his own son due to the supposed animality of the one and the proud overreaching of the other, Ulysses redeems them. And his counterpart and equal in the quick-wittedness necessary to elude permanent paralysis is Penelope, whose most famous ruse is the weaving and unweaving of a web.

As a stylistic mirror that takes reflection as one of its many subjects, "Circe" reveals the logic that leads from mirror to web, from Bloom's Odyssey to the domestic revolutions recorded in Molly's final monologue. But the web, as figural supplement to the mirror, is also complemented by the image of darkness, an implicit response to the most familiar metaphor of enlightenment, both rational and romantic. Darkness, like the web, takes on a specifically female character that exposes the implicit masculinity of classical and romantic epistemologies. Joyce's restoration of equal emphasis to darkness and light not only infuses *Ulysses* with an amoral Manicheanism, but it also demands a reappraisal of the grounds for categorizing sexual and racial relations according to the theological treatments of light and darkness. *Ulysses* traces anti-Semitism to a denial of darkness, fear of woman to the cultural tradition that compensates for the fall of Eve (eve) with the rise of

---

15 See his sketches from the Vollard Suite.

the Son (sun). The web – as an image of nonlinear connection – and darkness both illustrate the irrational power of language to unify and entrap, demonstrating, in highly specific ways, the more insidious and poetic aspects of the interpretive process.

PART III

MULTIPLE AUTHORITIES

4

TEXT STYLES, TEXTILES, AND THE TEXTURES OF *ULYSSES*

THROUGH "ITHACA," the dominant images and styles of *Ulysses* work to achieve an uneasy balance. That balance is represented, not only through the co-agency of light and shade moving literally and figuratively over the characters' heads, but through the mirroring of the first fourteen episodes in "Circe," their reversed reflection, and through the catechistic style of "Ithaca," its voices engaged in a regular, practiced antiphony of question and reply that duplicates, in mood and structure, the determined equanimity of Bloom (*U* 17.2177–94). The kind of balance that has been achieved to this point works like a large-scale chiasmus, in which the linear sequences developed through "Oxen of the Sun" reverse their order in "Circe." As postlude to such a grand pattern, the final episodes, with the exception of "Ithaca," seem merely to provide superfluous commentary on a completed design, partly affirming and partly disrupting that design through a miscellany of unassimilated details.

The grand pattern that is consummated on the level of style in "Circe" and on the level of plot in "Ithaca" is, of course, the pattern of departure and return. Departure and return is certainly the most frequently orchestrated movement in the book: not only does it harmonize the book's main narrative analogues – the *Odyssey*, the story of Shakespeare's life, the Bible – but it shapes a surprising number of individual sentences as well as the overall structure of the plot.¹ The pattern is reinforced not only through allusion, plot, and syntax, but also through Joyce's emphasis on the diurnal departure and return of light and the departure and return of images through the process of reflection.

If Bloom realizes the movement from departure to return, displaying its attendant satisfactions and dissatisfactions, it is Stephen who showcases its theoretical importance. In "Scylla and Charybdis," Stephen argues that Shakespeare, both in his life and his work, used the strategy of exodus and return as a way of finding "in the world without as actual what was in his world within as possible" (*U* 9.1041–2), seeing life and art as a double mode of recovering one's own alienated images. What any wanderer traverses, and returns to, is always the variousness and singularity of the self, as Stephen illustrates by citing Maeterlinck:

> Maeterlinck says: *If Socrates leave his house today he will find the sage seated on his doorstep. If Judas go forth tonight it is to Judas his steps will tend.* Every life is many days, day after day. We walk through ourselves, meeting robbers, ghosts, giants, old men, young men, wives, widows, brothers-in-love, but always meeting ourselves. (*U* 9.1042–6)

Departure and return, Stephen suggests, serves as a paradigm for all cognition.

Departure and return also serves most readers as a point of departure for their own critical exploration of *Ulysses*. However, one can't go far on such an Odyssey without realizing that the pattern represents at once a tautology and a figure of change, a change that represents both gain and loss. To follow the book's many departures and returns is to participate in a cognitive paradox of the most disconcerting kind, a paradox that forces us to experience the stress as well as the release of understanding. *Ulysses* not only recapitulates a congeries of motifs of exile that have been central to Western thought, but it reinterprets the relationship between departure and return as disturbingly complex, suggesting that the two actions, like all convenient oppositions, are identical as well as opposed.

1   See, for example, Kenner, *Ulysses*, pp. 7–8, for Joyce's use of chiasmus in key sentences and its effect. On return as a major motif in Western literature, see Jeffrey M. Perl, *The Tradition of Return: The Implicit History of Modern Literature,* especially chapters two and eight.

The movement of *Ulysses* splits the reader's mind in two, forcing it to travel in different ways at once. Although the book gains momentum through a protracted promise to bring its readers "home," it also affects its readers as an exercise in progressive alienation. As an imaginative Odyssey, written in the double shadow of Shakespeare, whom Stephen calls a playwright of banishment, and his counterpart suggestively known as "Homer," *Ulysses* treats exile and return as deceptively opposed names for the same disquieting and meaningful experience, a strained comprehension of centripetal and centrifugal motion, simultaneous loss and gain, intimacy and estrangement. As we see in "Ithaca," there is no reunion without separation, no "handtouch" without a "lonechill" (*U* 17.1249). Return necessarily involves estrangement, since the reversibility of space will always be offset by the irreversibility – and irreparability – of time (*U* 17.2024–7).

By questioning the separability of exodus and return, *Ulysses* implicitly challenges not so much the pattern itself as the way in which it is frequently interpreted and applied. Since the process of interpretation is itself a miniature Odyssey, a movement away from and back to a problem (compare Stephen's formula for apprehension in *Portrait*), the way that we interpret Odyssean structures affects not only our understanding of the book's subject, but our awareness of the constructed mechanisms that allow us to understand anything. Traditionally, the challenge of exegesis, in literature as in music, is to find the point of origin, the "key" signature, and to explicate the means of departure and return. Interpretation is a "departure" from the text that justifies itself as a means of redirecting readers back to the work with new attention. Such an interpretation gathers authority not only from the classical epic tradition, but also from religion, which, as Milton claimed, palliates our exile from Eden with hope of an imaginative return to a "paradise within us, happier far." The relationship between exodus and homecoming describes the movement of a day, from sunrise through sunset; a life, from birth through death; and biblical history, from genesis through apocalypse.

In *Ulysses,* Joyce's emphasis on metempsychosis as the Greek twin of parallax subtly undermines any desire to equate "return" and apocalypse, or to anticipate absolute closure. Joyce's apparent affirmation of reincarnation has little or nothing to do with mysticism; it is simply a compressed reminder of the simultaneous identity of and difference between beginning and ending, of the doubleness of each. In the Odyssey of interpretation, too, resolution is necessarily double; although we may think of it as single and final, the various meanings of the word itself illustrate the identity of difference, since "to resolve" is not only "to reduce by analysis," but also "to break up, separate." "Resolve" derives from the Latin *resolvere,* to unloose, although it has also come to denote its own antonym.

As *Ulysses* moves to its inconclusive conclusion, its language and narrative increasingly exceed the pattern of departure and return, thereby stressing the insufficiency of a single noncontradictory cycle to represent the complexity of verbal and human experience. The reassuring symmetry of Bloom's long-delayed return is spoiled by Stephen's unexplained departure, a departure that, he has vowed, will *not* be a return to home or tower. Similarly, Bloom recollects an experiment he once attempted with a marked florin, tendered "for circulation on the waters of civic finance, for possible, circuitous or direct, return" (*U* 17.983–4). Bloom's hopes were disappointed, his loss of the coin a reminder of the "imprevidibility of the future" (*U* 17.980): "Had Bloom's coin returned? Never." (*U* 17.997–8) In place of the simple reciprocity between going and coming, we find complex coinvolvement, and, more disturbingly, a diffusion of individuality amid the chaos of unknown and unknowable relations. The hope of return is strained by the reality of diaspora.

Stylistically, the uncertainty of symmetrical closure is represented through the growing diffuseness of the language, its increasing opacity; and it is this stylistic diffusion rather than the book's structural symmetries and asymmetries that has rendered criticism most helpless. The style of *Ulysses* has only become the focus of sustained critical attention in the last ten years, but curiously, some of the most stylistically extravagant episodes of the book – "Circe," "Eumaeus," and "Penelope," in particular – have resisted even the temporary critical containment that makes reevaluation possible. These episodes have not passed out of the domain of criticism, or even style, as some readers have suggested; they have simply overspilled the boundaries set by the first half of the book and by critical methods that define development in purely linear terms.

Another difficulty in writing about the styles of *Ulysses* is attributable to an almost imperceptible crosscurrent of critical procedure that has influenced the drift of Joyce criticism. Beginning in the late fifties, approaches to *Ulysses* began, like the book itself, to propel readers in two opposite directions: toward a general and distanced overview of character, fueled by Richard Ellmann's influential treatment of Joyce's own character, and toward a specific, disciplined knowledge of individual episodes, passages, words, and even letters – their interrelationship and their textual history. Hugh Kenner's approach in *Dublin's Joyce* (1956) was certainly more textual than biographical; but the "textual" approach had no real focus until A. Walton Litz's *The Art of James Joyce* appeared in 1961, followed by Philip Herring's edition of Joyce's notesheets (1972), Michael Groden's *Ulysses in Progress* (1975), and finally by the *James Joyce Archive* (1978) and Hans Walter Gabler's critical edition of *Ulysses* in 1984. Although the textual and biographical orientations have complemented each other in the larger arena of Joyce criticism, the concept of style that emerges from each is quite different. The biographical approaches tend to favor more transparent uses of language that help to reveal character; such approaches have been immensely valuable in establishing an understanding of the early works. The textual approach, in tracing the evolution of the style, necessarily underscores stylistic eccentricities by reavealing the logic of their development, and in that respect is oriented toward the later stages of stylistic discovery, towards the unmapped complexities of verbal "resolution."

Until recently, the emphasis given to the biographical approach has far outweighed that accorded to the textual one. Morever, Litz's book was too finely balanced in its treatment of Joyce's stylistic extremes to precipitate a critical dialectic; he understood and represented that dialectic far too well to position himself in opposition to a complementary critical tendency. But in the last decade the growing influence of linguistic theory, together with recent work on the text of *Ulysses*, has begun to shift attention back to the opacity and materiality of Joyce's mature style. It has become possible to bracket Joyce's style with a specific knowledge of its textual history, on the one hand, and an awareness of contemporary theories of language and their philosophical implications, on the other. Since 1975, several studies influenced by one or both of these critical poles have provided stimulating new perspectives on the styles of many of the later chapters, bringing us deeper into the book – Michael Groden on "Cyclops," Colin MacCabe on "Cyclops" and

"Sirens," Karen Lawrence on "Aeolus," Richard Brown on "Oxen of the Sun."[2] What is most noticeably missing, however, is what is also missing from *Ulysses* itself, at least until the end: a balanced and convincing representation of Penelope.

In 1956, Hugh Kenner wrote that "Molly in 'Penelope' has no direction but that imposed by the vagaries of her appetites, and no audience but herself."[3] By 1980, the tone of his treatment had changed, but not his insistence on the episode's formlessness; he asserts that in "Penelope," "there is no 'style': for once, no style. A style is a system of constraints; it denotes limits, and implies our sometimes amused complicity with the stylist who knows what those limits are."[4] A. Walton Litz asserts that "Penelope" "does not contribute to the sequence of styles which is one of our chief interests in *Ulysses*,"[5] and Karen Lawrence argues that its stylistic conception is "regressive," presenting "something denied by the rest of the book."[6] It is "Ithaca," not "Penelope," according to Lawrence, that provides the stylistic inspiration for *Finnegans Wake*. Even those who, like Bonnie Scott, defend the style as a viable alternative to approaches represented elsewhere in the book, end up characterizing it negatively, through its difference from the book's other voices, rather than positively, through a specific account of *how* Molly's way of seeing, interpreting, and expressing the world of *Ulysses* differs from and complements that of Bloom.[7] The best recent analyses of "Penelope" have found an unsteady structure in the paradoxical consistency of Molly's inconsistencies; but inconsistency, like inconstancy, is still too complicit with chaos to challenge the dominant view of the episode's formlessness. With few exceptions, "Penelope" has been placed in critical quarantine and examined in only the most clinical or personal ways. As a result, Molly's methods of interpretation have never been taken seriously, tested for their possible application to *Ulysses*, or com-

2 Groden, *Ulysses in Progress;* MacCabe, *James Joyce and the Revolution of the Word;* Brown, *Joyce and Sexuality* (Cambridge: Cambridge University Press, 1985); and Lawrence, *The Odyssey of Style in Ulysses.*

3 *Dublin's Joyce,* p. 244.

4 Kenner, *Ulysses,* p. 148.

5 "Ithaca," in Hart and Hayman, eds., *Ulysses: Critical Essays,* p. 404.

6 *The Odyssey of Style in Ulysses,* pp. 204, 206.

7 For Scott, Molly's is the voice of a female "other"; see *Joyce and Feminism* (Bloomington: Indiana Univ. Press, 1984), p. 183.

pared with Stephen's poetic strategies.[8] Molly, like Stephen in *Portrait,* has served not as a figure of meaning within the book, but as a catalyst for reactions *to* the book.

The diverse collection of responses to Molly makes one of the most astonishing archives in modern literary history. The particulars have been well documented by Philip Herring and Bonnie Scott, among others,[9] but what makes the accounts significant is not what they tell us about Molly, but what they reveal about the values of her readers. In *Dublin's Joyce,* Kenner mythologizes Molly as a repugnant blend of Francesca and the Minotaur:

> Some readers have over-sentimentalized the final pages of her monologue. They are in key with the animal level at which this comic inferno is conceived: and they are the epiphany of all that we have seen and heard during the day. The "Yes" of consent that kills the soul has darkened the intellect and blunted the moral sense of all Dublin. At the very rim of Dante's funnel-shaped Hell is the imperceptible "Yes" of Paola and Francesca; they are blown about by the winds, but Molly lies still at the warm dead womb-like centre of the labyrinth of paving-stones. Her "Yes" is confident and exultant; it is the "Yes" of authority: authority over this animal kingdom of the dead. (p.262)

Robert Martin Adams, in a similar spirit, identifies her with "the principle of fleshly existence, foul, frank and consciously obscene." He calls her "a slut, a sloven, and a voracious sexual animal as conceived by one of those medieval minds to whom the female can never be anything but a *saccum stercoris;* she is a frightening venture into the unconsciousness of evil." He adds, less convincingly and with noticeably less relish, that she is also holy.[10] Darcy O'Brien's easy dismissal of her in *The Conscience of James Joyce* is less poetic and more startlingly Boylanesque – "For all Molly's attractive vi-

---

8 Brook Thomas is one exception. In "Not a Reading of, But the Act of Reading *Ulysses," JJQ* 16: 81–93 (incorporated into *James Joyce's Ulysses: A Book of Many Happy Returns*), he proffers Molly as a figure of the reader, with some interesting results.

9 Herring, "The Bedsteadfastness of Molly Bloom," pp. 57–61, and Scott, *Joyce and Feminism,* pp. 156–161.

10 *James Joyce: Common Sense and Beyond* (New York, 1966), pp. 166–7.

tality, for all of her fleshly charms and engaging bravado she is at heart a thirty-shilling whore."[11] Even one of Molly's most sympathetic and insightful readers, Joseph Voelker, treats her more as a complex symbol than as a woman whose mode of apprehension, like those of her male counterparts, might provide a model for reading *Ulysses*.[12]

The only consensus to be found among the critics is the conviction that Molly represents that too, too solid/sullied flesh that most readers, like Hamlet, would apparently like to see melt and dissolve. Generally, the vivid and zestful controversy over Molly, like the now-moribund controversy over Stephen, testifies to the marginality of both characters to our understanding of *Ulysses*. Because both have, in different ways, been dismissed from the book that criticism has reconstructed, the disparities between the end of *Ulysses* and its beginning, between Stephen and Molly, are far more evident than any similarities between them. Despite the fact that *Ulysses* takes marginality as one of its main subjects, the book's human margins remain largely unexplored.

There are many reasons why criticism has focused on the relationship between Stephen and Bloom, or on the interplay between Bloom and Molly, rather than on the structural pairing of Stephen with Molly, but one of the primary reasons has to do with the apparent two-dimensionality of their characters. When considered apart from Bloom, the characters of Stephen and Molly slide almost imperceptibly into caricature; they become disturbingly one-sided embodiments of male and female tendencies as disseminated through Christian doctrine. He seems to represent the Word, she the material world; he plays the Son and she the earthly mother. Even Joyce's unorthodox insistence that the role of the Son is a doubling of Christ and Lucifer, and that the role of Mary encompasses the two Maries,[13] while challenging the assumption that

11 *The Conscience of James Joyce* (Princeton: Princeton University Press, 1968), p. 211.

12 " 'Nature it is': The Influence of Giordano Bruno on James Joyce's Molly Bloom," *JJQ* 14 (1976): 39–48.

13 The phrase "the two Maries" is one that Stephen uses when thinking of the two figures on the beach in "Proteus" (*U* 3.297), but an even clearer indication of Joyce's identification of the two is apparent in his treatment of Molly not only as a whore with obvious affinities to Mary Magdalen, but as a woman with equally strong ties to the Virgin,

obedience may be separated from rebellion and chastity from profligacy, still seems to posit a fundamental difference between men
and women as the respective representatives of word and world,
mind and body. Such a polarization might seem to realize a theory
that Stephen toyed with in *Stephen Hero,* "a theory of dualism which
would symbolise the twin eternities of spirit and nature in the twin
eternities of male and female" (*SH* 210).

Viewed from this oddly Cartesian perspective, Stephen and
Molly appear to be a full world apart; divided by the sheer bulk of
Ulysses, they mark the two poles between which the reader and
Ulysses must travel. They seem to represent all the oppositions
that the book explores: beginning and end, mind and body, youth
and maturity, man and woman. If she is the flesh that always affirms
(*Letters* I, 170), he is the intellect that always denies. However,
when viewed through the language used to designate each character
rather than against the backdrop of cultural tradition, the differences
dividing Stephen and Molly display a structural similarity. If Stephen plays Telemachus, Molly is the Gea-Tellus (*U* 17.2313), the
shared syllables stressing that both have something to "tell us."
Both characters are obsessed with communication as a means to
the elusive communion they are seeking, and they prefer systems
of signification that, although superficially different, operate in the
same manner. Stephen is preoccupied with language, the clothing
of thought, whereas Molly prefers clothing, the "language" of flesh.
The process of reading *Ulysses* is the process of bringing these two
preoccupations together, of recognizing their relationship to one
another, and in so doing to appreciate, in a newly specific way, the
complex interanimation of language, society, and sexual difference.

From "Oxen of the Sun" onward, *Ulysses* assumes a slightly
different shape if we read as Molly reads. If we see clothes as a kind
of language and language as a comparably material construct, unexpected coherences and incoherences emerge. As language takes
on more of the properties of cloth, as it grows in opacity, sensuality,
and self-referentiality, it increasingly resists interpretation as a reflection or illumination of some prior reality or style. Molly's conception of language is not a secondary reflection of Stephen's, but
an alternative version that ends up being strangely compatible, so

with whom she shares a birthday (September 8), and whose name is
enclosed in her own (Marion).

that each reflects the other, expanding our conscious awareness of the range of linguistic possibilities. Molly's monologue, far from being an escape from style, makes possible a "recovery" of the text's styles through its complex relationship to textiles, reestablishing, in the process, our awareness of the affinity between materiality and dream.

Ulysses provides us with a specific description of one aspect of Molly's way of reading, although it comes to us filtered through two mediating consciousnesses – that of the matter-of-fact Bloom, and that of the even more precise narrator of "Ithaca": "Unusual polysyllables of foreign origin she interpreted phonetically or by false analogy or by both: metempsychosis (met him pike hoses), alias (a mendacious person mentioned in sacred scripture)" (*U* 17.685–7). Like Stephen, who asks in "Aeolus," "Is the mouth south someway?", Molly uncovers a poetic – or humorous – "logic" in the correspondence of similar sounds. Her technique, though unconscious, is nevertheless more complex than Stephen's desultory search for "Rhymes and Reasons" in "Aeolus" (*U* 7.713–24). Her method of interpretation is closer to the formula for esthetic apprehension outlined by Stephen in *A Portrait*: she associates an unfamiliar word with other similar-sounding words – alias with Ananias – and automatically resituates those words into a narrative context that is more familiar to her – the Bible.[14]

Molly's unexpectedly appropriate "misreading" of "alias" reinforces the suggestion that Joyce makes throughout *Ulysses* and *Portrait,* that the Bible serves as an unconscious model for much of our understanding of language and narrative. The implicit dialogue between *Ulysses* and the Bible – the New Testament in particular – is especially important for an understanding of how *Ulysses* progresses, since that progression is in part a response to the progression of biblical narrative toward a final Revelation. Like the Bible, *Ulysses* moves toward revelation, but revelation read as Molly might read it – as "re-veilation," the opposite as well as the twin of its biblical counterpart. Whereas St. Paul describes revelation as the process of seeing through a glass darkly and then face to face (1 Cor. 13:12), and as a rending of the veil (2 Cor. 3:14–18), *Ulysses* approaches revelation through darkening the glass and multiplying the stylistic veils, presenting its close through clothes. We begin

14 See Acts 5, as noted by Don Gifford in *Notes for Joyce.*

Ulysses with a deceptively clear vision that is gradually occluded; the book grows progressively more shadowy, along with the day it parallels, a tendency that culminates in the deeper darkness of *Finnegans Wake*. In place of the naked truth we may have been seeking, we find only an arabesque of shadowy disguises.

Two passages represent in microcosm the larger movement of the book towards a stylistic re-veilation that is also, potentially, a revelation: the passage narrated by the voice of De Quincey in "Oxen of the Sun," and the dance of the hours that materializes in "Circe." The De Quincey passage (14.1078–1109) translates the stylistic evolution of the book into images that take shape against the night sky, showing how female "nightmare" turns into Pegasus, or poetic inspiration, a feminized constellation writing, not on white paper, but on the darkened heavens; not with a pen, but using the more flexible medium of cloth. De Quincey's "nightmare" begins with the twilight phantoms of a mare and her fillyfoal, thin verbal guises for *une mère* and her Milly. They fade, displaced by the stellar "beasts" of the zodiac, "murderers of the sun," only to reappear at dawn in the form of the constellation Pegasus. Like the twilight equine phantoms of mare and filly, Pegasus is female, a girl "shod in sandals of bright gold, coifed with a veil of what do you call it gossamer!" The narrator's attention shifts from her to her veil, "sustained on currents of cold interstellar wind," "winding, coiling, simply swirling, writhing in the skies a mysterious writing till, after a myriad metaphorphoses of symbol, it blazes, Alpha, a ruby and triangled sign upon the forehead of Taurus," heralding the dawn (*U* 14.1106–9). De Quincey's "nightmare" is, in essence, an extravagant and compressed version of the last half of *Ulysses,* retold against the backdrop of the heavens. It suggests that the late styles of *Ulysses,* like the "mysterious writing" in the sky in the De Quincey passage, all flow from a multicolored veil, taking the material world traditionally relegated to women as their subject and their medium.

In "Circe," too, Joyce represents the stylistic movement of the book toward veiled obscurity through the mechanism of hallucination. Here, the device for representing the book is that of a dance – the dance of the hours – arrested by nightmare: the apparition of Stephen's mother. The hallucination grows, with the suddenness of dream, out of an earlier recollection in "Calypso": Bloom's memory of the bazaar dance where Molly first betrayed an interest in Boylan to the tune of Ponchielli's dance of the hours (*U* 4.525–30). In "Calypso," it is Beaufoy's story that evokes Bloom's recollection, establishing in his mind an associative link between fiction, music, dance, time, and betrayal. The connection between narrative and dance is illustrated in "Circe" through clothes: when Maginni, the dancing master, appears to direct the dance, he is dressed in clothes that Beaufoy wore in an earlier hallucination: lavender trousers and patent boots (*U* 15.814–16). The sartorial identity of writer and dancing master suggests that the dance of the hours is a vehicle for Joyce's own narrative, a representation of its own stylistic features as they metamorphose through time.

Earlier in the day, Bloom had contemplated the allegorical beauty of Ponchielli's ballet: "Evening hours, girls in grey gauze. Night hours then: black with daggers and eyemasks. Poetical idea: pink, then golden, then grey, then black. Still, true to life also. Day: then the night" (*U* 4.534–6). In "Circe," his thought assumes strange independent life. The blue morning hours "balance" the gold noon hours, emphasizing the symmetrical structure of the first half of the book, but when the night hours appear, "*Morning, noon and twilight hours retreat before them.*" As night falls, the dancers disappear behind clothes; the night hours are "*masked, with daggered hair and bracelets of dull bells,*" weary and veiled (*U* 15.4081–3). Maginni acknowledges the change by directing the dance differently. Instead of ordering them to "*Balance!*" "*Avant deux!*" he calls for "*La corbeille*" (the basket), and the pattern changes: "*Arabesquing wearily they weave a pattern on the floor, weaving, unweaving, curtseying, twirling, simply swirling*" (*U* 15.4090–2). The weaving and unweaving of the dance realizes Stephen's earlier Paterian account of how an artist weaves and unweaves his image through style (*U* 9.376–85), and at the same time it anticipates the action of Penelope as she weaves and unweaves her shroud. The dance of the hours, like De Quincey's nightmare, is another representation of the way that *Ulysses* progresses from hour to hour. Like the night hours, its later episodes are masked and "weary" in every divisible sense of the word, and charged with weaving and unweaving the book's unstable coherences.

The emphasis on weaving in the later episodes helps to bring together the two halves of the book. Molly's weaving and unweaving of her thoughts in "Penelope" materializes the notion of material and verbal artistry that Stephen presents in "Scylla and

Charybdis," the idea that the artist weaves and unweaves his image in the same way that "we, or mother Dana, weave and unweave our bodies . . . from day to day, their molecules shuttled to and fro" (*U* 9.376–7). The romantic father of Stephen's understanding of artistic style is Walter Pater; his classical counterpart, whose cunning is expressed through her treatment of materiality, is Homer's Penelope. In *Ulysses*, Joyce brings them together to generate a more complex model of what Stephen described in *A Portrait* as the "rhythm of beauty" – the prolongation and dissolution of a set of relations – expressed as a perpetual weaving and unweaving of the self.

Weaving is a complex intermeshing of opposites to form a web, or network, that figures both interconnection and entrapment. As the Odyssean story of Penelope suggests, the final product of any human weaving is a shroud, since death is the fate of all that is "material," but a periodic unweaving of what has been woven delays that process. Walter Pater, in the conclusion to *Studies in the History of the Renaissance* (1873), appropriates the same metaphor for philosophical and aesthetic discourse. The first two paragraphs of Pater's conclusion outline an oscillation between external and internal experience, between coherence of phenomena and their dissolution.[15] He argues that as far as our physical being is concerned, we are intimately interconnected through "phosphorus and lime and delicate fibres" not only to each other but to the rest of the material world, so that "That clear, perpetual outline of face and limb is but an image of ours, under which we group them – a design in a web, the actual threads of which pass out beyond it." When, however, we turn to the inward world of thought and feeling, "the cohesive force seems suspended like some trick of magic," and "each object is loosed into a group of impressions." A sense of continuity with the world is replaced by the apprehension of individual isolation, "each mind keeping as a solitary prisoner its own dream of a world." Pater argues that this movement between connection and isolation, external and internal reality, is a continual weaving and unweaving of human identity that defines the experience of life. In a passage that reverberates through Stephen's thought, Pater concludes, "It is with this movement, with

---

15 Walter Pater, *The Renaissance: Studies in Art and Poetry: The 1893 Text,* ed. Donald Hill (Berkeley: California, 1980), pp. 186–8.

the passage and dissolution of impressions, images, sensations, that analysis leaves off – that continual vanishing away, that strange, perpetual, weaving and unweaving of ourselves."

Pater presents life as an intricate tissue of elements that we alternately weave and ravel, endlessly creating and destroying ourselves. Penelope's treatment of weaving and unweaving is less poetic, more cunningly pragmatic. Her stratagem is a defense against the importunity of her suitors, a subtle way of prolonging uncertainty and thereby resisting entrapment. Interpreted figuratively, her ruse is less an affirmation of life than a trick to forestall "death." The product of her art, once completely woven, will be a shroud, and for her personally it will signify entrapment, the necessity of pledging herself to a single suitor. Whereas Pater identifies unweaving with the experience of imprisonment, Penelope sees as well the entrapment implicit in weaving. Together, their visions of weaving and unweaving are perfectly complementary, each reversing the implicit preference of the other for one of the two poles of experience. Together, they generate an alternative paradigm for twentieth-century thought, a paradigm that is both idealistic and practical. It is the culmination of the epistemological revolution that began with the Romantics, a revolution aimed at toppling the dominant structure of value. Instead of viewing oppositions as hierarchical arrangements of values, we may arrange them horizontally, as interdependent alternatives. The alternative paradigm is not dialectical, since the two terms never fuse into synthesis. Instead, the relationship between opposites is defined as an alternating movement – not the alternation of rise and fall, but of expansion and contraction, construction and deconstruction, community and isolation.

Weaving is a particularly valuable metaphor when language is the chosen medium of communication, since "text" derives from *texere,* to weave. Joyce was interested in the contradictory pulsations of history, but he was also committed to the relationship between communication and community – with the power of language to serve as a model for all interrelationship – and the analogy of weaving inspired new practical strategies for complicating the linear progression of letters and words through the mind. Joyce found in the analogy of weaving practical ways of emphasizing the texture of language, the intricate interrelationships and differences that make up its unstable surface. In *Ulysses* and *Finnegans Wake,* in particular, Joyce plays variously on the interrelationship between language and cloth as coverings for and versions of thought and the body, using them to complicate and multiply the contradictory individualism represented by a naked human organism.

By moving from an echo of Pater in "Scylla and Charybdis" to the figure of Penelope in the last episode, Joyce mates the words of a "Latin" Father with the material cunning of his Greek foremother, thereby producing the margins of *Ulysses*. In structuring *Ulysses*, Joyce reverses the progression of historical time by moving *toward* rather than away from Penelope, as he reverses the movement of the Bible by moving toward rather than away from Eve. Consequently, women become increasingly prominent as the sun falls and eve approaches, and clothes, too, begin to proliferate as we near the book's close. The "logic" of the late *Ulysses* is determined by connections illogically forged by language, coincidental similarities of sound and meaning laden with latent significance.

In *Finnegans Wake*, many of the connections that influenced the development of *Ulysses* are pursued still further. In the Mime of Mick, Nick, and the Maggies, for example, Joyce plays more heavily on the homophonic interrelationship between clothes, a journey's close, and the close of day; between Eve and eve; and between dying and dyeing, when describing Isa's "gloom":

> She is fading out like Journee's clothes so you can't see her now. Still we know how Day the Dyer works, in dims and deeps and dusks and darks. And among the shades that Eve's now wearing she'll meet anew fiancy, tryst and trow. (*FW* 226.11–14)

In *Finnegans Wake*, more obviously than in *Ulysses*, women represent the process of aggregation and dispersal that counterbalances and revitalizes social and verbal constructions that have become too exclusively male. Maleness, as Joyce suggests more directly in the *Wake*, tends to be defined by the twin possibilities of rigidity and flaccidity, its erections singular or repetitiously double. Joyce parodies the "male" through the agency of the "mail," representing Shem and Shaun, Earwicker's double double, as pen and post. Women, by contrast, are multiple and everflowing, miscellaneous and schizophrenic. In them is vested a variable understanding of material artistry: they have the power to gather together and disperse, or in the metaphor current in *Ulysses,* to weave and unweave.

In *Ulysses,* as the texture of language gains density, the references and allusions to clothing as a symbol of intermediation begin to swell. In "Nausicaa" clothes provoke and express sexual climax, invading Bloom's brief half-dream as they mingle with the clothes in *Sweets of Sin* and Molly clothed as he dreamed of her the night before:

> O sweety all your little girlwhite up I saw dirty bracegirdle made me do love sticky we two naughty Grace darling she him half past the bed met him pike hoses frillies for Raoul de perfume your wife black hair heave under embon *señorita* young eyes Mulvey plump bubs me breadvan Winkle red slippers she rusty sleep wander years of dreams return tail end Agendath swoony lovey showed me her next year in drawers return next in her next her next (*U* 13.1279–85)

In "Circe" costume changes replace narrative explication, as plot literally yields to disguise, and in "Penelope" Molly's thoughts return obsessively, comically, to the clothes she considers essential to any kind of intercourse, whether sexual ("if its going to go on I want at least two other good chemises" [*U* 18.438]) or intellectual:

> Id love to have a long talk with an intelligent welleducated person Id have to get a nice pair of red slippers like those Turks with the fez used to sell or yellow and a nice semi-transparent morning gown that I badly want or a peachblossom dressing jacket like the one long ago in Walpoles (*U* 18.1493–7)

Clothes increasingly displace people as the subject of the characters' thoughts, drawing our attention from the unique to the patterned, from individuality to custom, and finally, to the importance of complex relationship as a determinant of individual identity.

AGE, GENDER, AND THE MATRIX OF RELATIONSHIP

When viewed as a class, Joyce's male characters seem, stereotypically, to be preoccupied with problems of language and with the nature of social and religious institutions, whereas his female characters seem absorbed in the more domestic interests of romance and fashion. In "Ithaca," Bloom reflects on "the deficient appreciation of literature possessed by females" (*U* 17.1411) and contemplates Molly's "deficient mental development"(*U* 17.674). Bloom seems to see women's clothes and the sensuality they represent as a refuge from the more pressured world of public affairs, as is apparent not only in "Nausicaa," but also in his fond memory of Nelly Bouverist's "non-intellectual, non-political, non-topical expression of countenance" and her "white articles of non-intellectual, non-political, non-topical underclothing" (*U* 17.437–40). Gerty and Molly, moreover, seem to promote the fetishistic identification of their bodies with clothing, and particularly underclothing. Gerty, a "votary of Dame Fashion," readily displays her undergarments to Bloom's desirous eyes, and Molly represents herself as a more knowing exhibitionist obsessed from childhood with the donning and doffing of clothes:

> that winter when I was only about ten was I yes I had the big doll with all the funny clothes dressing her up and undressing that icy wind skeeting across from those mountains the something Nevada sierra nevada standing at the fire with the little bit of a short shift I had up to heat myself I loved dancing about in it then make a race back into bed Im sure that fellow opposite used to be there the whole time watching (*U* 18.916–21)

Joyce, however, undermines what seems to be a stereotyped portrayal of gender differences by crossing that opposition with others that fail to support it. He refines the outlines of his characters by defining each in varying contrast to at least three others, creating a character matrix that can be broken down into different triangles and linear segments by differently interested readings, but which, when regarded as a whole, frames the partiality of such analyses.

The model for Joyce's complex characterizations of Stephen, Gerty, Bloom, and Molly is his treatment of Beatrice, Bertha, Richard, and Robert in *Exiles*. Each character is defined in relationship and opposition to other characters, and no single opposition is sufficient to define the resulting network of kinship and incompatibility. These multivalent interrelationships are conveniently illustrated through the patterning of letters in the characters' names. Alliance of gender is indicated by alliteration, but an opposition of tendency, established through verbal and literary associations, challenges and undermines that alliance. "Bertha" suggests earth (and birth), whereas "Beatrice" evokes both beatitude, and, through the allusion to Dante, death. Similarly, Richard and Robert are initially bonded together by gender, a tie literally represented by a shared initial, but that bond is complicated by a difference of position and preference that distinguishes a "rich" man from one who "robs." Joyce attempts to dramatize that implication of their names in Act I, through Richard's otherwise unmotivated discussion of riches and robbery with Archie.[16] The common earthiness of Robert and Bertha is again reflected onomastically in the shared syllable "bert," although the opposite positioning of the syllable stresses the diametrical opposition between Robert's stealth and Bertha's openness. Similarly, "Richard" and "Beatrice" share the letters "ric," representing their shared intellectual riches, although once again the letters occupy different positions in their respective names to emphasize the sharp difference between Richard's intellectual generosity and Beatrice's cold reserve. The only characters unlinked by nomenclature are brought together by blood: Robert and Beatrice, who are cousins, and Richard and Bertha, united in Archie.

RIChard   BeatRICe

RoBERT   BERTha

With the possible exception of Bertha, Joyce does not recognizably import any of the characters of *Exiles* into *Ulysses,* despite the similar emphases on betrayal, uncertainty, and human freedom that mark both works. Instead, *Exiles* provides a model for character definition through multiple pairings, a strategy that both evokes and blurs stereotypical features. Each different pairing of an individual character highlights a different brace of qualities and a new opposition, all framed by the oppositions between and within genders – of openness versus stealth, of intellection versus sensuality,

---

16 Archie asks, "Are there robbers here like in Rome?" and Richard replies, "There are poor people everywhere."

of internal versus external reality. The weblike matrix that results from these different pairings of the four characters creates iridescent characters who are both susceptible to and resistant of simple categorization or definition.

Joyce uses this model of complex characterization to fashion the interrelationship of Stephen, Gerty, Molly, and Bloom in *Ulysses,* although he abandons the contrivance of reflecting it onomastically. Initially, it seems possible to define the pair of male characters as artistically inclined, in contrast to the more fashionably inclined Molly and Gerty. However, a slight shift in the way that the characters are paired disrupts the neatness of such a conclusion: Gerty shares Stephen's susceptibility to language; like him, she patterns her inner narratives on those she has read. Bloom shares a passion for clothes with Molly and Gerty; it is precisely this shared passion that allows him to engage in an "affair of the eye" with Gerty in "Nausicaa" – as Bloom reflects, "Still it was a kind of language between us" (*U* 13.944). The difference between Bloom and Gerty in their attitude toward clothes is essentially the difference between the voyeur and the exhibitionist (or reader and author), and is best illustrated by their parallel attempts to catch a glimpse of a stylishly clothed woman. Bloom hopes to "Watch! Watch! Silk flash rich stockings white" (*U* 5.130) when the well-dressed woman in front of the Grosvenor mounts her cab, but his "watch" is stopped by a heavy tramcar. Bloom longs to see beneath the outer clothing to the "understandings," whereas Gerty is interested in clothing as display rather than concealment: she "knew by the style it was the lord and lady lieutenant but she couldn't see what Her Excellency had on because the tram" (*U* 10.1208–9).

By means of such ever-shifting character pairings, Joyce suggests that sexual conditioning alone is insufficient to account for the differences between someone absorbed in language and someone interested in clothes, between intellectual and sensual proclivities. Such tendencies are also influenced by age: in addition to opposing men to women, Joyce opposes youth to maturity. Moreover, as a way of further undermining the comforting fiction that oppositions are simple and clear-cut, Joyce reverses the prevalent cultural assumptions attached to each term. Instead of portraying men as dominant and women as subservient, Joyce attributes activity to females and passivity to males; instead of presenting youth as a time of uninhibited delight in newly discovered physicality, Joyce implies that the young, such as Stephen and Gerty, use language and clothes to dress up and conceal the facts of physical existence, transporting themselves – body and narrative – into the illusory worlds of other people's fictions.

Both Stephen and Gerty use clothes to identify themselves with the kinds of artistic beauty they admire, thereby disguising and even denying the reality of the flesh beneath, with its desires and imperfections. Gerty dresses herself to take an imagined place on the Woman Beautiful page of the Princess novelette (*U* 13.87–9), and imaginatively transforms herself into a Greek statue like the ones Bloom so admires:

> The waxen pallor of her face was almost spiritual in its ivory-like purity though her rosebud mouth was a genuine Cupid's bow, Greekly perfect. Her hands were of finely veined alabaster. (*U* 13.87–9)

Gerty's willingness to transform herself into a work of art might seem to invite feminist criticism. However, her manipulation of appearances to fictionalize herself resists simple classification as an activity programmed exclusively by gender, because Stephen does the same thing. For Stephen, too, dress is a means of veiling flesh and advertising fiction: his black clothes and Latin-quarter hat proclaim his sense of affinity with Hamlet; the crown of vine leaves that he drunkenly assumes in "Oxen" (*U* 14.1116–7) dramatizes the meaning of his name (*Stephanos*, garlanded) and signals his affectation of the character Ejlert Lövborg in *Hedda Gabler*; his ashplant marks him as Wotan and Siegfried by turns. Stephen, like Gerty, uses clothes to display his aesthetic preferences, which are pretentiously literary rather than popular, but which serve to display an equally contrived image. Bloom instinctively understands that Stephen's clothes express a preference for literary over human communities, thinking to himself that Stephen, "a youthful tyro in society's sartorial niceties, hardly understood how a little thing like that could militate against you" (*U* 16.1832–3), and he reflects that "it would afford him very great personal pleasure if he would allow him to help to put coin in his way or some wardrobe, if found suitable" (*U* 16.1618–20).

Gerty and Stephen use language as they use clothes, to conceal their physical desires and fears. Their self-consciously stylized thoughts serve to disguise their sexual urges and their bodily weak-nesses, hiding them from themselves and in the process revealing them to those engaged in the voyeuristic act of reading. In *Portrait,* Stephen's composition of the villanelle best showcases his prefer-ence for euphemism, for using language to spiritualize and disguise physical ecstasy. His assertion that "His soul was all dewy wet" (*P* 217) anticipates through its delicate substitution of "soul" for "body" Gerty's avowal that Bloom could "read her very soul" (*U* 13.413). The comedy of youth's romantic misconstruction of sex-uality as spiritual revelation climaxes in "Nausicaa," when Gerty looks up to see Bloom's emission as a "heavenly" event: fireworks. Gerty ignores the sexual desire fueling her romantic flights as de-terminedly as she conceals her limp, and the physical imperfection and fragility it betokens.

Stephen and Gerty's appropriation of narrative styles is consistent with their respective styles of dress, suggesting that the two kinds of style are complementary reflections of a single impulse: the im-pulse to inhabit a world of art. Unlike the poetic speaker of Yeats' "Sailing to Byzantium," they regard the world of "whatever is begotten, born and dies" as uncongenial not to the old, but to the young. As characters, they are not "self-authored" in any sense; lost in a world of signifiers, they are strangely isolated figures in the solid world they find so alien. Their private, derivative fictions are highly colored, intense, and sterile; indulgently self-referential, they lose all meaning when challenged by the mundaneness of everyday life.

In contrast, Bloom and Molly inhabit a palpably different world. As a couple, they are as preoccupied by physicality as Gerty and Stephen are inhabited by fictions. Instead of concealing and feeding on sexual desire, the art that they prefer stimulates it: *Ruby, Pride of the Ring, Sweets of Sin,* Aristotle's *Masterpiece,* Greek statues of Venus and Narcissus. Instead of turning herself into a statue, like Gerty, Molly imaginatively transforms statues, such as the statue of Narcissus, into flesh:

> that lovely little statue he bought I could look at him all day
> long curly head and his shoulders his finger up for you to
> listen theres real beauty and poetry for you I often felt I wanted
> to kiss him all over also his lovely young cock there so simple

I wouldnt mind taking him in my mouth if nobody was looking as if it was asking you to suck it (*U* 18.1349–53)

Bloom, like Molly, blurs the distinction between flesh and marble, slipping into the library museum to see if the Venus has an anus (*U* 8.920–32; also 9.615). Any contemplation of art slides almost imperceptibly into physical desire, and conversely, the body's productions take on the characteristics of art. In one of Bloom's letters to Molly, he implies that for him, her feces have the inspirational power of the "thing of beauty" Keats celebrates at the beginning of *Endymion*: "my Precious one everything connected with your glorious Body everything underlined that comes from it is a thing of beauty and of joy for ever" (*U* 18.1176–8). All of the supposed "perversions" of Bloom and Molly stem from his secretive and her open delight in physicality.

Unlike Stephen and Gerty, Molly and Bloom treat clothes as fetishized equivalents of the very flesh that their younger counterparts attempt to deny. They regard both language and clothes as exaggerated representations of physical reality, as the narrator of "Eumaeus" sententiously implies when he relates that one of Bloom's trouser buttons "had, to vary the timehonoured adage, gone the way of all buttons" (*U* 16.36–7). The way of all buttons is the way of all flesh; yet *The Way of All Flesh* represents a body of words, Samuel Butler's novel, as well as a physical process. By replacing "flesh" with "button" in this familiar phrase, Joyce primes a recognition that language, clothes, and flesh all participate in a single mortal rhythm of freshening and decay.

At the structural center of the book, the "Wandering Rocks" section, Joyce presents a fiction such as *Ulysses* as easily divisible into a variety of more salacious narratives, all of which purport to "reveal" hidden sexual perversions. Seeking to procure a book for Molly, Bloom is unexpectedly assaulted by a series of titles that isolate and sensationalize different aspects of his social and sexual situation. Humorously, the titles jostle one another as competing indications of what a book like *Ulysses* might be said to be about, and their authors' names attribute masochism to men named "James" and "Leopold." We could extract from *Ulysses* a smaller book that might be called *Fair Tyrants,* by James Lovebirch, an autobiographical account of female sadism and male masochism in sexual relations, the oxymoronic title suggesting that it is "fair" for the fair to tyrannize such men. Similarly, we could concentrate on the source of Bloom's masochism, tracing it to his ethnic background, in which case our *Ulysses* could be called *Tales of the Ghetto,* by Leopold von Sacher Masoch. The book Bloom ultimately chooses to bring home to Molly is *Sweets of Sin,* by a gentleman of fashion. The title of this book emphasizes the dulcet pleasures of forbidden desires rather than pain and persecution, an emphasis more in keeping with that of *Ulysses,* but even more revealing is our glimpse of what is happening between its covers. *Sweets of Sin* focuses its attention on two systems that are both social and sexual in nature: language and clothes.

Sweets of Sin showcases the capacity of both language and clothes to pander to sexual desire. Written by a "gentleman of fashion," it takes clothing as its ostensible subject, as an obvious vehicle for the body that it simultaneously exaggerates and conceals: "*All the dollarbills her husband gave her were spent in the stores on wondrous gowns and costliest frillies. For him! For Raoul!*" (U 10.608–9) The titillating power of the book is enhanced by its lingering attention to every detail of the woman's clothing – her *deshabille,* her sable-trimmed wrap, her heaving embonpoint. Bloom is reading about the way that clothes stimulate desire, but Joyce complicates that recognition by showing us how the book's language is producing the same effect on Bloom that clothing has on Raoul. As Bloom continues to read, the narrative devoted to him begins to display its affinities with the book being read. The narrative dissolves the distinctions between the characters being read about and the characters reading, a parallelism that potentially works three ways, since Bloom is also a character being read about as well as a character reading. As the woman in *Sweets of Sin* gradually unveils herself beneath Bloom's gaze, Joyce, too, sheds proper nouns, and then pronouns, intermingling the two narratives and the two sets of characters until it is virtually impossible to disentangle them:

> Warmth showered gently over him, cowing his flesh. Flesh yielded amply amid rumpled clothes: whites of eyes swooning up. His nostrils arched themselves for prey . . . Sulphur dung of lions!
> Young! Young! (U 10.619–24)

The "flesh" cowed by warmth seems to be Bloom's, but the second "Flesh" that immediately follows it seems to be that of the adulterous couple, although the repetition of the same word without a pronoun clouds any differentiation. Language and clothes work together to collapse the distinction between physical and imagined realities; all perceivers become participants through the equalizing power of a shared vehicle and a mutual desire.

As a representation of *Ulysses* as Bloom or Molly might read it, *Sweets of Sin* illustrates the power of language and clothes to dissolve difference and collapse distance. In *Portrait*, Stephen, too, finds the erotic potential of language comparable to that of clothes, so that when the director of the college makes reference to both at once, through the phrase "*Les jupes*," it kindles a "tiny flame" on Stephen's cheek, for "the names of articles of dress worn by women or of certain soft and delicate stuffs used in their making brought always to his mind a delicate and sinful perfume" (*P* 155). In *Ulysses*, too, Bloom thinks of perfume as the olfactory equivalent of a dress or web: "Tell you what it is. It's like a fine fine veil or web they have all over the skin, fine like what do you call it gossamer, and they're always spinning it out of them, fine as anything, like rainbow colours without knowing it. Clings to everything she takes off." (*U* 13.1019–22) He adores the "cobweb hose" of the wax model Raymonde, and in "Lestrygonians" he sees "silk webs" as part of a woman's promised land: "High voices. Sunwarm silk. Jingling harnesses. All for a woman, home and houses, silkwebs, silver, rich fruits spicy from Jaffa. Agendath Netaim. Wealth of the world." (*U* 8.634–6)[17]

As emblems of comparably sensual networks, language and clothes have the power to excite desire, which is always the desire to resolve difference in union, whether that union is physical or intellectual, an act of consummation or communication. However, only an intense awareness of *difference* can render the transient experience of unity desirable. When perceived as complex systems, language and cloth illustrate the intricate fabric of relationship, but in their particulars, words and garments serve to depict and exaggerate the very differences that create desire. Eroticism feeds on the illusion of strangeness; in "Nausicaa," Gerty is attracted by the

17 Compare Giacomo's appreciation of his pupil's "cobweb handwriting," her "soft web of stocking," and the "websoft edges of her gown" (*GJ* 1, 9, 7).

foreignness of Bloom's appearance, and Bloom thinks of Gerty, "See her as she is spoil all" (*U* 13.855). Clothing, in particular, exaggerates the difference between the sexes, and Bloom is sharply aware of the role that clothing plays in pandering to sexual desire. In "Eumaeus" he reflects that immorality is "largely a matter of dress and all the rest of it," thinking wearily of the repetitious necessity of dressing up in order to undress: "Ladies who like distinctive underclothing should, and every welltailored man must, trying to make the gap wider between them by innuendo and give more of a genuine filip to acts of impropriety between the two, she unbuttoned his and then he untied her, mind the pin" (*U* 16.1207–11). In "Penelope," Molly clearly understands the relationship between dress and excitation, thinking, "Ill start dressing myself to go out presto non son piu forte Ill put on my best shift and drawers let him have a good eyeful out of that to make his micky stand for him" (*U* 18.1508–10). Bloom, too, sees sexual excitement as a game of dress-up that is as predictable, brief, and natural as a sneeze: "Dress up and look and suggest and let you see and see more and defy you if you're a man to see that and, like a sneeze coming, legs, look, look and if you have any guts in you" (*U* 13.993–5).

The kinship between sexuality, language, and clothing is clearest in "Nausicaa," since Bloom owes his climax not only to the care with which Gerty clothes her body ("*Lingerie* does it . . . Fashion part of their charm" [*U* 13.796–804]), but also to her readiness to "dress" her thoughts and perceptions of reality in the language of romantic fiction. Bloom's pleasure in contemplating Gerty is the natural equivalent of Gerty's fictionalization of herself; both depend for their effect on the interposition of distance between themselves and what they contemplate. In *Finnegans Wake,* it is Issy who is most aware of the way that clothes inspire a desire for closeness. She repeatedly draws attention to the semantic as well as the aural affinity between fashion and passion: "Mind my duvetyne dress above all! It's golded silvy, the newest sextones with princess effect. For Rutland blue's got out of passion" (*FW* 148.7–9). She ends her verbal display of the particulars of her dress by asking incredulously, · "Did you really never in all our cantalang lives speak clothse to a girl's before?" (*FW* 148.22–24) To an ear attuned to harmonies of sound, and to a mind disposed to take those harmonies seriously, the substantive and adjectival meanings of the word "close" bear an important relationship to one another, a paradoxical relationship reflected in their homonym – clothes.

Joyce presents the Blooms' fetishistic attitude toward clothing as natural, and even, in part, inevitable, since clothing affects the mind as well as the eye. Clothes are opaque to the eye, but they are transparent to the human imagination, as Magritte so startlingly illustrates in "Philosophy in the Boudoir" (1947). In their power to exchange opacity for transparency, clothes complement language, which we learn to regard as transparent, but which, as Freud has shown, betrays its materiality to the imagination through jokes, slips, and dreams. The body, as the most familiar fact of human existence, achieves new appeal when translated into clothing. Clothing then becomes a readily apprehensible fact that transforms the body back into an elusive and desirable fiction. As Joyce suggests more directly in *Finnegans Wake,* the interchangeability of fact and fiction is the basis of all appeal, whether sexual or esthetic; this is his ripest contribution to the esthetic theory he devoted his life to evolving:

> Who in his heart doubts either that the facts of feminine clothiering are there all the time or that the feminine fiction, stranger than the facts, is there also at the same time, only a little to the rere? Or that one may be separated from the other? Or that both may then be contemplated simultaneously? Or that each may be taken up and considered in turn apart from the other? (*FW* 109.30–6)

Clothes are to the body what context is to text; we may be seduced by the illusion that they are separable and stable in their differences, when in fact they constantly exchange roles in the imagination. Clothes and the body, like fiction and fact, context and text, are alluringly different terms for a reality that is both unified and multiple, systematic and chaotic, but necessarily double. As a narrator of *Finnegans Wake* warns,

> to concentrate solely on the literal sense or even the psychological content of any document to the sore neglect of the enveloping facts themselves circumstantiating it is just as hurtful to sound sense

as imagining as naked a lady to whom one had just begged an introduction (*FW* 109.12–15).

Sexuality depends upon the interplay of fact and fiction; the interplay is constant, although the identification of which is which can never be finally fixed. Dress and undress, address and message, frame and picture, signifier and signified, author and reader have a disquieting tendency to exchange places, despite our attempts to stabilize their differences through names. Sexuality and death, closeness and closings, beginnings and endings have a similarly troubling tendency to reverse themselves, as Joyce shows in both "Proteus" and "Hades," where thoughts of death intertwine with reminders of consummation and birth, "seawrack" with "seaspawn," drowned men with midwives.

The desire for communion, community, and communication is sparked by a need for sameness but sustained through the mechanisms of difference. The experience of difference is the experience of isolation, the imaginative equivalent of death. That isolation, however, as a by-product of the same process that periodically dissolves isolation in unity, is the reversed reflection of communication, cooperation, and sexual union. In *Ulysses,* Joyce expresses the interdependence of connection and disconnection, sexuality and death, by portraying clothes – and language – as shrouds as well as fetishized objects. Bloom is forced to rediscover the identity of sexuality and mortality when he unveils the nun in "Circe"; when he removes her "habit," and her "plaster cast" begins to crack, she exudes the stench of mortality, the same stench Bloom associates with sexuality in "Wandering Rocks": "Rut. Onions. Stale. Sulphur. Grease." (*U* 15.3477–8) Like St. Anthony in Flaubert's *Tentation,* one of the sources for "Circe," Bloom has been made to recognize that death (the nun) and lechery (the whore) are sisters (see *Tentation,* chapter 7).

Zoe, too, when transformed in "Circe" into a picture of the "life" her name denotes, illustrates not only the interrelationship of clothing and narrative, but also the kinship of sexuality and mortality. Zoe's body and clothes cooperate to produce a landscape that also realizes a promise of scripture. The sapphire slip closed with three bronze buckles that she was wearing earlier (*U* 15.1279–80) is newly described as "*a sky of sapphire, cleft by the bronze flight of eagles. Under it lies the womancity, nude, white, still, cool, in luxury*" (*U* 15.1326–28). Her lips unexpectedly blossom into "*Mammoth roses"* which *"murmur of scarlet winegrapes. A wine of shame, lust, blood exudes, strangely murmuring"* (*U* 15.1329–30). However, beneath the allure of a sexuality doubly enhanced through material and verbal ornamentation lies a royal burial ground, as we see when her gold-filled mouth opens to reveal a seriocomic image of death through tooth decay: *"The roses draw apart, disclose a sepulchre of the gold of kings and their mouldering bones"* (*U* 15.1340–1). Bloom's hallucinogenic vision of Zoe is a picture of "life" colored by the sensual and morbid language of the Judeo-Christian tradition. It was called forth by his forlorn memory of a line from Thomas Moore he had once inscribed on a valentine for Mrs. Breen, "I never loved a dear gazelle but it was sure to . . ."die (*U* 15.1323, 15.435), and it appropriately depicts the interdependence of sexuality and mortality as twin conditions of physical existence.

Words, and more particularly clothes, represent for the Blooms the range of physical experience, from sexual flowering, contact, and reproduction to the gradual isolation of age that eventuates in death. However, clothes also have the potential to bind – and blind – as surely as their fictional counterparts. Molly and Bloom are blinded by the fictions created by clothes just as Stephen and Gerty are blinded by verbal fictions – both the younger and the older characters are seduced by texts and textiles into falsifying reality by oversimplifying it. The fiction that clothes help to fashion and maintain is the social fiction that role constitutes identity, that "clothes make the man." Like literary fictions, clothes define and classify character, turning living beings into mere representations. They constitute a visual reminder of the way society tailors its citizens, turning them into stock characters in a human comedy. To identify an individual with a single suit of clothes, a single role, or even a single gender is to encase her or him in a "habit," paralyzing perceiver and perceived alike. In the second half of *Ulysses*, Joyce plays on the rhythm of dressing and undressing, weaving and unweaving to suggest that clothes both make *and unmake* not only man, but woman too: sexual identity is one among many roles that clothes can translate into fact and dissolve as fiction. In *Ulysses*, clothes, like words, represent social and sexual identity, which can be confining, but which is also subject to the process of continual change. That process, for Joyce as for a number of his literary precursors, both constitutes and veils human consciousness, which can know only one unmediated or "naked" truth: the final and irreversible reality that puts an end to knowing.

WOR(L)D AS CLOTHES

> Then Ozymandias said the spouse, the bride
> Is never naked. A fictive covering
> Weaves always glistening from the heart and mind.
>
> Wallace Stevens,
> "Notes toward a Supreme Fiction"

Ulysses resuscitates the ancient notion that language and clothes comprise comparable systems of signification. Both are composed of what Carlyle called "symbols," in which "there is concealment and yet revelation."[18] What they reveal is difference (and *différance*), in its tantalizing play; what they conceal is sameness, an awareness of our common mortality. Together, these signs make up a comprehensive, everchanging system which weaves and unweaves itself from moment to moment, from day to day. The purpose of both words and clothes is to facilitate social and sexual interaction – they promote plurality, just as they themselves are useful mainly in the plural – but the interconnections they inspire are necessarily makeshift, devised to fit a temporary situation. The moments of social cohesiveness, interpersonal communication, and sexual union, although brief and sporadic, help to veil the isolation and meaninglessness that lie between and beyond such moments. The panoplies of costume and custom create society, as they create identity, and as Bloom is directed to see in "Circe," only decay lies beneath the veil. (See Bloom's unveiling of the nymph/nun [*U* 15.3465–70].)

In "Penelope," Molly reflects, "sure you cant get on in this world without style" (*U* 18.466–7). Style is indispensable "in this world"; even nudity, which is sometimes perceived as a symbol of the "thing in itself," is simply another style of presentation, for as Bloom reminds himself in "Ithaca," the "thing in itself" is intangible (*U* 17.2212–3). Humanity is always clothed, even when naked, just as language always works by metaphor, even when it creates the illusion of directness. Intangible feelings, thoughts, convictions

18 *Sartor Resartus,* Book Third, Chapter III.

can only be conveyed – however imperfectly – through analogy to sensory forms; this is the "ineluctable modality" of the visible and the audible.

Joyce certainly isn't the first to adopt the philosophical view that "clothes" are all that we can know. Shakespeare turned the third act of *King Lear* into a complex dramatization of the inevitability of disguise, a drama that grows from Lear's feeling of having been stripped of his social and personal identity. Lear externalizes his feelings of "exposure" by exposing his body to the storm, addressing the equally exposed Poor Tom in these well-known tones of angry compassion:

> Thou wert better in a grave than to answer with thy uncover'd body this extremity of the skies. Is man no more than this? . . . Thou art the thing itself: unaccommodated man is no more but such a poor, bare, fork'd animal as thou art. Off, off, you lendings! Come, unbutton here. (III.iv)

Lear proffers his body as a symbol of unadorned truth, freed from the clothing that has disguised it, and in so doing dramatizes the view that our common humanity is animalistic, lying beneath the trappings of society and culture. He seems unaware of the irony that when he uses his body as a symbol, it becomes a kind of "clothing" for an intangible insight. His own nakedness, like that of Edgar posing as Poor Tom, is simply another disguise.

Shakespeare draws attention to the omnipresence of "clothes" by exposing nakedness as a lonely illusion. Two hundred years later, Carlyle compels a similar recognition using strikingly different techniques.[19] Instead of subtly undermining a minimalist view of bare reality, Carlyle subjects a philosophy of clothes to comic, pseudo-pedantic, discursive exaggeration and stolid editorialization to reinforce the realization that there is no such thing as unmediated reality. In *Sartor Resartus,* the entire purpose of Teufelsdröckh's philosophy of clothes is to demonstrate the "grand Proposition"

19 In *Finnegans Wake,* the tailor – a conception clearly indebted to Joyce's reading of Carlyle – is the complement of the sailor in the multiple characterization of HCE: "so sartor's risorted [Sartor Resartus; tailor's resorted] why the sinner the badder! [Sinbad the Sailor; the sooner the better]" (*FW* 314.17–18).

that our earthly interests "are all hooked and buttoned together, and held up, by Clothes" (Book First, Chapter VIII). Teufelsdröckh goes on to show that the world as we know it is constituted entirely by clothes: nature, language, society all serve as "garments" for other, less tangible, realities. Such "clothes" are the primary agents of connection. In social terms, "hooks and buttons" represent the possibility of communication, and even community; in philosophical terms, material represents materiality, our only alternative to the Void: "Society sails through the Infinitude on Cloth, as on a Faust's Mantle, or rather like the Sheet of clean and unclean beasts in the Apostle's Dream; and without such Sheet or Mantle, would sink to endless depths, or mount to inane limboes, and in either case be no more" (Book First, Chapter VIII). Peter's dream of a "great sheet" to which Teufelsdröckh alludes (Acts 10:9–20) represents the continuity of human society. It teaches Peter not to call any man common or unclean (Acts 10:28), persuading him, a Jew, to keep company with a gentile, and thereby to attain a new appreciation of the notion of community. Teufelsdröckh's implication is that the study of clothes can give birth to a stronger social conscience and a more cohesive society, a possibility also raised in *King Lear*.

Ibsen picks up the motif of clothing as a metaphor for earthly reality, and he too emphasizes its power as an agent of connection. In *Peer Gynt,* which was one of Joyce's models for *Ulysses,*[20] Peer insists that he can somehow dissociate himself from his clothes, and thus from the way he presents himself to others. When, in his guise as a Turkish prophet, he discovers that he has been betrayed by Anitra, his first act is to strip himself of his Turkish costume, congratulating himself on the ease with which he is able to separate himself from his assumed role:

> There lies the Turk, then, and here stand I!–
> These heathenish doings are no sort of good.
> It's lucky 'twas only a matter of clothes,
> And not, as the saying goes, bred in the bone. (IV.ix)

20 In 1907 Joyce told Stanislaus of his intention to expand "Ulysses," originally intended as a short story for *Dubliners,* into a book that he would turn into a Dublin "Peer Gynt" (*JJ* 11,265).

What Peer fails to see is that he *is* his clothes; there is no kernel of self which lies beneath them, an insight that Ibsen dramatizes by showing Peer his image in a wild onion. He peels the onion, stripping off "one coat after another," seeing in each "coat" one of his former roles. Eventually, he becomes impatient, exclaiming,

> What an enormous number of swathings!
> Is not the kernel soon coming to light?
> *(Pulls the whole onion to pieces.)*
> I'm blest if it is! To the innermost centre,
> It's nothing but swathings – each smaller and smaller. –
> Nature is witty! (V.v)

Peer's refusal to learn nature's lesson leaves him totally unprepared for his sudden recall to the divine button factory. When the button-moulder tells him that he was "designed for a shining button / On the vest of the world," but that his "loop" has given way and he must be recast (V.vii), he has no idea why the characterization of himself as a button is fitting. Peer has consistently refused to understand that he lives in a world of "cloth," in which individuals serve as buttons, a refusal that has severed him, not only from others, but from the "vest of the world." As he is forced to discover, the "hidden" reality he was always seeking is death.

From the perspective of writers like Shakespeare, Carlyle, Ibsen, and Joyce, the crucial philosophical problem is not to define the nature of the world, since from Plato onward earthly existence has repeatedly been defined in terms of "veils," and language itself encodes an awareness that the material world is comprised of "material," or fabric. The more pressing problem is rather to determine what these veils conceal, and the most familiar and accepted answer has been that they clothe some form of the ideal. However, for those who, like Joyce and Ibsen, insist on the identity of extremes, that ideal also constitutes a perversion. Pursuit of the one necessitates flight from the other: every higher world calls a lower one into being, every God calls up a devil, every virtue a vice, as the pattern continues to reproduce itself with deadening regularity. Stephen Dedalus falls into this pattern in *Portrait* as he swings between obedience and apostasy; Bloom acts it out more personally in his relationship with Molly, who alternately appears before him as Calypso and Circe, goddess and whore. *Ulysses* suggests that the only way out of this pattern is to redirect attention away from *any* fantasy of a world "beyond the veil," and back to the world itself, in its motley, many-colored guises.

In *Ulysses*, Lear's "Come, unbutton here" is replaced by the costume changes of "Circe," followed by the "Bip" of Bloom's back trouser button as it snaps, and finally, by the easeful unbuttoning, "process of divestiture," in "Ithaca" (U 17.1434–91). As in *King Lear*, this unbuttoning signals an altered attentiveness to the language of clothes. Both Lear and Bloom begin to apprehend the inadequacy, and the danger, of rigidly defined, single roles, whether assumed oneself or assigned to others, since every role implies and even comprehends its opposite. Haughty king is powerless beggar; cuckhold is bawd; whore is virgin. Such dichotomizing kills; as Stephen remarks during his discussion of Shakespeare, the "Lover of an ideal or a perversion, like José . . . kills the real Carmen" (U 9.1022–3). The directive to choose Scylla *or* Charybdis, to choose between opposites, is a dangerously misleading one, since, as the *Odyssey* shows, the traveller will invariably be propelled toward the other extreme by the flux and reflux of time.

"CIRCE": FIXED VERSUS MIXED IDENTITY

"Circe" is the first episode to be not only informed but shaped by the relationship between clothes and identity. Clothes in "Circe" signal the play of psychic as well as social roles, roles that, like the clothes that represent them, are both restrictive and variable. The episode owes its structure not to any sequence of external actions – and the plot of "Circe" can be described in a brief paragraph – but to the unacknowledged contradictions about the nature of identity that divide the minds of characters and readers alike. "Circe" presents characters in the double focus of costume and custom, emphasizing the individual *and* social nature of identity, both its amenability and its resistance to type. In "Circe," Joyce focuses not only on the paradoxical nature of identity, but also on our unreflective mimicry of its inconsistencies in our attitudes toward ourselves and others. "Circe" shows that the "double standard" is, in effect, a thoughtless reaction against the doubleness of identity, an attempt to preserve freedom for ourselves by denying it to others. However, since identity is social as well as individual, the attitude that an individual adopts toward others defines subject as well as object, a law that frames Bloom's judgment of Molly and the reader's judgment of both.

In "Circe," Bloom's constant costume changes illustrate not only the variousness of his identity, but the importance of that variousness to his personal freedom.[21] Throughout the day, Bloom has betrayed a sadomasochistic desire to divide Molly into her individual roles, only to discover, disquietingly, a counterpart of each of those roles in himself. He discovers that he has been paralyzed, not by Molly herself, but by the stereotypical views of her that Joyce identifies in a letter as Penelope's "apparitions": the immortal nymph, represented by the photograph over his bed (Calypso), the virgin (Nausicaa), and the whore (Circe).[22] In "Circe," Bloom tries to avoid being categorized as he has categorized Molly, constantly changing roles in a protean attempt to avoid the persecution that inevitably dogs those who allow themselves to be "typed," but he fails to realize the hypocrisy of his stance. Only gradually does he begin to suspect that by typing his wife, he types and restricts himself; to see her as the immortal Calypso is to admire himself as a comparably faultless god; to preserve her as a young virgin is to escape nostalgically into an illusionary youth; to portray her as a barren mother is to legislate his own impotence; to see her as a faithless whore is to cast himself as the grovelling swine she dominates and defiles.

Mesmerized by the apparent purity of the nymph over his bed and by the obscenity of his secret desire to subject himself to sexual degradation and defilement, Bloom is the captive of Calypso and Circe by turns, and cannot return home to the mortal, complex woman who is his equal in every way. His impotence is a product of the unacknowledged fact that he must see himself as he sees her, as *either* a bawd or a cuckold, when in fact, as Stephen says of Shakespeare, "he is bawd and cuckold. He acts and is acted on" (*U* 9.1018–19). But Bloom can only sense this when he sees that

---

21 Joyce told Budgen that "Circe" was a "costume episode" in which "Bloom changes clothes half a dozen times" (the number is actually closer to two dozen times); see Budgen, *James Joyce and the Making of Ulysses*, p. 228.

22 See *Letters* I, 180: "I have rejected the usual interpretation of her as a human apparition – that aspect being better represented by Calypso, Nausikaa and Circe, to say nothing of the pseudo Homeric figures."

the woman he loves is neither totally etherial nor totally sensual, but as changeable as the words and habits that variously clothe her. The impulse behind "Circe" is the drive to show Bloom his own reflection in a whore's mirror, and it is only after seeing his unacknowledged treacheries reflected there that "the spell," in the form of his trouser button, is broken (*U* 15.3449), and he can return home.

Molly reflects not only Bloom but the reader in her mirror, although the relationship between her image and ours has been notoriously difficult to recognize. Bloom is not the only character to appear in a variety of costumes, a fact conspicuous by its absence from critical accounts of "Circe." Molly, too, is present in disguised form throughout the episode, her volatile identity reflecting and illuminating Bloom's own; she is reflected in every woman Bloom encounters, subsuming, in her variousness, all of them. In her imperious despotism, she has usurped the role of mother, as her voice shows when it dominates and dispels the image of Bloom's mother with its peremptory summons: "Poldy!" (*U* 15.294) An image of Molly as he had dreamed of her, in Turkish costume, immediately materializes to link the image of motherhood with the tempting images of youth that follow. Bloom is presented with a succession of virgins, all of whom remind him of Milly, her virginity wavering in the balance in Mullingar. Milly, too, is a transparent disguise for Molly, for as he reflected earlier in the day, "Molly. Milly. Same thing watered down." (*U* 6.7) Bloom's encounters with the virgins in "Circe" remind him that although a knowing virginity is not innocent, neither is he in his response to it, past and present. He, too, has played an active role in deflowering virgins, both in his life and in his dreams. The first virgin the Bawd offers him, who like Milly is only fifteen, turns out to be Bridie Kelly, Bloom's first lover (*U* 15.358–62; see 14.1069–75 for his memory of the encounter). She is followed by a whorish Gerty MacDowell, reminding him through her gestures of the fantasies he entertained about her in "Nausicaa," re-presenting her genitals not in the form of white linen, but as a bloodied physical reality (*U* 15.372–3).

The vision of the knowledgeability possible in innocence is followed by an illustration of the innocence compatible with adultery. Mrs. Breen succeeds the "virgins," illustrating through the pleasure with which she responds to Bloom's attentions how devoid of romance and illusion her life has become. Bound in marriage to a harmless but determined man who has lost his connection to reality, a man whom coincidence and narrative have intermittently linked to Bloom, she embodies the aspect of Molly that is starved for romance, a hunger that Bloom shows, in odd ways, that he shares. He gives her a ruby ring, reenacting his procurement of *Ruby, Pride of the Ring* for Molly. He offers her his hand with the words "*Là ci darem la mano*," thereby playing not only Don Giovanni but Boylan to Mrs. Breen's Molly. Bloom tries out on her the excuse he plans to give Molly for his lateness, and her disbelief anticipates Molly's (*U* 15.495–8, 15.521). As they are exchanging reminiscences, she fades away, repeating the famous words that punctuate the end of "Penelope": "Yes, yes, yes, yes, yes, yes, yes" (*U* 15.576). Even the wreaths·of tobacco remind him of his wife, as they chant the title of the book he borrowed for Molly in "Wandering Rocks": "Sweet are the sweets. Sweets of sin" (*U* 15.655). The ease of recapturing the past with Mrs. Breen shows Bloom how innocently he could slip into Boylan's clothes, with Mrs. Breen in Molly's, thereby transforming the "villainy" of adultery into a human yearning for closer contact.

Bloom's encounter with Mrs. Breen has forced him toward an understanding of Molly's position that is immediately heightened when he is detained by the watch. Suddenly, he finds himself accused of what he has mentally charged Molly with. Martha upbraids him for "breach of promise" (*U* 15.765; the phrase emerges as "beach of promisck" in *FW* 323.11); the scullerymaid accuses him of assaulting her. Mrs. Yelverton Barry testifies that he wrote to her under the name James Lovebirch and offered to send her a book by Paul de Kock (*U* 15.1016–24; see also 10.601–2); Mrs. Bellingham alleges that he addressed her as a Venus in Furs, like Leopold von Sacher Masoch, and castigates him for urging her to commit adultery; and Mrs. Mervyn Talboys reveals that he sent her an obscene photograph and begged her to horsewhip him. Bloom has certainly looked on a woman to lust after her, and by the judgment of Christ, he "hath committed adultery with her already in his heart" (Matthew 5:28; Joyce noted this saying as early as *SH* 189–91). By the judgment of Christ, Bloom shares the guilt of adultery, and he has been sentenced to hang when Zoe accosts him at Mrs. Cohen's.

The whores, Zoe and Bella in particular, complete the composite portrait of Molly that Bloom has segregated into discrete images in his mind. Zoe represents the promise of sexuality, which is also the promise of his mother and his race: she bears the name "Higgins," which is Bloom's mother's maiden name, and she is described as a realization of the landscape of paradise, Solomon's Jerusalem, which recalls the association Bloom made in "Calypso" between Molly's body and his hopes for the "promised land" of Agendath Netaim (*U* 3.191–203). If Zoe embodies the promise of sexuality, Bella represents its concomitant threat, a threat that Bloom can only control when he knows that she, too, is a mother.

The whores remind Bloom that they are all animated exaggerations of his perceptions of Molly, repeating the phrase, "You'll know me the next time." When Bloom gazes into Zoe's eyes to the refrain of oriental music, his smile softens and she assures him that he won't mistake her again: "You'll know me the next time" (*U* 15.1321). He doesn't know her the next time, however, which is when Bella plays the nymph; and after Bella reappears, she repeats the formula (*U* 15.3481). When Bloom first meets Bella, her fan greets him as if he were a familiar acquaintance, asking, "Have you forgotten me?" (*U* 15.2764) Bloom answers, "Nes. Yo." The Fan then suggests that for Bloom all women, imagined or real, are the same:

> Is me her was you dreamed before? Was then she him you us since knew? Am all them and the same now me? (*U* 15.2768–9)

Molly and Bloom both incorporate a variety of identities, play a number of roles, wear an impressive array of costumes. But the challenge for Bloom, and for the reader, is to recognize the unity in multaeity, and the multaeity in unity. It is a woman's activity, weaving and unweaving an alluring web of disguises around her body, that shows Bloom that he too assumes a variety of roles in a double attempt to escape responsibility and to preserve freedom. Just when Bloom feels that he is most securely trapped in Circe's web, a sudden revelation frees him and the web is unwoven. Literally, it is a popping button on his clothes that suggests to him that he has been spellbound by a dazzling array of costumes. He has learned that a traitor is only a "turncoat" (*U* 15.791), as he himself is. In the vision of apocalypse that almost, but not quite, puts an end to the chapter, Joyce suggests that the difference between good and evil is also a matter of clothes: the only differences between the saved and the damned on the last day are the direction in which they read and the color and material of their assumed "skins" – the saved wear white sheepskin, the damned black goatfell (*U* 15.4671).

"Circe" suggests that what differentiates both Bloom and Molly from many of their contemporaries is their ability to try on different roles. Their transvestism represents their willingness to try on the "clothes" – the prerogatives and restraints – culturally assigned to the opposite sex,[23] and at the same time it signals their courage to transgress social codes in order to understand them. When Bloom's button bursts, it signals a momentary and partial release from the constraints of "male" costume and custom, constraints that he increasingly comes to regard as "unsuitable." In "Ithaca," his gradual divestiture is prompted by his irritation at the tightness of his collar and waistcoat:

What caused him irritation in his sitting posture?

Inhibitory pressure of collar (size 17) and waistcoat (5 buttons), two articles of clothing superfluous in the costume of mature males and inelastic to alterations of mass by expansion. (*U* 17.1430–3)

Joyce emphasizes the constrictiveness and superfluity of male articles of clothing, but he also stresses their variousness: when Bloom rises to go to bed, he does so "gathering multicoloured multiform multitudinous garments" (*U* 17.2063–4).

Bloom's new awareness of the constraints imposed by male clothing results from his experience of the greater cruelty of female garments in "Circe," when Bello orders him to don a punishment

23 This argument is diametrically opposed to Sandra Gilbert's in "Costumes of the Mind: Transvestism as Metaphor in Modern Literature," in Abel, ed., *Writing and Sexual Difference*, pp. 193–219. Gilbert argues that "male modernist costume imagery [including that of Joyce] is profoundly conservative [whereas] female modernist costume imagery is radically revisionary in political as well as a literary sense, for it implies that no one, male or female, can or should be confined to a uni-form, a single form or self" (p. 196).

frock and become a possession, "a thing under the yoke" (*U* 15.2965–6). Bello points to "his" whores, warning:

> As they are now so will you be, wigged, singed, perfume-sprayed, ricepowdered, with smoothshaven armpits. Tape measurements will be taken next your skin. You will be laced with cruel force into vicelike corsets of soft dove coutille with whalebone busk to the diamondtrimmed pelvis, the absolute outside edge, while your figure, plumper than when at large, will be restrained in nettight frocks, pretty two ounce petticoats and fringes and things stamped, of course, with my houseflag. (*U* 15.2973–80)

Bloom's partly masochistic imprisonment in female garments produces thoughts about the constraints of gender that Molly reinforces in "Penelope" when she thinks of Lily Langtry's confinement in a chastity belt – the jealous old husband "he made her wear a kind of a tin thing round her and the prince of Wales yes he had the oyster knife" (*U* 18.486–7) – as well as her own handicapped condition in stays: "these clothes we have to wear whoever invented them expecting you to walk up Killiney hill then for example at that picnic all staysed up so you cant do a blessed thing in them" (*U* 18.627–9); "whoever suggested that business for women what between clothes and cooking and children" (*U* 18.1129–30).

After having experienced the constricting power of clothes, Bloom is able to see Molly's change of suitors as little more than Bloom's changes of suits; both are engaged in what Pater called "that strange, perpetual weaving and unweaving of ourselves" as an attempt to forestall entrapment. Exchanges of suits and suitors are strategies for resisting the paralysis of "habit," but if they continue indefinitely, they come to represent the inertia of never-ending motion, counterpart to the inertia of stasis, the perpetual evasions characteristic of irresponsibility. The only deadly deceptions are those that change arbitrarily, and those that are resistant to change, the deceptions of Mulligan and Murphy, respectively, who represent the Charybdis and Scylla of interpretive technique.

"EUMAEUS": ANCHOR AND FOOL

Mulligan treats costume – and identity – as a toy: "Primrosevested he greeted gaily with his doffed Panama as with a bauble" (*U* 9.489–

90). Self-denominated "Mercurial Malachi," his perpetual playacting is always mockery. He sees the world of clothing, of style and mannerism, as the only world; for him, life consists solely in the interplay of signifiers, an everchanging panoply of difference that is humorous because it is meaningless: in short, he is a postmodernist. Joyce dramatizes his role in the human drama as that of the fool – acutely intelligent, entertaining, and irresponsible. His own "suit," patched together as it is out of the assumed guises of others, is, appropriately, motley, as is clearest in "Circe," where he appears *"in particoloured jester's dress of puce and yellow and clown's cap with curling bell"* to gape at the apparition of Stephen's dead mother (U 15.4166–7; see also 9.486 – "blithe in motley"). At the end of "Circe," he materializes in the guise of Father Malachi O'Flynn, the black priest of ballad who is not only a fool in the Shakespearean sense, but a maker of fools (U 15.4693).

Structurally, the *"soi-disant* sailor" (U 16.620) who styles himself Murphy is the counterpart of Mulligan, just as "Eumaeus" mirrors "Telemachus" in the tripartite structure of *Ulysses.* Mulligan's light mockery finds its reversed reflection in Murphy's lurid tales of violence, Mulligan's heroic action of saving a man from drowning in the suspicion that Murphy might have knifed someone (U 16.835–8, 16.589). Whereas Mulligan regards appearances as purely exterior, changing his "clothing" whenever there is advantage in doing so, Murphy wears a human face *beneath* his clothing, indelibly imprinted on his skin. His assumption is that one name or even different names denominate a single reality, so that when he hears the name "Dedalus" he can "identify" him as a sharpshooter virtually indistinguishable from the other characters Murphy describes, or finally from "Murphy" himself. If Mulligan's emblem is motley, Murphy's is the anchor that forms part of his tattoo; despite the apparent variousness of his anecdotes, they are all anchored in a single narrative of violence, the violence of Roman history that Stephen sees reflected in the table knife. Paradoxically, the man who calls himself a traveller has an imagination that is utterly settled, never prompting him to sound the "lie of the land" or interrogate language as a tissue of lies. He defines life as easily penetrable, by anecdote or weapon, ignoring the plethora of possible interpretations that any profile – verbal or human – invites, impervious to any "hocuspocus of conflicting evidence that candidly you couldn't remotely" (U 16.1109–10). Like the others in the cabman's shelter, and like the citizen of whom Bloom is reminded, the sailor is one of those "pretending to understand everything, the why and the wherefore, and in reality not knowing their own minds" (*U* 16.1531–2), a temperament that, like his name, is far commoner than Mulligan's. The immobility threatened in "Eumaeus" is the paralysis of ignorance posing as knowledge, summed up in the image of Gumley, sleeping through his "watch." The narrator links his sleep to the more figurative blindness of Murphy by characterizing him as wrapped in "the arms of Morpheus" (*U* 16.947–8), "Morpheus" mutating into "Murphy" near the end of the episode (*U* 16.1727). The surroundings depict the nightmare of immobility: the fourwheeler that shows no sign of "budging a quarter of an inch" (*U* 16.28); the apprehension of Murphy apparently "glued to the spot" (*U* 16.1626–7); Bloom's realization that "a move had to be made" (*U* 16.1625) and his decision to eschew "hidebound precedent" (*U* 16.1621); the description of the encounter as a "*séance*" (*U* 16.1702), appropriate not only because of the evocation of the spirit of Parnell, but also literally, since "*séance*" *means* "sitting." The paralysis of the entire episode is expressed in the closing image of a pair of black-clothed figures, talking on various subjects and walking past a miring horse, "while the man in the sweeper car or you might as well call it in the sleeper car who in any case couldn't possibly hear because they were too far simply sat in his seat near the end of lower Gardiner street *and looked after their lowbacked car*" (*U* 16.1891–4).

"Eumaeus" explores the potential "lie" of a common name, whether that name is common to many, like Murphy, or common to a man and a woman in marriage (Bloom characterizes the plight of the O'Sheas by thinking, "nothing in common between them beyond the name" [*U* 16.1380–1]). The word "coffee" can be applied to vastly different-tasting concoctions, and the word "roll" can be used to designate something that may more closely resemble a brick (see the narrator's skeptical reference to Stephen's "mug of coffee or whatever you like to call it" [*U* 16.1169–70]). A name can be a lie and a truth, and it takes a shrewd observer to discern the contexts in which letters can express meaningful relations. The lie is always broadcast by "type," like the slander of Parnell published in "the *Insuppressible* or was it *United Ireland*" (*U* 16.1334–5, 16.1500–1), and the first step in sounding the lie of the land is always to break up the type, as Bloom helped to do in the Parnell incident. Parnell's supporters broke up the typecases with hammers, but the option of breaking up "type" is always open to a reader in the act of reading characters. To break up type is to eschew stereotypes, whether of words or personages, to note the literal relationship between "Murphy" and "Morpheus," the imagistic logic of attributing *Ham*let to Bacon (*U* 16.783), and to hear the unfinished promise of the name *Telegraph* to "tell a graphic lie" (*U* 16.1232). "Eumaeus" constitutes a map of place through a careful sounding of the placename, parenthetically defining Dublin, Ireland, through the interrelationship of dubbing and ire, the privilege of naming and the violence that ensues when names are regarded as the fixed anchors of a predictable reality. (See also "Bloom (properly so dubbed)" [*U* 16.1307]; and the keeper "(completely regardless of Ire)" [*U* 16.1685].)

"Eumaeus" is framed by Bloom's admonitions against Mulligan (*U* 16.264–7, 16.279–86, and 16.1868–73), whom Bloom distrusts as a doublefaced equivalent of Murphy, a man who literally wears two faces, both of which can be made to smile or frown (*U* 16.673–89). Instead of putting himself in Stephen's shoes, Mulligan has put Stephen quite literally in his own shoes; and Murphy, too, casts everyone in his own mold, pulling all anecdotes out of his own "chamber of horrors, otherwise pocket" (*U* 16.588). Mulligan denies all authority ("To me it's all a mockery and beastly" [*U* 1.210]), and Murphy has installed himself as the only authority. An alternative to the alternatives that Mulligan and Murphy represent is the one represented in Bloom: to see authority as variable, yet confined by the boundaries of the human systems that produce it; to see it as something that, like words or clothes, both invest and divest an individual of power and of freedom.

PENELOPE AND THE MATERIALITY OF DREAM

If you say on the hautboy man is not
   enough,
Can never stand as god, is ever wrong
In the end, however naked, tall, there is still
The impossible possible philosophers' man,
The man who has had the time to think
   enough,

Text Styles, Textiles, and Textures

> The central man, the human globe,
>   responsive
> As a mirror with a voice, the man of glass,
> Who in a million diamonds sums us up.
>   Wallace Stevens,
>   "Asides on the Oboe"

Whereas "Circe" restores a kind of balance by literally materializing Bloom's thoughts, effecting an equally material release through the popping of a button, "Penelope" moves in the opposite direction, tracing Molly's thoughts as they flow from clothes to poetry, from materiality to vision. Like Bloom, she uses clothing as a kind of language, and like Stephen, she has an almost superstitious belief in the power of names. If Stephen is a man of letters, she is, more literally, a woman of letters in all senses of the word: obsessed with letter writing as a form of lovemaking, liberal with letters in her mental orthography, and literal in her approach to foreign words. As her thoughts weave in and out among her "suitors," they create in their very inconsistency a consistent pattern. Her lovers, like Bloom's, line up along a spectrum bounded by sentimentality and bestiality; her "Calypso" is Mulvey, her "Circe" is Boylan. Yet the one person most nearly capable of spanning that spectrum, of wearing the "suits" of each of her suitors, is Bloom. Although unfaithful to him in body, she is faithful to her multifaceted idea of him in spirit, as her network of allusions to names and clothes makes clear. It is her memory and her vision of him as Tweedy-Mulvey-Gardner-Simon-Boylan-Stephen Bloom, a man that Wallace Stevens would call "impossible possible" since he never is and always is, that she imaginatively and sensually re-espouses at the end of the book. As a conglomerate of men, Bloom is to Molly an abstraction that she can only experience fully through living representations of his different aspects. Her adultery is a form of faith, her obsession with suits and suitors a kind of lonely poetry comparable to Stephen's, as she brings the book and the day to a close.

To Molly, men are both endlessly exciting in their variousness and always the same ("theyre all so different" [U 18.246]; "theyre all made the one way" [U 18.483]). In their difference, they emerge as Boylan, Mulvey, her father, Bloom, Stephen, Simon, Gardner; in their sameness, as Bloom, who is "always imitating everybody" (U 1205). Stylistically, the part of speech that best expresses

Bloom's unity in multaeity is the pronoun "he," a variously inflected word that attracts a cluster of unexpectedly changing referents throughout "Penelope."[24] A memory of Bloom glides imperceptibly into anticipation of Boylan via a comparison with Gardner: "I liked the way he [Bloom] made love then he knew the way to take a woman . . . but he never knew how to embrace well like Gardner I hope hell [Boylan] come on Monday" (*U* 18.328–32). Repeatedly in Molly's train of thought men succeed one another behind the veil of a pronoun, as when Molly is thinking of Bloom's antics on a train and quietly exchanges him for Boylan with a deft change of tense: "a good job he [Bloom] was able to open the carriage door with his knife or theyd have taken us on to Cork I suppose that was done out of revenge on him O I love jaunting in a train or a car with lovely soft cushions I wonder will he [Boylan] take a 1st class for me he might want to do it in the train by tipping the guard" (*U* 18.364–8).

The consistency in Molly's inconsistency becomes apparent only when we read her thoughts as she reads life, attending to the "language" of appearances as well as to the appearance of language. In *Exiles*, Joyce touched on the device of representing a change of allegiance through a change of costume, linking Robert with different women through the changing colors of his clothes.[25] In *Ulysses*, however, Joyce plays more subtly on a more various array of garments, fabrics, and accessories to dramatize changing relationships. To Bloom, Boylan is never more than clothes and a name: in "Hades," he is a white straw hat in salute (*U* 6.199); after lunch, he appears as a "straw hat in sunlight," "tan shoes," and "turnedup trousers" (*U* 8.1168); and his "gay hat" returns to mock Bloom's lugubriousness in "Sirens" (*U* 11.302). As a suitor, Boylan is first and foremost a suit, and the appeal of that suit is its power to replay love's old sweet song. Boylan's white hat reinforces the suggestion embedded in his name that he acts as an avatar of lost youth. His suit recalls that of a younger Bloom, his hat the straw hat that Bloom wore on Howth (*U* 18.1573), and, more distantly, the hat

24 See Kenner, *Ulysses*, p. 147.

25 In Act I, Robert appears in a dark blue suit like that of Beatrice, but at the end of the play he signals his new rapport with Bertha and the earth by wearing dark brown, the color Bertha had worn to his cottage the evening before.

Molly wore with Mulvey high on the rock of Gibraltar, "leaning over him with my white ricestraw hat to take the newness out of it the left side of my face the best my blouse open for his last day transparent kind of shirt he had" (*U* 18.797–9). Boylan attracts her through a boyishness that recalls Bloom's and Mulvey's, but its appeal is gradually surpassed by the greater youth – actual and remembered – of Stephen.

Hats synecdochically represent suits – doubly experienced as garments and lovers' entreaties – that can be idealized and infused with nostalgic sentiment or relegated to the economy of wear, as Molly does when she deflates Boylan to a new hat: "in any case God knows hes a change in a way not to be always and ever wearing the same old hat" (*U* 18.83–4). Mulvey's hat, like Boylan's, helps to elucidate the role he plays in Molly's imagination; its legend links him with "Calypso," an immortal, idealized vision of youth: "he didnt know what to make of me with his peak cap on that he always wore crooked as often as I settled it straight H M S Calypso" (*U* 18.835–7). Mulvey's "Calypso" hat signals his place in Molly's mythology, a place occupied by the nymph (Calypso) in Bloom's. Boylan at first appears to be a version of Mulvey, but in the end he reveals his alliance with the other extreme, acting as Molly's "Circe." Her impressions of him in retrospect are predominantly bestial, as "a Stallion driving it up into you . . . with that determined vicious look in his eye" (*U* 18.152–3), or, more tellingly, a lion: "sure you might as well be in bed with what with a lion God Im sure hed have something better to say for himself an old Lion would" (*U* 18.1376–8).

Molly's view of Boylan as a lion, and particularly a Lion, once again recalls Bloom through the chain of association initiated by the "Leo" in "Leopold." Bloom too is an animal as well as a lost dream, but within those borders he contains a comprehensiveness Boylan lacks. Boylan is implicitly what both Mulvey and Gardner are explicitly – a lieutenant (*U* 18.818, 18.389), literally, someone holding a place (*lieu* + *tenant*, from *tenir*). Gardner, Mulvey, and Tweedy are all holding a place for Bloom, foreshadowing different aspects of his name and wardrobe, just as Boylan, Rudy, and Stephen echo him. Bloom's attempts to make Molly imagine him as other men are for this reason comically redundant, since it is precisely her readiness to see him in others that constitutes her "infidelity," along with her quickness to see the "otherness" in Bloom.

Bloom is impossibly protean, a glass man, and at the same time oddly unique: "I suppose there isnt in all creation another man with the habits he has look at the way hes sleeping at the foot of the bed ... its well he doesnt kick or he might knock out all my teeth" (*U* 18.1197–1200).

In "Penelope," names and clothes intertwine to create a texture of interconnection that is also, paradoxically, an affirmation of loss, since, as Mr. Duffy observes when breaking off intercourse with Mrs. Sinico, "every bond ... is a bond to sorrow" (*D* 112). What Mr. Duffy only belatedly realizes is that those bonds are ineluctable, linking the living to the dead, the present to the absent. In "Penelope," too, Joyce stresses that every "woven" structure is also a memorial to something that no longer exists, every weaving also a shroud for the unwoven reality it drapes and buries. Such a weaving, more pragmatically represented as language and clothes, enmeshes Bloom with Molly's dead father, Major Tweedy. She confesses to desiring a "ghostly father," or someone in the guise of a father, when thinking about priests and their habit of burying physical reality in euphemism: "O Lord couldnt he say bottom right out and have done with it ... I always think of the real father ... Id like to be embraced by one in his vestments" (*U* 18.110–19). Molly's desire to embrace a father dressed as a father resurfaces more subtly through her recollection of Howth, where Bloom's grey tweed suit fulfilled the promise of her father's name (*U* 18.1573), making him a "Tweedy" and offering at the same time a new name and a new poetry, the promise of "Bloom."

Molly celebrates the materialization of dream through marriage, but she also laments that realization, periodically seeking to recover the lost poetry of youth. As unlikely as it may initially seem, Molly, with her sensitivity to the figurative dimension of words and names, is a poetic figure, a counterpart to Stephen, Echo to his Narcissus. Appropriately, her idea of poetry is best represented by the naked statue of Narcissus: "theres real beauty and poetry for you" (*U* 18.1351). Molly's longing for poetry surfaces in her dreams, in her memories, in her literal approach to words as microcosmic expressions of the poetic impulse, and in her attraction to Stephen. In contrast to Bloom's dream of the night before – which featured Molly's clothes, the materialization of desire – Molly's dream has "something about poetry in it" (*U* 18.1321). The allure of poetry, and particularly romantic poetry, had initially drawn her to Bloom, who "made me the present of lord Byrons poems and the three pairs of gloves," being "very handsome at that time trying to look like Lord Byron" (*U* 18.185–6; 18.208–9). Her marriage to Bloom substituted a more prosaic reality for her poetic dream, as she recalls: "I always liked poetry when I was a girl first I thought he was a poet like lord Byron and not an ounce of it in his composition I thought he was quite different" (*U* 18.1323–6). Her growing dissatisfaction with Boylan repeats and exaggerates her earlier disillusionment with Bloom, until she denounces him as an "ignoramus that doesnt know poetry from a cabbage" (*U* 18.1370–1). She eventually rediscovers the poetic aspect of Bloom's sensibility, partly through her ruminations about Stephen, who seems to offer anew the youth and poetry that initially attracted her to Bloom. Molly is faithful to her dream of love, a fidelity paradoxically inseparable from betrayal. The final irony of *Ulysses* is the realization that Molly, so frequently regarded as a "great lust-lump" preoccupied with exclusively material concerns, uses the material world to live out a private poetry, trying to keep faith with her memory of a dream.

Molly's poetic sensibility is apparent not only in her attraction to poets, but also in her literal approach to words and names. As the narrator announces in "Aeolus," the name "Penelope" envelopes the word "pen" as well as designating a mythological weaver – and "Pen is Champ" (*U* 7.1034). Like Stephen, another proponent of pens and signatures, Molly has a feel for the texture of language, an instinct undisguised by Stephen's patina of arcane knowledge. Like the child whom she remembers as "an innocent boy then and a darling little fellow in his lord Fauntleroy suit and curly hair like a prince on the stage" (*U* 18.1311–12), and whom we remember puzzling over the meaning of words and names at the beginning of *Portrait*, Molly attends to the metaphorical possibilities of names, deriving "bloomers" from "Bloom" (*U* 18.839–40), affirming Bloom's desire to denominate her a "flower of the mountain" by taking his name, and recording her preference for the name "Bloom" as "better than Breen or Briggs does brig or those awful names with bottom in them Mrs Ramsbottom or some other kind of a bottom" (*U* 18.843–5). Like Stephen as a child, she muses over the strangeness of his name, linking it back to the foreign names in Gibraltar – "they had the devils queer names there" (*U* 18.1464).

Her concern with names highlights the figurative potential of names such as "Tweedy," "Boylan," and "Bloom," their power to turn protean humanity into mere signatures, or into the suits they so much resemble.

Bloom's name achieves new meaning in a variety of contexts – as a euphemistic curse ("It was too blooming dull" [*U* 10.1124–5]); as bloomers, sign of the "new woman" the bishop was preaching against (*U* 18.837–9); as a rhyme on "womb," "tomb," and "loom," a rhyme with reason of the sort that Stephen is always pursuing;[26] as a sob (Bloo-who); and as accidental catastrophe, a casualty of print – "L. Boom." But Molly is most deeply impressed by the most obvious association of his name, its evocation of flowers. She espoused the idea of bloom before she ever met Leopold, when she told Mulvey that she was engaged to a man named Don Miguel de la Flora (*U* 18.772–4), and when she formed an attachment to a man named "Gardner." She unconsciously connects the organic rhythms of gardening with the artistic rhythms of weaving, "male" sowing with "female" sewing. Moreover, she intuitively uncovers and responds to the metaphorical poetry of Christian lore, feeling its movement from a garden to a man that rose as a poetic tribute to human bloom that helps to compensate for the certainty of wear, the knowledge that people, like garments, are eventually "laid on the shelf" (*U* 18.1022). Her attraction to men is always bordered by references to gardening, whether the emphasis is upon the planting or the flowers, earthy sexuality or etherial lyricism. Molly's thoughts of Lily Langtry exemplify her awareness of the figurative suggestiveness of her name, its "tree" and its "lily," and when she thinks of the Prince of Wales' visit to Gibraltar in the year she was born, she reflects, "I bet he found lilies there too where he planted the tree he planted more than that in his time he might have planted me too if hed come a bit sooner" (*U* 18.501–3). Boylan's sexual prowess, too, reenters her thoughts as an energetic gardening: "poking and rooting and ploughing" (*U* 18.1106).

26 Stephen uses the metaphor of dress to describe the verbal phenomenon of rhyme, picturing rhyme as "two men dressed the same, looking the same," and "three by three, approaching girls, in green, in rose, in russet, entwining" (*U* 7.715–6, 7.720–1).

When Molly's feelings become more lyrical she stresses not the planting but the bloom, thereby renewing her commitment to a name and all the "music" it represents for her. Many of her allusions to flowers are, like Bloom's, musical: she sings "shall I wear a white rose" when anticipating an appointment with Mulvey (*U* 18.768), a song that recurs to accompany her fantasy of a musical evening with Stephen (*U* 18.1553–4), and she remembers singing "O Maritana wildwood flower" with Stephen's father (*U* 18.1297). Her view of herself as a flower endows the flow of her thoughts with a more stable form, verbally bridging the distance between Molly and ALP in *Finnegans Wake*, as the "-er" in "flower" metamorphoses into a suffix of the verb "flow," turning momentary bloom to neverceasing motion. Molly's return to nature is inseparable from her return to dream, her impossible return to childhood and youth ("I used to love myself then" [*U* 18.922–3]), since what she returns to is the *idea* of nature, and the *idea* of Bloom, the interwoven garment of appearances and language that mediates all experience. Her final affirmation is not so much an affirmation of Bloom as it is of bloom, since his name and his blood (a connection that Bloom makes in "Lestrygonians": "Bloo... Me? No. Blood" [*U* 8.8–9]) are all she can have of him: "I love flowers Id love to have the whole place swimming in roses God of heaven theres nothing like nature the wild mountains then the sea and the waves rushing ... and colours springing up even out of the ditches primroses and violets" (*U* 18.1557–63). Bloom's gift is blooded language, his assertion that she is "a flower of the mountain yes so we are flowers all a womans body yes that was one true thing he said in his life" (*U* 18.1576–7).

In *Ulysses*, Bloom and Molly's unfaithfulness to one another is inextricable from their faithfulness to dream. Both chafe against the tailoring of their desires and the straitening of their potential that marriage implies; both regard their mutual "suitability" as a kind of closing to the openness of their youth. Both express their protests against the constraints of custom through an obsession with costume: Molly once ran a used clothing business, and Bloom fetishizes underclothing as a material substitute for understanding. Yet what makes their attitudes toward clothes significant is not the peculiarities of their respective attitudes, but their instinctive recognition of the way that cloth lays bare the mechanisms of communication, figuring connection and isolation by turns.

DRAPERY AND *FINNEGANS WAKE*: THE NORWEGIAN CAPTAIN EPISODE

As Joyce's works move from the "drapery" sold at Father Flynn's in *Dubliners* to the drapery of letters that obscures *Finnegans Wake*, they generate an increasing awareness of the interrelationships between language and cloth, while at the same time they mark a progression from one to the other. The development of Joyce's style suggests that human communication evolves from narrative to display, from spun yarns to woven ones, a tendency that culminates in the complex fabric of *Finnegans Wake*. As the last of Joyce's works, *Finnegans Wake* is also the one most dedicated to the revelatory potential of verbal drapery. If the medium is indeed the message, the main "subject" of the book is obscurity and "reveilation" – the perpetual, ever-changing enigma of human and verbal disguise. Words, like clothing, serve both as decoration and camouflage, flaunting the seductiveness of meaning through the vanity of style; and *Finnegans Wake* both advertises and deprecates the cleverness of "a word as cunningly hidden in its maze of confused drapery as a fieldmouse in a nest of coloured ribbons" (*FW* 120.5–6). If "In the beginning was the Word," "In the becoming was the weared" (*FW* 487.20–1). "French" yields to "frenge," "translate" to "translace"; journey's close is more aptly "journee's clothes"; and what paper is made of and in need of is gaily clothed girls, as textual mishaps become "miss shapes": "For that (the rapt [wrapped] one warns) is what papyr is meed of, made of, hides and hints and misses in prints" (*FW* 20.10–11). Language has turned to cloth.

The view that communication begins in telling and ends in tailoring, as the individual trades his isolated wanderings for society in the form of publichouses, serves as a larger frame for the individual maturation of HCE in the Norwegian Captain episode (*FW* 311.5–332.35), his change of state from single sailor to married "tailor." Appropriately, the Norwegian Captain episode is one of the most densely veiled narratives in the *Wake*. The Norwegian captain's foreignness is underscored not only by the language of the tale, but also by the strangeness of its narrative precursors, both personal and mythic. Joyce's account of HCE's marriage takes the particulars of its plot from a story told to his father by one of his friends, but it takes its mythic outlines from Wagner's *The Flying Dutchman*, reread as a parable of marriage and a subtle analysis of the the faithlessness of keeping faith with a dream. In addition, the story of the Norwegian captain is a counterpart of the story that succeeds it, the account of how Buckley shot the Russian general, in which HCE is undone by a younger generation much as he was "kerssed" by an older one in the Norwegian Captain tale. The parallels between Kersse and Buckley are emphasized when the ship's husband asks Kersse to "make and shoot" (make a suit) for the Norwegian captain (*FW* 311.27; see also 329). Finally, the captain's story is a version of the Prankquean episode from a male point of view: the first of three tailors tells the captain's story in the rhythm of her thrice-repeated question to van Hoother: "Nohow did he kersse or hoot alike the suit and solder skins" (*FW* 317.22).

The version of the story that Joyce heard from his father focuses on an argument between a hunchbacked Norwegian captain and a Dublin tailor over a suit that didn't fit, with the captain blaming the tailor's craftsmanship and the tailor blaming the captain's irregularity of form (see *JJ* II, 23). Joyce frames his version of the story with a description of the way that radio broadcasts penetrate the labyrinth of the ear, thereby implying that this is a tale about storytelling, listening, and the "magic" of conception, one that celebrates the impossibility of perfectly suiting any one listener. The "tailor" is in this regard a "taler," someone who tells tales. Yet the multi-referentiality of language suggests that the opposite is also true: the sailor is also someone who "says," a spinner of yarns, as a mutation of spelling points out ("he sayled," 325.25; see also the description of one of the sailor's voyages: "the baffling yarn sailed in circles" [*FW* 320.35]).

The Norwegian captain asks simultaneously for "a suit and sowterkins [sooterkins, sweetheart]" (*FW* 311.22–23), establishing himself as a version of the tailor through his desire to be a suited "suitor" (see *FW* 326.27, "sutor"), and through his "wooving [weaving; wooing]" (*FW* 318.32). If the sailor is a kind of tailor, the tailor is also, reciprocally, a sailor, since his services are for "sale." (HCE as "landlord" [*FW* 316.6] is also telling [310.30, 313] – or counting – coins received in return for the "liquid courage" [313.29] that he sells in "Publin" [315.24].) The narrator substitutes "talerman" for "tillerman" in a line of "tea for the tillerman" (*FW* 319.8), reinforcing the identity of sailor and tailor and at the same time suggesting that the tailor is a spectator, since *taler* means "spectator" in Norwegian – again like the sailor, who is described as a "seelord" (*FW* 325.16). Joyce suggests through the network of linguistic links that intertwine "sailor" and "tailor" that the two men are versions of each other, and versions of Shem and Shaun, Tom, Dick and Harry as well. These different men are all reconciled through the captain's wedding to the tailor's daughter, when the sailor, as a "faulter-in-law" (*FW* 325.15), takes the tailor as father-in-law. The sailor is a sinner, a "Sinbad," a soiler (*FW* 327.25, 325.24; *sale* is "dirty" in French), a seaman personifying homeless semen (see "seoman," *FW* 331.29–30). His maritime life is a "merrytime" of life (*FW* 325.30), but it is also a time to marry. His wedding is depicted as a soiler's cleansing, a "wetting," and a baptism (*FW* 314.33, 326) that enters history as our "kristianiasation" (*U* 331.32), or the discovery that "drouth is stronger than faction" (*FW* 336.20). Cleansed and suited (or "groomed") by ALP, his "streamstress" (*FW* 324.33) who approaches him as Nausicaa approached another profligate and naked sailor, he exchanges his boat for a coat, his "loudship" for a "landshop," his "sails" for "sales," intent on "playing house of ivary dower of gould" (*FW* 327.28). He yearns to be close to someone, and in that way to bring his tale to a close and clothes to his tail (see the narrator's version of "When a man marries" as "When a tale tarries" [*FW* 336.9]). ALP is "the lappel of his size" that suits the captain (*FW* 314.33–4); this is Joyce's version of *Sartor Resartus*: "so sartor's risorted why the sinner the badder!" (314.17–18) But since no tailored suit (or suitable tale) can ever really fit the eccentricities of the human state, being suited becomes its own "kersse," and every tailor a "breachesmaker."

The Norwegian Captain episode defines the complicated interrelationship of its characters by literally interchanging verbal characters, creating a complex network of words. Joyce called the episode a "wordspiderweb" (*Letters* III, 422), working on the logic that there is no revelation without entrapment, no "emprisoming" without imprisonment. In *Finnegans Wake* Joyce subjects narrative, as well as individual words, to the refractory action of a prism by telling more than one version of a story at once, and in that way deprivileging the authority of any simple interpretation. In the Norwegian Captain episode, he complicates the outlines of McCann's story (as retold by John Joyce) by crossing it with another maritime story touched on in *Ulysses*, the story of the Flying Dutchman (as retold by Wagner). As Joyce interprets the story in the Norwegian Captain episode, Wagner's *The Flying Dutchman* comes to illustrate the interdependence of faith and treachery, while at the same time challenging the view that spinning is a purely "material" activity, bringing it back, by a "commodius vicus of recirculation," to the world of dream.

Structurally, Wagner's *Der Fliegende Holländer* is itself a musical "web" spun entirely out of Senta's ballad, the spinning song of Act II. Throughout, spinning is associated with illusion; as Senta spins, she dreams, and gazes on the Dutchman's portrait. The Dutchman, in turn, confesses that he has often dreamed of her image. Both she and the Dutchman pledge their troth to an illusion, and Senta literally sacrifices herself to prove that she has always been faithful to him, "saving" him by killing herself, so that he too may die. Nietzsche scorned this as pure "Senta-mentality,"[27] but Joyce's reading of the story, as it informs *Ulysses* and *Finnegans Wake*, emphasizes the ironic contradictions expressed in the subplot. By keeping her word to the Dutchman, who is to her the apparent incarnation of a dream, a portrait, and a song, Senta breaks faith with her first lover, Erik. When Erik reminds her of the day he gathered mountain flowers for her and she confessed her love for him anew, the Dutchman thinks she has betrayed him, and all is lost. Like Molly Bloom, Senta has always been faithful to her youthful dream, and that faith has caused her to betray her real lover for a "phantom shape" (*FW* 327.25–6). Moreover, that shape is a version of her father, Daland, who has "sold" her to the Dutchman at the expense of the dispossessed Erik. As in the Norwegian Captain episode, where the captain and Kersse, the betrothed and the father, are versions of each other, Daland and the Dutchman live out different forms of the same torment, as is apparent in Act I, when Daland is blown away from home:

> Curses!
> I have already seen my house on the shore,

27 Nietzsche, *The Case of Wagner*, trans. Anthony Ludovici, vol. VIII of *The Complete Works of Friedrich Nietzsche*, ed. Oscar Levy (1909–11: rpt. New York: Russell and Russell, 1964), p. 4. Joyce owned a copy of this translation in Trieste; see Ellmann, *The Consciousness of Joyce*.

Senta, my child, was nearly in my arms;
then this devilish wind blows up.[28]

Near the end of the act, Daland sells Senta to his counterpart, cementing the identity between husband and father: "May she continue so to love her father! / True to him, she will be true to her husband."[29] The father betrays his daughter to ensure the vicarious fulfillment of his own dream, just as Senta betrays Erik to pledge faith to the dream she inherited. The different strands of plot all suggest that marriage to a mutual dream is a kind of death.

In the Norwegian Captain episode, ALP is presented as having spun a dream similar to Senta's:

> when it's summwer calding and she can hear the pianutunar beyant the bayondes in Combria sleepytalking to the Wiltsh muntons, titting out through her droemer [dormer; dreamer] window for the flyend of a touchman [the flying dutchman] over the wishtas of English Strand, . . . Where our dollimonde sees the phantom shape of Mr Fortunatus Wright (*FW* 327.20–26)

HCE appears to her as a "bugganeering wanderducken" [Vanderdecken, the name of the Dutchman], "voyaging after maidens" (*FW* 323.1, 323.6–7), and they marry, "her youngfree [jungfrau] yoke stilling his wandercursus" (*FW* 318.9–10). With their mutual pledge of faith, the dream they had composed decomposes into memory. As ALP tells HCE near the end of her journey, "You make me think of a wonderdecker [Vanderdecken] I once. Or somebalt thet sailder, the man megallant, with the bangled ears" (*FW* 620.6–7). The dream is materially passed on as Issy, their "spindlesong aside" (*FW* 336.14), but ALP never abandons her original "creation." "Like the queenoveire [Queen of Eire, Guinevere]" (*FW* 28.1), she is forever "sewing a dream together, the tailor's daughter, stitch to her last" (*FW* 28.7–8).

28 Richard Wagner, *Der Fliegende Holländer*, Chicago Symphony Chorus and Orchestra, conducted by Sir Georg Solti (London: Decca Record Company Ltd., 1977), p. 17.
29 Wagner, *Der Fliegende Holländer*, p. 22.

CONCLUSION

The growing opacity and obscurity of Joyce's style, accompanied by an equally marked adulteration of the authorial voice, is the natural culmination of a lifetime of experimentation with the politics of style and the "biology" of artistic reproduction. Joyce sought, not merely to redirect our attention to the "female" dimension of language, the texture that subtly comprehends its authoritarian impulses, making it more democratic, but to restore awareness of the complicated interdependence of revealing and reveiling by emphasizing the equal agency of the mother in any "genesis." He saw that our habits of interpretation tend to highlight sameness at the expense of difference, the general to the detriment of the particular, the author rather than the authored, the past regardless of a future. His fiction works to correct this cultural imbalance through an increasing attention to the interrelationship of language and cloth, of "male" and "female" styles.

Ulysses is haunted by the three greatest barriers to human understanding – difference of age, difference of gender, and difference of race or creed. Those differences can only be bridged, and preserved, by systems of mediation, such as language and clothes, but the interconnective and disconnective capabilities of these particular systems have been straitened by the way that they have been segregated from one another. By regarding language and clothes as complementary versions of a single communicative system, Joyce is able to draw attention to the opacity, as well as the transparency, of language, and to emphasize the transparency, as well as the opacity, of clothes. Stylistically, Joyce attempts to restore wholeness of perception by drawing attention to the *texture* of words as well as their meaning. He prompts his readers to look *at* individual words, and not just to peer through them; he emphasizes the comic way that words thwart and misdirect our attempts to channel them toward a straightforward goal. Grammar may be linear, but language is weblike, constantly suggesting a network of connections between similar sounds and images that subvert our desire to turn language from a truly communal art form into an instrument. As Hillis Miller argues, narrative proffers a labyrinth as well as a line.[30]

30 J. Hillis Miller, "Ariadne's Thread: Repetition and the Narrative Line," pp. 57–77; and "Ariachne's Broken Woof," pp. 44–60.

Both "text" and "textile" come from the Latin *texere*, "to weave." Joyce attempted to recover the threads of connection between texts and textiles, and in so doing to restore the awareness that "weaving," as an expression of the rhythm of fabrication and wear, interconnection and gradual isolation, is a dynamic process common to both life and art. This oscillating movement between the coherence and dissolution of disparate phenomena is the neglected partner of logocentrism, its natural spouse. It is the variegated play of impressions that Pater referred to as "that strange, perpetual weaving and unweaving of ourselves," the movement that to Pater constituted the essence of life. And it is the pattern that Penelope translates into action by diurnally weaving and unweaving Laertes' shroud, thereby resisting the pressure to confine herself to a single suitor, or a single "suit" – which is always, by implication, a shroud.

The process of weaving and unweaving becomes a new – or at least a recovered – model of the way that both language and perception can and should operate. This is a view indebted to the ancient past and prophetic of the future; it is born of the symmetrical relationship between Odysseus and Penelope in *The Odyssey*, nurtured by the perceptual theories of Pater, and it anticipates some aspects of theoretical positions that postdate *Ulysses*: feminist critiques of patriarchal epistemologies; Todorov's descriptions of the critical *praxis*; Hillis Miller's analyses of the "threads" of narrative; Derrida's play on the fluctuations of discourse, its power to deconstruct its own constructions. And it is a movement that defines the borders of *Ulysses*, its fundamentally identical margins of word and world.

Weaving and unweaving is a process of fabrication. What every text fabricates anew is human and literary history, on the one hand, and language, on the other. Moreover, as T. S. Eliot asserted in "Tradition and the Individual Talent," the reverse is equally true: history and language, together with the history *of* language, also fabricate every text, serving as reconstructed context and pretext. There is a complex "logic" to the interrelationship between a character and his or her refabricated precursors, a logic that is always reinforced by the unexpected interconnections among sounds, images, and letters that are the "illegitimate" offspring of the attempt to manipulate meaning.

As a pattern for thought, Penelope's cunning strategy of weaving and unweaving a shroud in order to remain "faithful" yields several insights into the nature of physical and mental activity:

1. It suggests that reality is neither hierarchical nor dialectical; instead, it is an alternating movement between coherence and incoherence. In the language of *Finnegans Wake*, "The untireties of livesliving being the one substance of a streamsbecoming. Totalled in toldteld and teldtold in tittletell tattle . . . Why? It is a sot of a swigswag, systomy dystomy, which everabody you ever anywhere at all doze. Why? Such me." (*FW* 597.7–22) Joyce's "answer" to the challenge of human existence is not male logocentrism and identity-building alone, nor does it center around female prescience in dismantling male structures; rather, it takes as its pattern the continuous, diurnal oscillation between coherence and destabilization, between day and night. This emphasis on life as a *process* of interconnection between complex extremes also reaffirms the importance of deconstructing any proposition in order to remain "faithful" to a reality in which the opposite of any given proposition is also true.

2. The Penelope model emphasizes the labyrinthine interconnectedness and disconnectedness of *any* created system.

3. It suggests that *all* systems are, in a sense, shrouds woven to conceal the ugly and inescapable incoherence of death. Alternately, these shrouds, or systems, must be periodically unwoven or else they turn the intimation of death into a present reality, since any ossified system kills the process of life.

4. It affirms the value of inconsistency, which has been culturally designated as a "female" trait.

5. Finally, the process of weaving and unweaving serves as a paradigm for the labyrinthine interconnectedness and disconnectedness of all phenomena on the one hand, and as an image of intimate physical "connection" in the form of dressing, undressing, and redressing, on the other. But it also serves as a model for human identity, in which each individual is, like Odysseus, both everyman and noman; this is the sense in which Pater used the metaphor. For him, the "strange, perpetual weaving and unweaving of ourselves" was a way of defying the encroachment of death upon life; a way of admitting the contradictions of human experience as something that oscillates between community and isolation; and finally, a metaphor for the human individual, who possesses an entire world and no world within the circumference of a single flesh-case.

The implications of Joyce's affirmation of weaving and unweaving as a metaphor that can describe the process of both physical and mental life are important: the issues he raises and the metaphor he adopts to "resolve" them, through an admission of the insufficiency of any final resolution, continue to haunt and even divide numerous schools of contemporary thought. What are "structuralism" and "deconstruction" but weaving and unweaving, applied not to the material world but to the linguistic one, clothed not in a "female" metaphor but in a metaphor culturally determined as "male"? Hillis Miller has responded to the logocentric implications of structuralism and deconstruction by restoring the female analogy for the workings of language. Feminist critics such as Mary Daly have announced their intent to restore the original dualism of traditionally female activities such as weaving and spinning. In *Gyn/Ecology*, Daly exhorts women to rediscover the interconnectedness of existence, arguing that women "must be able to weave and unweave, dis-covering hidden threads of connectedness."[31] The labyrinth, along with the thread or narrative necessary to penetrate it, has even become a dominant metaphor in the works of several post-modernist writers, including Borges, Barthelme, and Pynchon.

The fact that so many writers are preoccupied in so many ways with weaving and unweaving suggests that the issues that Joyce raised are still very much alive. Joyce suggests that the problems of gender-defined identity will never be resolved until we adopt different attitudes toward *all* the oppositions that our culture has appended to the opposition between "male" and "female" principles. In Joyce's view, the most fundamental of "weighted" oppositions is the supposed dominance of spiritual over physical truth. He suggests that spirituality, that language, must have a symbiotic relationship to physicality, to Aristotelian appearances; if this relationship lapses or fails to be renewed, then the spirit becomes a mere phantom (this is one of its meanings), and the body a *corpus*, or corpse. Joyce's most memorable contribution to this debate is not theoretical, however, but practical: he uses language in such a way that we are forced to explore the relationship between its texture, its rich metaphoric potential, and its textuality. We are asked to look at words, to hear them, to dissect and reassemble

31 *Gyn/Ecology*, p. 400.

them, as well as to use them as windows in the always voyeuristic attempt to gain knowledge. In the language of clothes, we are asked to look again at our tendency to treat words as mere signs and not as artifacts with a wantonly sensual referentiality. With this perspective in mind, it becomes easier to appreciate the irony and appropriateness of Joyce's plays on "Pen" and "Penelope"; his pairing of "sailors" and "tailors" as people who deal with yarn/yarns, and as those who *say* and *tell*; his association of Molly with breeches as well as breaches; his insistence that Molly is both a flower and a "flow-er." Finally, it reawakens us to the power of literature to reach out and encompass life in its fictionally coherent yet comically unstable webs. Joyce's fictions certainly grew out to meet the coincidences of his own life: the Fates, those original spinners, gave Joyce as his most faithful and consistent benefactress, a feminist woman of letters named Weaver.[32]

32 Harriet Shaw Weaver's association with Joyce began when she became editor of the *Egoist*, which published *Portrait* in serial form in 1914–15. Miss Weaver began making anonymous bequests to Joyce in 1917 to help him through the war, and she continued to support him in a variety of ways throughout his life: serving as his most frequent correspondent during the years when he was composing *Ulysses* and *Finnegans Wake*; taking care of Joyce's daughter Lucia after Lucia's madness was apparent to everyone but Joyce; even paying for Joyce's funeral and acting as his literary executor. There is some evidence that he saw the "Penelope" episode as a tribute, in part, to her: he tells her in a letter that the name of the chapter "by other strange coincidence is your own" (*SL* 289). See *JJ* II, pp. 352–3 and *passim*; Bonnie Scott, *Joyce and Feminism*, pp. 88–97; and Jane Lidderdale and Mary Nicholson, *Dear Miss Weaver* (New York: Viking, 1970).

POSTSCRIPT:
"PRESEEDING" AUTHORITIES:
READING BACKWARD

I F A TEXT, like a shroud, is something that must be both woven and unwoven, read and unread, then the literary language that comprises it must necessarily be solid and ephemeral by turns. The process of shuttling between a constructed reality and a deconstructed nothingness dictates an awareness of the reversibility of a created artifact, a reversibility that reflects a view of time as likewise reversible, periodically moving backward as well as forward, bringing the past as well as the future to new life. The action of unweaving and reweaving dead realities to give them fresh imaginative life is a strategy for changing the "habits" of the present. The reciprocity of past and present, living and dead, is best illustrated by the processes of reading and writing: a present reader and an absent author are asked to exchange places, so that the author becomes imaginatively present and the reader absent, until the reader reasserts his or her presence through criticism that can potentially reshape our image of the written reality, making that writing once again contemporaneous.

In *Positions*, Jacques Derrida alludes to the identity and reciprocity of writing and reading by directing those who would understand his writings to his readings: "You know, in fact, that above all it is necessary to read and reread those in whose wake I write, the books in whose margins and between whose lines I mark out and read a text simultaneously almost identical and entirely other."[1] Derrida's statement not only undermines the distinction between writing and reading; at the same time it plays with the oppositions of text and context, message and margin. Most strikingly, it stresses the double nature of interpretation: in the process of reading, the reader both adjusts himself to the text and adjusts the text to him in the space around the writing. Reading is an activity both ambivalent and implicitly marginal, but it has the power to generate the centripetal activity of writing. Writing is the complementary process of centralizing what was marginal, a process engendered by reading and animated by the vital interplay between what is present and what is absent, between text and context, between the writer and those whose works he or she has read, assimilated, and found wanting.

Writing, seen as an Odyssey that begins with reading, the process of imaginatively filling the margins of other books, can be read as a process first described by Homer. The dependence of writing on the digressions of reading can be seen to follow the "logic" of the *Odyssey*, which Bloom pithily sums up in *Ulysses*: "Longest way round is the shortest way home" (*U* 13: 1110–11). The insight that the *Odyssey* expresses in spatial terms as the necessity of circumspection and circumnavigation, *Hamlet*, the other major precursor of *Ulysses*, explores in terms of heredity: straightforward movement is equally impossible through space *and* time. We create our past as surely as it creates us; as Stephen insists through his theory, *Hamlet* illustrates the way that characters father their authors, who in turn father their forefathers. In Mulligan's words, Stephen's argument is "that Hamlet's grandson is Shakespeare's grandfather and that he himself is the ghost of his own father" (*U* 1.555–7). Expressed more simply, Stephen's insight is this: when seen as an imaginative as well as a biological process, "heredity" works its influence in both directions. Alpha and omega, center and margin, must be treated as interchangeable doubles if change is ever to occur.

Joyce suggests that the concept of influence, of pressure exerted by an author on a reader who is also an author, must be seen as a

---

1 Derrida, *Positions*, trans. Alan Bass, p. 4.

reciprocal operation, a fruitful dialogue between the living and the dead in which neither interlocutor can be sure which role he or she is playing. This reciprocity also pertains to individual works, for, as T.S. Eliot asserts in "Tradition and the Individual Talent" (1917):

> What happens when a new work of art is created is something that happens simultaneously to all the works of art which preceded it. The existing monuments form an ideal order among themselves which is modified by the introduction of the new (the really new) work of art among them. The existing order is complete before the new work arrives; for order to persist after the supervention of novelty, the whole existing order must be, if ever so slightly, altered. . . . Whoever has approved this idea of order, of the form of European, of English literature, will not find it preposterous that the past should be altered by the present as much as the present is directed by the past.

What Eliot calls "an ideal order" formed by artistic "monuments" is, from the point of view of *Ulysses*, simply a habit of interpretation that has made temporary sense of cultural "tradition." Consequently, the change that any new work has the capacity to produce is a change in the way that "traditional" works may be interpreted. The function of literature, then, resembles that of criticism, to unravel and recombine our privileged habits of interpretation.

Ulysses is not only a piece of writing partly based on the *Odyssey*; it is also an implicit reading of the *Odyssey* that transforms it from a heroic tale of adventure into a collection of ancient parables about the double nature of reality, both created and found. Similarly, Joyce's implied reading of *Hamlet* transforms it into a play that differs sharply from the play that Sir Laurence Olivier brought to life in his well-known portrayal of Prince Hamlet. Instead of suggesting that tragedy results when a man cannot make up his mind, Joyce's *Hamlet* implies that it makes relatively little difference whether an individual listens to or ignores the demands of the past. What is tragic about Joyce's *Hamlet* is its view of the past itself – an importunate ghost of fatherhood, seeking to influence without being influenced in turn. The relationship between past and present is decidedly not a reciprocal one for Prince Hamlet: the ghost's command to "List! List! O List!" can never be turned back on the ghost himself, since one of the things that he will not entertain is a dialogue. But Joyce's treatment of men and women in *Ulysses*, together with the verbal and material styles associated with each, does have implications that extend backward. Genesis, the *Odyssey*, legends associated with virginity, *Sartor Resartus*, and *Peer Gynt* are all subjects of Joyce's reading that alter their shape in the light of his writing: *Ulysses* has changed them as much as they may have directed *Ulysses*.

GENESIS

Seen in the light of *Ulysses*, with as much attention paid to the metaphorical implications of its language as to the possible intentions of its author, Genesis proffers not one but two metaphors for the process of creation, representing the different roles of the female and the male in biological reproduction and illustrating different aspects of the way that language and narrative reproduce meaning. The first mode of reproduction to be presented is modelling, in which the model is brought to life by imaginative inspiration: God shapes his own image in dust and breathes life into it. Such divine creation, represented in natural as well as artistic terms, is also a kind of divine dissemination in which God's "seed" is an idea brought to life by the earth; but in either case, the "author" of the creation is represented as single, divine, and male. The second mode of fashioning is human rather than divine, and precipitated by the actions of a woman: the postlapsarian activity of gathering together, or sewing. The two modes of fashioning illustrate complementary processes and values: the first is individualistic, the second social; the first legislates conformity and continuity; the second assimilation; the first is a reading of the male role in reproduction, the second a view of the female role.

Much recent criticism and theory converges around the discovery that our culture tends to favor "male" modes of acculturation over "female" ones, imitation over the more uncertain alchemy of exploration and assimilation. Colin MacCabe, in the wake of Lacan, depicts the dominance of narrative over discourse, language as "plot" over language as wilderness, as a version of the dominance of the father over the mother, of the need for ultimate control over the wayward pleasures of desire.[2] In feminist criticism, the hegemony of a male self over a female "other" is seen as one characteristic feature of a patriarchal system. The term "patriarchy," however, although accurate in an anthropological sense, tends to be misleading when used more generally because of its suggestion that the social structure is modelled on a family in which the father, or *pater*, is dominant. A careful reading of the metaphors for creation presented in Genesis suggests that any culture that locates its "beginnings" here will be more onanistic than paternal, sowing homunculi rather than engendering children. Culture reproduces its values onanistically if the frame of reference is sexual, through the casting of seed if it is organic, and through modelling if it is artistic. The pattern for such reproduction is not familial, but authoritative, and its clearest expression is in the Pygmalion myth, which outlines a program for creating an "other" who can act as object, child, and lover. At the end of his career, in *When We Dead Awaken*, Ibsen exposed the darker side of the Pygmalion myth, its hidden role in producing stultification and living death. Ibsen's last play is a relentless inquest into the implications of realistic representation, of "modelling" as a means of self-perpetuation. Joyce reviewed it at the beginning of his career (*CW* 47–67), and Ibsen's end point became the starting point of Joyce's lifelong search for alternative means of producing and reproducing human experience.

Genesis suggests that our notions of authority and origination are rooted in the Garden of Eden, and specifically in the activity of sowing. The first four chapters of Genesis tell two different stories (those of Adam and Eve and Cain and Abel), both of which define male productivity and labor in agricultural terms. Adam's curse, which is presented as comparable to Eve's curse of menstruation and childbirth, changes his relation to the ground. God tells him, "Cursed is the ground for thy sake; in sorrow shalt thou eat of it all the days of thy life; Thorns also and thistles shall it bring forth to thee; and thou shalt eat the herb of the field; In the sweat of thy face shalt thou eat bread, return unto the ground; for out of it wast thou taken: for dust thou *art*, and unto dust shalt thou return" (Genesis 3:17–19). Similarly, when Cain offers the fruit of the ground to the Lord and the Lord prefers Abel's offering of lamb, Cain kills his brother, only to learn that his curse is to be

2 *James Joyce and the Revolution of the Word*, esp. pp. 52–68.

an even greater alienation from the ground: "When thou tillest the ground, it shall not henceforth yield unto thee her strength; a fugitive and a vagabond shalt thou be in the earth" (Genesis 4:17).

Sowing, as it turns out, is an apt figure for much of the activity generated by males: not only is it linked to male sexuality (semen: seed), but it is also a means of husbandry and a metaphor for increase through authorship. Moreover, as a paradigm, it orients all phenomena along a "vertical" axis. The fluctuation between planting (a downward movement) and growth (its upward corollary) becomes the model for any fall and rise, and ultimately for a weighted conflict of "lower" and "higher" values. According to the Judeo-Christian tradition, the father of humanity was a gardener and a namer, a *sator* and an author, who in a garden initiated the pattern of rise and fall, growth and decay that would dominate all human history. Joyce conveys his awareness of the traditional relationship between gardening, authorship, masculinity, and the comically obsessive "plot" of rising and falling most economically in his portrayal of the dead Finnegan, with "a barrowload of guenesis hoer his head" (*FW* 6.27).

The Latin word "sator" reflects the interrelation of values that Genesis sets forth: it means "sower, planter," and also "father, promoter, author." An author is an individual male originator, single, yet productive. He sows, and in so doing defines what we know as our "culture." All of *Finnegans Wake* is a comic inquest into his "original sin": his presentation of himself as "original" and his confused reading of an "original hen" as the original "sin." HCE is a gardener who embodies paternal authority, an authority that is constantly being challenged and reaffirmed. For human complexity, Joyce invites us to thank Our Mother, "Bringer of Plurabilities, haloed be her eve" (*FW* 104.2). *Finnegans Wake* repeatedly prompts us to reread our beginnings, to reexamine our authorities and the "sators" who implanted them: "all old Sators of the Sowsceptre highly nutritius family histrionic" (*FW* 230.28).

The order of events as it is presented in Genesis suggests that the male "sower" is able to arrogate authority by claiming priority, despite the fact that the precedence of one gender over the other can never be incontrovertibly proven. Women give birth to men, but men impregnate women, so the question of priority is as insoluble as the conundrum of the chicken and the egg, which insinuates itself into *Finnegans Wake* through recurrent references to

Humpty Dumpty and the hen. However, the myth of primacy presented by Genesis has persisted for thousands of years; according to the Bible, man not only precedes woman but he gives birth to her through his body, in a startling reversal of the only empirically familiar mode of reproduction. In *Finnegans Wake*, Joyce emphasizes the essential identity of Eve and Adam by frequent references to Eve as "madam," Adam's palindrome, and presents the difference between them as the difference between earth and water essential to the continuance of life. *Finnegans Wake* begins, like the earth, with water, and the unexpected precedence of Eve before Adam. However, "riverrun, past Eve and Adam's..." brings us *back* to HCE, reversing the first reversal. By turning reversals back on themselves, Joyce implies that the very concept of origin is a fiction, and that understanding is invariably circular. The first half-sentence of the book suggests that all beginnings, including this one, represent a continuation of some prior or subsequent "end."

To give man priority, and therefore authority, over woman, is also to accord word authority over world. "Sator" means author as well as sower, and the word "author" denotes not only a writer, but any originator. Once again, the Bible is a central authority for the view that the realm of language is a male dominion. The word of a male God precedes and creates the world; as St. John proclaims, "In the beginning was the Word, and the Word was God." Christ's role as the Logos, God's Word incarnate, and Adam's responsibility to name the creatures of the earth further strengthen the links between men and language. Woman, by contrast, is always associated with that which is allegedly created by men and language – the material world. Her world is clearly a lower one, since it is she who brings about man's "fall" from his ideal state into "her" world of reproduction and death.

The metaphors that inform Genesis suggest that we have sown our culture from the seeds of "male" values, all of which stem from the power of origination, the source and meaning of authority. This authority includes the privilege of authorship, a privilege infrequently extended to women, who tend to be associated with the mute – and fatal – flesh. ("In the beginning was the gest he jousstly says, for the end is with woman, flesh-without-word" [*FW* 468.5–6].) This "male" chain of being was initiated by the "author of all things," an omnipotent culturer who created men and texts in his own image, whom Stephen Dedalus alludes to as "the playwright who wrote the folio of this world and wrote it badly (He gave us light first and the sun two days later)" (*U* 9.1046–8).

The *action* of "sowing" and its correlatives define male prerogatives, yet the *word* "sowing" points the way to an alternative action which is specifically "female." A sensitivity to homophones turns "sowing" into "sewing," a traditionally female activity which illustrates a rival organization of values. The view of sewing as a female occupation acknowledges woman's relegation to the material world, even while emphasizing her power over it. Sewing is the act of creating and shaping material, in the form of both cloth and bodies. Two of the most immediate consequences of the fall reinforce the bondage of women to materiality: sewing and reproduction, making material and becoming *mater*. Once fallen, one of the first cooperative acts of Eve and Adam is to sew clothes for themselves: "And the eyes of them both were opened, and they knew that they *were* naked; and they sewed fig leaves together, and made themselves aprons" (Genesis 3:7). Sewing is also presented as a "divine" activity: God sows the garden, but he also sews, making coats from skins to clothe postlapsarian Adam and Eve (3:21). In the King James translation, the language of sewing and sowing is even intermingled: God puts Adam into the garden of Eden to "dress" it and keep it (2:15).

It is possible to see sewing and sowing as equal and comparable activities, signs of the parity of male and female labor, a parity reflected in John Ball's famous couplet,

> When Adam delved and Eve span,
> Who was then the gentleman?

In *Finnegans Wake*, Joyce continues this tradition, presenting delving and spinning as interdependent processes necessary for the maintenance of life and the creation of every new year's "eve." Adam delves devilishly, while "madameen" twiningly produces watered silk together with the watery silt of her riverbed: "It was of a night, late, lang time agone, in an auldstane eld, when Adam was delvin and his madameen spinning watersilts . . . " (*FW* 21.5–6). Joyce emphasizes the interdependence of planting and spinning as analogous to the productive potential of earth and water; but historically, sewing and sowing seldom balance on the scale of cultural value. Literally, sowing seems to be the more significant activity because it results in the creation of life, whereas sewing produces a mere artifact. Figuratively, however, the priority is reversed: sowing as a metaphor for authorship results merely in the production of texts, whereas sewing traditionally represents the female capacity for giving birth, or creating life.

Just as sowing may be seen to figure the male role in reproduction, sewing signifies the female role. If men sow, women reap, or gather together, whether in the form of Isis gathering the limbs of Osiris, or the gnarlybird scratching through the litter in *Finnegans Wake*. Moreover, since birth is an incarnation into the physical world, spinning, or the creation of material, becomes an apt metaphor for the female power of giving birth, and with the power to give birth comes the responsibility for death. The Fates, for example, illustrate the power of the female over materiality, since their spinning represents the creation and destruction of human life. Blake picks up this traditional association between mothers, material, and materiality in his depiction of Enitharmon, who weaves bodies on her looms at Luban's Gate.[3] In "For the Sexes: The Gates of Paradise," Blake identifies the creative and destructive female principle with a "Worm Weaving in the Ground," whom he addresses as the type of all female relations:

> Thou'rt my Mother from the Womb,
> Wife, Sister, Daughter, to the Tomb:
> Weaving to Dreams the Sexual strife,
> and weeping over the Web of Life.

Activities defined as "male" seem to have evolved differently from those assigned to the female, as the physical activity of sowing was supplanted by its mental corollary, authorship. The similarity between sowing and plotting is expressed by the various meanings of the word "plot," which, like "author," has an agrarian as well as a literary meaning. A plot can be "a small area of planted ground," "a secret plan," or "the plan or main story of a literary work." By contrast, the "female" activities of sewing and giving

---

3 See Morton D. Paley, "The Figure of the Garment in *The Four Zoas, Milton,* and *Jerusalem,*" in *Blake's Sublime Allegory: Essays on The Four Zoas, Milton, Jerusalem,* ed. Stuart Curran and Joseph Anthony Wittreich, Jr. (Madison: University of Wisconsin Press, 1973).

birth are both physical. As a result, the difference between male and female "styles," the difference between writing and weaving, texts and textiles, mimics the difference between mind and body, and their relative valuation. This difference is even apparent in the ways that the products of the two occupations are used: textiles clothe the body, whereas texts stimulate the mind. Such simplistic contrasts encourage us to regard "men" as the root of "mentality," and to see "men" and "texts" as the verbal "seeds" that engender "women" and "textiles."

Out of a division between male and female labor came the view that there is a different "style" appropriate to each gender. The art of writing was appropriated by men; the art of fashion assigned to women. Such divisions turn both arts into weapons in the war between the sexes, restricting their artistic potential to encompass and reflect the fullness and rhythm of life. Writing, however, need not be regarded as a product of male parthenogenesis, since *two* metaphors, not one, serve as its progenitors: texts are intricately interwoven as well as authored. The principle of interconnection is as important as the principle of authority: if writing presents itself as sheer authority, it becomes propaganda, a means of oppression; if weaving presents itself only in its finished form, as interconnected material without an "author" to unravel or replace it, it becomes a symbol of oppression through entrapment. A recognition that both arts are dependent upon the individual imperative to create *and* destroy defuses the opposition between them, and erodes the traditional privilege of "male" over "female" artistry.

The English language bears witness in a variety of ways to the similarities between, and the parity of, weaving and plotting; many words do double duty by describing both imaginative and material weaving. A "fabrication," for example, is an invention or creation, but such a meaning grows out of an awareness that imaginative invention is akin to making fabric. A "yarn" can be a narrative of adventures or a strand used in weaving. "Smart" and "sharp" signify a potentially "painful" precision, whether of intellect or appearance; a "design" is a pattern, equally applicable to plots and dresses; and "material" can denote cloth or a writer's subject matter. To "address" is to present directly, whether through words or, in its archaic meaning, appearance. What vertical and material fabrications share is their dependence on design, pattern, and "order," related to the Latin *ordiri* – to lay the warp, or begin. Genesis gives additional evidence that the activity of sewing is comparable to the activity of naming, but the fact that it is practiced only after the fall underscores its association with bodily shame, thus tainting its value. Ancient literature, by contrast, depicts the activities of plotting and sewing as mutually illustrative, comparable in value as well as in nature.

THE ODYSSEY

In Greek literature, cloth-making is represented as a female domestic activity, whereas more public activities such as speaking, warring, and commercial trading are depicted as male. In *The Odyssey*, Telemachus clearly marks the difference between male and female privilege when he dismisses Penelope in Book I: "Go, then, within the house and busy yourself with your daily duties, your loom, your distaff, and the ordering of your servants; for speech is man's matter, and mine above all others – for it is I who am master here."[4] However, despite the clear demarcation between male and female roles apparent in the *Odyssey*, the differences between their respective occupations are not pejorative. Helene Foley argues that women can play a powerful, highly valued role in *The Odyssey* largely because the spheres that men and women control are very separate, with women (like poets) having the responsibility to preserve what men produce:

> It is of parenthetical interest to an evaluation of women's role in Greek literature that their work – weaving, cooking and the guardianship of the household – is present even on Olympus and in utopia. Household economics does not require men or the establishment of a sexual hierarchy and women's control over this sphere is seen as natural, unproblematic. . . . Cooking and weaving on Ithaca are activities dependent on prior agricultural production. The household, as in the analysis in Xenophon's *Oeconomicus*, processes and makes useful and permanent goods produced by men through agriculture and herding. Because both cooking and weaving retard or

4 *The Odyssey of Homer*, trans. Samuel Butler, ed. Louise Ropes Loomis (Roslyn, N.Y.: Walter J. Black, 1944), p. 11. Butler's translation is one of the two translations Joyce used, according to W. B. Stanford.

conquer change they logically have a more primary association with the divine and eternal than male-controlled agriculture. Thus the products of weaving are in Homer sometimes forms of art comparable to poems.[5]

In *The Odyssey*, Odysseus' travels "clarify the nature and range of
female power over the inner sphere of household production, and
of the male power over the external world of agriculture, diplomacy
and exchange."[6] The poem itself enforces a realization that these
two worlds are interdependent, and intertwined.

Despite Homer's emphasis on the boundary separating male plotting and story-telling from female weaving, and despite Telemachus' assertion that men are "masters," Homer also suggests that
male hegemony is one of the fictions men are known for, one that
owes its survival to the continued tolerance of Greek women. Both
story-telling and weaving are expressions of ingenuity, an ingenuity
independent of gender. In the *Odyssey*, for example, Penelope's
ability to deceive through weaving is clearly equal to Odysseus'
facility in plotting narrative fabrications. One of the ways that
Homer draws attention to the analogies between Odysseus' strategies and those of Penelope is through the use of what Helene Foley
calls "reverse similes": similes comparing women to men, and men
to women. According to Foley, these similes "suggest both a sense
of identity between people in different social and sexual roles and
a loss of stability, an inversion of the normal."[7]

Samuel Butler also draws attention to the unusual parity between
men and women in *The Odyssey*, but he does so by exaggerating,
in a way that is both comic and startlingly credible, the importance
of women in the poem. In *The Authoress of the Odyssey*, one of the
volumes in Joyce's Trieste library, Butler proposes that the poem
was written by a young woman, basing his argument on a recognition of the similarity between the traditionally "male" and
"female" arts. He argues, "If a woman could work pictures with
her needle as Helen did, and as the wife of William the Conqueror

5 Foley, " 'Reverse Similes' and Sex Roles in the *Odyssey*," in *Women
   in the Ancient World: The Arethusa Papers*, ed. John Peradotto and J. P.
   Sullivan (Albany: SUNY Press, 1984), pp. 65–6.
6 Ibid., p. 68.
7 Ibid., p. 60.

did in a very similar civilisation, she could write stories with her pen if she had a mind to do so."[8] Butler stresses the control that women exercise over men throughout the poem, and his translation supports his suggestion that the stratagems of Ulysses and Penelope are perfectly comparable. His rendition of Book XVIII highlights the mutual enjoyment that Ulysses and Penelope derive from each other's wiles. Penelope is complaining to the suitors that they aren't wooing her properly with rich presents, and Butler writes, "Odysseus was glad when he heard her trying to get presents out of the suitors, and flattering them with fair words which he knew she did not mean."[9]

In *The Odyssey*, weaving exemplifies a "craftiness" as potentially dangerous as that of Ulysses. Women's webs have the uncannily double nature more often recognized in language: they can display an alluring beauty, or conceal a deadly snare. All of the women who take Ulysses as lover – Calypso, Circe, and Penelope – engage in weaving, and all are presented as exceptionally clever. Each has Penelope's power to "bring any number of men to her feet, hoodwink them, spoil them, and in the end destroy them."[10] Calypso is first introduced as weaving – "busy at her loom, shooting her golden shuttle through the warp and singing beautifully"[11] – and Circe is presented in almost exactly the same way, "singing most beautifully as she worked at her loom, making a web so fine, so soft, and of such dazzling colors as no one but a goddess could weave."[12] Penelope's "web of wiles" is more obviously an image of her power to deceive and even paralyze her suitors; she prevents them from taking action until she finishes her weaving, but since she unravels nightly what she has worked during the day, she is able to arrest the progress of time for three years.

The association between women, weaving, and clothes in *The Odyssey* signifies the female power over sexuality as well as over death. Appropriately, many of the references to cloth in *The Odyssey* fortify or dissipate erotic expectations. Helen's parting gift to Te-

---

8   Butler, *The Authoress of the Odyssey*, 2nd ed. (London: Jonathan Cape, 1922), p. 13.
9   Butler, *The Odyssey of Homer*, p. 231.
10 Butler, *The Authoress of the Odyssey*, p. 128.
11 Butler, *The Odyssey of Homer*, p. 60.
12 Ibid., p. 122.

lemachus is a dress for his bride on their wedding day (Book XV), and when Odysseus first encounters Nausicaa, she is washing linens in anticipation of her betrothal. Webs can represent erotic promise and also the frustration of that promise. When Telemachus asks whether his mother has remarried and abandoned Odysseus' bed, he asks whether it is webbed, "without bedding and covered with cobwebs" (Book XVI).[13]

Perhaps the most convincing evidence of the parity between male and female arts in *The Odyssey* is found in Book XIII, when Athena presents herself as Ulysses' counterpart. She changes back into a woman whom Cowper's translation describes as "Beauteous, majestic, in all elegant arts accomplished" (11.343–4), and tells Ulysses that he and she are two of a kind. Both are plotters, skillfully interweaving lives, lies, and threads, as Athena concedes when she tells him that they both excel in "ingenious shifts" of discourse: "For thou of all men in expedients most / Abound'st and eloquence, and I, throughout / All heaven have praise for wisdom and for art" (Bk. XIII, 11.354–6).[14] The weaving, plotting Athena is one of the many female versions of Penelope in the poem, as Samuel Butler was the first to observe: all are cunning, seductive, and formidable practitioners of a female art which rivals the complementary art

13 Ibid., p. 198. See also Cowper's translation, in which Telemachus asks whether Ulysses' bed is "To be by noisome spiders webb'd around" (Bk. XVI, 1. 44). *The Odyssey of Homer*, trans. William Cowper, in *The Works of William Cowper, comprising His Poems, Correspondence, and Translations*, ed. Robert Southey, vols. 13 and 14 (London: Baldwin and Cracock, 1837). The only translations that Stanislaus remembers Joyce using are Butler's and Cowper's; see Hugh Kenner, *The Pound Era* (Berkeley: California, 1971), p. 46; and W. B. Stanford, *The Ulysses Theme: A Study in the Adaptability of a Traditional Hero* (1954; 2nd ed. Oxford: Blackwell, 1963), p. 276, note 6.

14 Cowper, *The Odyssey*, p. 15. The relationship between weaving and plotting is even more explicit in Robert Fitzgerald's translation, which of course postdates Joyce. Fitzgerald describes Athena as a woman "tall and beautiful and no doubt skilled / at weaving splendid things" (XIII, 1. 284–5), and has Athena commend Odysseus' skill "in plots and story telling" (XIII, 1. 296). Odysseus, in turn, asks Athena to "weave" him a way to pay the suitors back (XIII, 1. 391). *Homer: The Odyssey*, trans. Robert Fitzgerald (New York: Doubleday-Anchor, 1963).

of Odysseus. In *The Odyssey*, men and women are equal in the exercise of craft.

Reread from the vantage point of *Ulysses*, the *Odyssey* shows that texts and textiles, verbal constructs and material ones, mirror one another as products of "male" and "female" style. The separation of textual and verbal weaving, like the separation between the men and women who traditionally practice them, is a heuristic separation that has become rigid and oppressive. In the *Odyssey*, however, textiles and text styles represent a pattern of thought that offers an alternative to war, much as the domestic impulse fueling the *Odyssey* counters the martial ferocity of the *Iliad*. If, as the analogy of the mirror suggests, opposites are always heuristic constructions, reflections of the self that make self-consciousness possible, then war between opponents – whether the opponents are man and woman, mind and body, fact and fiction, or Greeks and Trojans – is always civil war. In the *Odyssey*, the parallels between storytelling and weaving enforce an awareness of the formal similarities between verbal and material artistry, an awareness that is also reflected in a variety of ways in the English language. Moreover, the *Odyssey* portrays storytelling and weaving as *processes* that must be undone and redone if they are to retain their strategic effectiveness in the art of living. Just as Penelope must weave and unweave her web, Odysseus must tell and retell his story, altering its particulars to "suit" the everchanging contexts in which he finds himself.

DISANIMATION

Classical authors used the association between women and textiles to signify both the ingeniousness and the power of female sexuality. Christianity invested the ties between women and cloth with a dramatically different meaning: women were portrayed less frequently as creators, and more frequently as the products of creation. Clothes encase the body, and women, like the clothes they fashioned and wore, came to be seen as vessels. Instead of signifying the power of female creativity, spinning came to represent the oddly asexual purity associated with motherhood, motherhood defined not as the power to create, but as the willingness to serve as an instrument. Fittingly, the Virgin Mary was noted for her work with fabric; as the Abbé Orsini wrote in his nineteenth-century *Life of the Blessed Virgin Mary*,

The Virgin surpassed all the daughters of her people in those beautiful fabrications so highly prized by the ancients. We learn from St. Epiphanius that she excelled in embroidery and the art of working in wool, in byssus, and in gold. The proto-gospel of St. James represents her seated before a distaff of purple wool, which moved under her taper fingers like the trembling leaf of the poplar; and the Christians of the West have perpetuated the traditional opinion of her unrivalled skill in spinning the flax of Pelusia, by giving the name of *Virgin's thread* to that net-work of dazzling whiteness, and of almost vaporous texture, which floats over deep valleys in the damp mornings of autumn. The chaste and modest brides of the early Christians, in memory of these domestic avocations of the Queen of Angels, never failed to consecrate to her a distaff adorned with fillets of purple, and charged with spotless wool.[15]

Orsini also notes that in the Middle Ages, weavers worked under the banner of the Annunciation as a tribute to the Virgin's works in flax, and the Church of Jerusalem kept Mary's spindle as one of its treasures, until it was later placed in the Church of the Guides in Constantinople.

Spinning, weaving, and sewing signify the power to give birth, the *potential* to bear life, which explains why the activity of working with cloth can suggest either virginity or profligacy. Cloth artistry as a preparation for motherhood is depicted as righteous, but as a substitute for motherhood it is presented as sinister. The word "spinster" exemplifies the opprobrium of spinning instead of giving birth, and it testifies to the almost occult strangeness with which the rejection of instrumentality is invested. As numerous commentators have noted, Christianity allows women to choose between two roles, that of the proverbial virgin mother or that of the whore; but as Joyce recognized, these are essentially the same role. The virgin mother is an earthly vessel, a body to house the divine, male Word. Carried to its logical extreme, her role becomes that of universal vessel – or promiscuous whore. The natural counterpart of the virgin Mary is Helen of Troy, whom Stephen describes as "the wooden mare of Troy in whom a score of heroes

15 Abbé Orsini, *Life of the Blessed Virgin Mary* (1897), p. 68.

slept" (*U* 9.622–3). *Mère* or mare – a woman so conceived is a mere casing for men, a womb or a tomb. Consequently, the same skill with cloth can signal virginal obedience or the sexual capaciousness of someone like Chaucer's Wife of Bath: "Of cloth making she had such an haunt / She passed them of Ipres and of Gaunt."

The two "styles" that have become characteristic of female and male artists are two versions of a single imaginative activity, but Christianity played down female artistry and authority by conflating women with the coverings they created. Women – like clothes, wombs, and their phonetic counterparts, tombs – were seen as something that enclosed a more essential reality. Women became housings, identified with the inanimate aspects of the home they had once dominated, a "house of fiction" incarnate. Women, as workers of cloth, face the danger of becoming "hemmed in," with "hims" and "hymns" as their "hems." Joyce counters such threats by presenting women as flowers, those who "flow," praying of "our mother" that "her singtime [be] sung, her rill be run, unhemmed as it is uneven!" (*FW* 104.2–3)

The problem of female enclosure has been a focus of much recent feminist criticism. Mary Daly, Adrienne Rich, Sandra Gilbert, and Susan Gubar, in particular, have probed woman's confinement to the material world and her exclusion from the world of language; they have shown how women are encouraged to express themselves mutely, through necessarily ephemeral appearances, in contrast to men, who have been challenged to adopt the supposedly more powerful and permanent mode of articulating through language. Feminist critics have examined the straitening of female creativity, showing how it has been defined as the act of turning one's body into a work of art, suggesting that the "female" arts are not only seductive, but also potentially self-destructive. According to this view, Tennyson's Lady of Shalott serves as the archetype of the female artist, who exchanges the isolation and unreality of weaving for an artistry practiced on her own body, an artistry that transforms her into a verbal corpus (the poem itself), and a corpse.

According to this line of argument, there is a significant difference between male and female "styles," a difference which is far from innocent. The activity and the products of weaving have the power to destroy the lives of the very women who are urged to create and wear them. The culturally imposed restrictions on female style have made it possible for women themselves to be fetishized and framed, their expressiveness constricted as abnormally as their waists once were. This view presents the traditionally "female" arts as those with the power to transform the artists who practice them into artifacts which can be wholly possessed. "Sleeping Beauty" has often been read as an anti-feminist tale, but it also contains a subversive warning against the practice of "female" arts such as spinning: the mere touch of a spindle is enough to send a young woman into a senseless trance for a hundred years. The story of Arachne, too, contains a similar warning: Arachne's extraordinary skill in weaving becomes, quite literally, a mode of suicide. In *The Madwoman in the Attic*, Gilbert and Gubar show how dramatically the difference between male and female artistry has served to underscore the power of men and the helplessness of women. They analyze two versions of "Little Snow White" which suggest that male and female children respond to maternal aggression in opposite ways, concluding that

> The male child's progress toward adulthood is the growth toward both self-assertion and self-articulation, . . . a development of the *powers* of speech. But the girl child must learn the arts of silence either as herself a silent image invented and defined by the magic looking-glass of the male-authored text, or as a silent dancer of her own woes, a dancer who enacts rather than articulates.[16]

The association between women and materiality has worked to silence women, branding them as interlopers in the world of language. The relegation of women to a world of fashion showed its destructive potential most powerfully in the nineteenth century, when the physical movement of upper-class women was most inhibited by their clothing, and that of lower-class women by the factories – many of them textile factories – in which they worked long hours. But weaving can also be a means of protest and empowerment, as the myth of Philomela suggests. Philomela is both raped and mutilated, her tongue cut out to prevent her from telling her story. When deprived of the power of speech, she uses weaving as an alternative means of communication, making her story into the tapestry that works her revenge. Philomela's weaving, like

16 Gilbert and Gubar, *The Madwoman in the Attic*, p. 43.

Penelope's, becomes a powerful stratagem allowing her to protest her violation. Eventually, the woman who had been rendered mute was transformed into the bird with the most beautiful song of all.

At first, male word-weaving seems far preferable to female weaving, since it allows for greater freedom. Words, being more ambiguous and more elusive than thread, unravel themselves much more quickly than clothes, and for that reason seem less confining. Writers, however, face a different if complementary danger in the exercise of their craft: if weavers tend to practice their art on themselves, rendering themselves inanimate, writers face the possibility that their work is insubstantial, a mere phantom. If "female" art threatens to turn life into cloth, "male" art threatens to turn it into air, into ghosts or dreams. *A Midsummer Night's Dream* does not categorize the arts by gender, but it does probe the interrelationship between weaving and dreaming. Bottom, the most fanciful dreamer and most accomplished actor of all the rude mechanicals, is a weaver by profession, a dreamer by avocation, and an ass by implication. He is comic precisely because he is too heavy-handed, especially in contrast to the fairies, one of whom is fittingly named Cobweb. The playwright implicitly avoids both the clumsiness of worsted and the insubstantiality of cobwebs by encompassing both of them, although he presents himself as closer to the fairies than to Bottom, since his "weak and idle theme" is "no more yielding but a dream." In Shakespeare's plays, materiality is always the stuff of comedy, assuming a status subservient to the magic of words; Prospero will always prefer Ariel to Caliban.

Carlyle, too, favors the ideal world over the material one, but he nevertheless recognizes that ideals lapse back into chaos without the shape that material prototypes give them. In *Sartor Resartus*, Carlyle stresses the interdependence of the material and the divine, even while favoring the divine. He champions both tailors and creators and reasserts the mystical power of clothes, making them a universal symbol for the entire phenomenal world. Teufelsdröckh concludes his philosophy of clothes by asserting that "the Tailor is not only a man, but something of a Creator or Divinity," asking, "What too are all Poets and moral Teachers, but a species of Metaphorical Tailors?" (Book Third, Chapter XI). Carlyle seems to be celebrating the world of cloth less for its own sake than for the intangible divinity it makes manifest. Still, he recognizes that with-

Postscript

out metaphor, without the phenomenal world to give shape to abstractions, the divine world turns to vapor.

Late nineteenth- and early twentieth-century literature subtly challenges the assumption that the weaver of words and dreams, although not uncommonly classed with weavers of cloth, practices a "higher" kind of craft. Writers such as Ibsen and Woolf make the sexual polarity of cloth-weaving and word-weaving more explicit, and they place greater stress on the dangers of "male" artistry, its uneasy pact with nothingness. Ibsen, in particular, suggests that "male" artistry, while analogous to "female" artistry, is more destructive, and potentially delusory, whereas the art of material weaving is the art of social and interpersonal connection. In *Peer Gynt*, in particular, he presents the female spinner of cloth as far preferable to the male spinner of lies.

In *Peer Gynt*, Ibsen consistently links and contrasts Peer Gynt's imaginative notions to the "notions" of tailoring: a lad bids a button for Peer's palace in the Ronde, and Peer offers to sell his dream of a silver-clasped book for an old hook and eye (V.iv). Peer deals in illusion, whereas Solveig – and God – work through materiality. Throughout the play, Peer's wandering, posturing opportunism is counterpointed by Solveig's faithful, sedentary spinning and waiting, Penelope-style. The action of the play gradually diminishes Peer's initial appeal. Ultimately, he who sought to play so many roles discovers himself a nonentity, "No One" (V.x), whereas he discovers in Solveig a much more versatile personality, one truly able to encompass the various roles of mother, wife, and innocent woman (V.x). Peer argues, "*Man mus sich drappiren*" (one must drape oneself) (V.v), but as the devil (dressed as a priest) reminds him, "there's a right and wrong side to the jacket" (V.x). Peer inverts "the jacket" by using clothes to escape responsibility and to multiply his identity (much as Bloom does at the beginning of "Circe"), until finally confronted with a vision of his own nothingness, the troll-like offspring of stories and dreams.

Although Ibsen valorizes the female spinner, he does so in a nineteenth-century spirit. She is idealized in her capacity as wife or lover; like Margaret in *Faust* or Senta in *The Flying Dutchman*, she embodies the eternal feminine. Unlike Margaret or Senta, however, she doesn't draw her lover upward; instead, she draws him home, to domestic realities, away from rather than toward death. Virginia

Woolf de-romanticizes the relative positions of male and female artistry still further in *Mrs. Dalloway*. As in *Peer Gynt*, a "female" world of sewing and fashion is juxtaposed with a "male" world of imaginative intensity, literary sensibility, and destructiveness through the characters of Clarissa Dalloway and Septimus Warren Smith. Woolf presents these worlds as importantly analogous, but the woman is no longer assigned the responsibility of "saving" the man; instead, she reveals an independent, solitary understanding of his plight. The opposition that Clarissa and Septimus present is only a superficial one; philosophically, the extremes that they define are identical. Separately, in rhythmic syncopation, Clarissa and Septimus weave and unweave their worlds. The paradigm that Woolf endorses is that of Penelope or of Pater: she presents a view of life as a pulsating movement between isolation and connection, whether that movement is expressed through words or through the more traditionally "female" mode of fashionable society. Woolf insists upon the "gap" between all individuals, even while she presents in Clarissa a means of momentarily weaving together the fragile webs of connection that bind them.[17] Woolf's Penelope weaves and unweaves the fabric of polite society, whereas Joyce's Penelope takes the physical world as her material. Woolf and Joyce interpret the "female" world differently, taking their women from different social classes, but both writers attempt to subvert the view that "female" weaving is in any way inferior to the art of writing.

Both Ibsen and Woolf intimate that "female" spinning, weaving, and sewing metaphorically produce the fabric of society. Ibsen suggests that the human relationships created by women are more vital than the more ephemeral yarns spun by men, whereas Woolf posits a more truly revolutionary view. Like Joyce, she refuses to weigh the two activities against one another on a traditional or antitraditional scale; instead, she invests with value a quality that both activities share: their participation in the natural rhythm of cohesion and dissolution. Both the social world and the literary work are systems, or webs, and like all systems they alternately emphasize the harmony and the incompatibility of their components. Both Woolf and Joyce recognized that preserving or even

17 See Peggy Kamuf, "Penelope at Work: Interruptions in *A Room of One's Own*," *Novel* 16 (Fall 1982): 5–18, for a different application of the model of Penelope's weaving to Woolf's work.

reversing the hierarchy of traditionally "male" and "female" arts validates the artificial distinction between the two. It effectively limits both women and men, so that the wholeness, the interconnectedness and autonomy that is the goal of both weaving and writing, becomes a mirage. The fundamental identity of the two systems can only become apparent when clothes emerge as a figure, not only of enclosure and disguise, but of transient interconnection as well.

WORKS CITED

Abel, Elizabeth, ed. *Writing and Sexual Difference.* Chicago: University of Chicago Press, 1980.

Almeida, Hermione de. *Byron and Joyce through Homer: "Don Juan" and "Ulysses."* New York: Columbia University Press, 1981.

Aristotle. *The Basic Works of Aristotle,* trans. Richard McKeon. New York: Random House, 1941.

Attridge, Derek and Daniel Ferrer, eds. *Post-Structuralist Joyce: Essays from the French.* Cambridge: Cambridge University Press, 1984.

Bakhtin, Mikhail. *Problems of Dostoyevsky's Poetics,* ed. and trans. Caryl Emerson. Minneapolis: University of Minnesota Press, 1984.

Barthes, Roland. "The Death of the Author," in *Image–Music–Text,* trans. Stephen Heath. New York: Hill and Wang, 1977, pp. 142–8.

Beja, Morris, Phillip Herring, Maurice Harmon, David Norris, eds. *James Joyce: The Centennial Symposium.* Urbana: University of Illinois Press, 1986.

Benjamin, Walter. *Illuminations,* ed. Hannah Arendt, trans. Harry Zohn. New York: Harcourt, Brace & World, 1968.

Brown, Richard. *Joyce and Sexuality.* Cambridge: Cambridge University Press, 1985.

Budgen, Frank. *James Joyce and the Making of "Ulysses."* 1934; rpt. Bloomington: Indiana Univ. Press, 1960.

Butler, Christopher. "Joyce and the Displaced Author," in *James Joyce and Modern Literature,* ed. W. J. McCormack and Alistair Stead. London: Routledge and Kegan Paul, 1982.

Cixous, Hélène and Catherine Clément. "Sorties," in *La Jeune Née.* Paris: Union générale d'éditions, 1979, pp. 114–275.

Works Cited

Culler, Jonathan. *On Deconstruction: Theory and Criticism after Structuralism.* Ithaca: Cornell Univ. Press, 1982.

Daly, Mary. *Gyn/Ecology.* Boston: Beacon Press, 1979.

Derrida, Jacques. *Of Grammatology,* trans. Gayatri Chakravorty Spivak. Baltimore and London: Johns Hopkins Univ. Press, 1974.

Positions, trans. Alan Bass. Chicago: Univ. of Chicago Press, 1981.

Ellmann, Maud. "Disremembering Dedalus," in *Untying the Text: A Post-Structuralist Reader,* ed. Robert Young. Boston, London and Henley: Routledge & Kegan Paul, 1981, pp. 189–206.

"Polytropic Man: Paternity, Identity and Naming in *The Odyssey* and *A Portrait of the Artist as a Young Man,*" in *James Joyce: New Perspectives,* ed. Colin MacCabe. Sussex: Harvester, 1982, pp. 73–104.

Ellmann, Richard. *The Consciousness of Joyce.* Toronto and New York: Oxford Univ. Press, 1977.

"Ulysses" on the Liffey. New York: Oxford Univ. Press, 1972, 1973.

Foucault, Michel. "What is an Author?" in *The Foucault Reader,* ed. Paul Rabinow. New York: Pantheon, 1984. Reprinted from *Textual Strategies: Perspectives in Post-Structuralist Criticism,* ed. and trans. Josue V. Harari. Ithaca: Cornell, 1979.

Gallop, Jane. *The Daughter's Seduction: Feminism and Psychoanalysis.* Ithaca: Cornell Univ. Press, 1982.

Gilbert, Sandra and Susan Gubar. *The Madwoman in the Attic: The Woman Writer and the Nineteenth-Century Literary Imagination.* New Haven: Yale Univ. Press, 1979.

Goldman, Arnold. *The Joyce Paradox: Form and Freedom in His Fiction.* London: Routledge & Kegan Paul, 1966.

Gorman, Herbert. *James Joyce.* New York: Rinehart, 1939.

Groden, Michael. *Ulysses in Progress.* Princeton: Princeton Univ. Press, 1977.

Hart, Clive, and David Hayman, eds. *James Joyce's "Ulysses": Critical Essays.* Berkeley: Univ. of California Press, 1974.

Herr, Cheryl. *Joyce's Anatomy of Culture.* Urbana and Chicago: Univ. of Illinois Press, 1986.

Herring, Phillip F. "The Bedsteadfastness of Molly Bloom." *MFS* 15 (1969): 49–61.

Herring, Phillip F., ed. *Joyce's "Ulysses" Notesheets in the British Museum.* Charlottesville: Univ. Press of Virginia, 1972.

Joyce's Notes and Early Drafts for "Ulysses": Selections from the Buffalo Collection. Charlottesville: Univ. Press of Virginia, 1977.

Irigaray, Luce. *This Sex Which Is Not One,* trans. Catherine Porter. Ithaca: Cornell, 1985.

Kenner, Hugh. *Dublin's Joyce.* Bloomington: Indiana Univ. Press, 1956.

Ulysses. London: Allen & Unwin, 1980.

Lane, Jeremy. "His master's voice? The questioning of authority in lit-

Works Cited

erature," in *The Modern English Novel: The Reader, the Writer and the Work*, ed. Gabriel Josipovici. New York: Harper and Row, 1976.

Lawrence, Karen. *The Odyssey of Style in Ulysses*. Princeton: Princeton Univ. Press, 1981.

Levenson, Michael. "Stephen's Diary in *Portrait* – The Shape of Life." *ELH* 52: 1017–35.

Levine, Jennifer. "Originality and Repetition in *Finnegans Wake* and *Ulysses*." *PMLA* 94 (1979): 106–20.

MacCabe, Colin. *James Joyce and the Revolution of the Word*. London: Macmillan, 1978.

MacCabe, Colin, ed. *James Joyce: New Perspectives*. Sussex: Harvester Press, 1982.

McCormack, W. J. and Alistair Stead, eds. *James Joyce and Modern Literature*, London: Routledge & Kegan Paul, 1982.

McHugh, Roland. *Annotations to "Finnegans Wake."* Baltimore and London: Johns Hopkins. 1980.

Miller, J. Hillis. "Ariadne's Thread: Repetition and the Narrative Line." *Critical Inquiry* 3 (1976): 57–77.

"Arachne's Broken Woof." *Georgia Review* 31 (1978): 44–60.

Norris, Margot. *The Decentered Universe of "Finnegans Wake": A Structuralist Analysis*. Baltimore: Johns Hopkins, 1974.

Perl, Jeffrey M. *The Tradition of Return: The Implicit History of Modern Literature*. Princeton: Princeton Univ. Press, 1984.

Philip, J. A. *Pythagoras and Early Pythagoreanism*. Suppl. vol. 7 of *Phoenix: Journal of the Classical Association of Canada*. Toronto: Univ. of Toronto Press, 1966.

Potts, Willard, ed. *Portraits of the Artist in Exile: Recollections of James Joyce by Europeans*. Seattle: Univ. of Washington Press, 1979.

Riquelme, John Paul. *Teller and Tale in Joyce's Fiction: Oscillating Perspectives*. Balitmore and London: Johns Hopkins Univ. Press, 1983.

Scott, Bonnie. *Joyce and Feminism*. Bloomington: Indiana Univ. Press, 1984.

Senn, Fritz. *Joyce's Dislocutions: Essays on Reading as Translation*, ed. John Paul Riquelme. Baltimore and London: Johns Hopkins Univ. Press, 1984.

Solomon, Margaret C. *Eternal Geometer: The Sexual Universe of "Finnegans Wake."* Carbondale: Southern Illinois Univ. Press, 1969.

Thomas, Brook. *James Joyce's "Ulysses": A Book of Many Happy Returns*. Baton Rouge: Louisiana State Univ. Press, 1982.

Young, Robert, ed. *Untying the Text: A Post-Structuralist Reader*. Boston, London & Henley: Routledge & Kegan Paul, 1981.

INDEX

Index

doubling, technique of (*cont.*)
83, 93, 99, 102; in *Ulysses*, 8, 49, 109, 126–8, 136, 165
dualism: and authority, 23–6, 43–4; in Christianity, 15–18, 42, 44, 85 (*see also* Christ and Lucifer); in criticism, 3–4, 24–6, 60, 85, 102–3, 146, 190–1; in *Finnegans Wake*, 6, 7, 34–5, 39–41, 49; and gender, 45, 46, 48–9, 195–6 (*see also* gender roles); in Greek philosophy, 39–41; Joyce's general attitudes toward, 4–6, 12–13, 43–4, 49–50, 86, 87, 164, 189–91; in *Portrait of the Artist as a Young Man*, 63, 69, 102; in religion, 8–9; in *Ulysses*, 10–11, 15–17, 105, 108–9, 116–19, 127, 128–30, 134, 140–1, 164–6, 169–70; *see also* authority
Dublin, 50, 67–8, 96–101; *see also* Ireland
Dubliners (Joyce): authority in, 27–32, 50; doubling in, 50, 53; Father Flynn, 26–31; fatherhood in, 30–2; female imagery in, 32; and mainstream Joyce criticism, 2–3, 27–8; puns and language play, 29, 31, 69, 71; reading in, 31–2; reflection in, 106; social criticism in, 4
Dumas, Alexandre *père*, 90

Eagleton, Terry, 3n
Einstein, Albert, 49
Eliot, T. S., 47–8, 188, 194
Ellmann, Richard, 137
Exiles (Joyce), 110, 119n, 149–50, 176

fatherhood: in *Dubliners*, 30–2; in *Portrait of the Artist as a Young Man*, 12, 16, 103; in *Ulysses*, 8, 16, 47, 48
Finnegans Wake (Joyce): authority in, 33, 47, 184; clothing in, 147, 157–9, 162n, 182–6; doubling in, 33, 49–50, 54; dualism in, 6, 7, 34–5, 39–41, 49; gender roles in, 147–8; and Genesis, 197–200; incest in, 122; and Irish history, 14; language as subject in, 2, 4, 10, 14–15, 19, 54, 61, 182–4; and mainstream Joyce criticism, 2, 3; reading and learning in, 14–15, 37–8; sexual anatomy in, 32–4, 36–9, 43, 147; and *Ulysses*, 138, 143, 147, 181
Flaubert, Gustave, 122–3, 159

Foley, Helene, 202–3
Foucault, Michel, 25–6
Freud, Sigmund, 14

gender roles: and authority, 23–4, 45, 46, 47–9, 196, 197–202, 212–13; in Christianity, 196–9, 206–8; and clothing, 148–9, 152, 157, 160, 170–1, 199–212; and dualism, 45, 48–9, 195–6; in *Exiles*, 149–50; in *Finnegans Wake* 49, 197–8, 199; in the *Odyssey*, 202–6; in *Stephen Hero*, 141; in *Ulysses*, 140–1, 148–9, 151, 157, 160, 170–1
Genesis, *see* Bible; Christianity
Ghent, Dorothy van, 56n
Giacomo Joyce (Joyce), 80–1
Gilbert, Sandra, 119n, 170n, 208, 209
gnosticism, in *Ulysses*, 9
Goldman, Arnold, 55n
Groden, Michael, 7
Gubar, Susan, 208, 209

Hamlet, in *Ulysses*, 5, 31, 47, 111, 113, 135, 165, 193, 194–5
Homer, *see Odyssey*

Ibsen, Henrik, 152, 163–4, 196, 211, 212
Ireland: history of, 14; and *Ulysses*, 110, 120–1, 122; *see also* Dublin
Irigaray, Luce, 3n, 23–4, 45

"James Clarence Mangan" (Joyce), 86
Jameson, Fredric, 3n
Joyce, James: attitudes toward female style, 10, 19, 187, 189, 190, 208; author's image derived from his characters, 26–9, 32, 102–3, 119n, 137; critical reactions to, 1–3, 26–9; literary styles, 1–2, 27–8, 56, 61, 96–7, 136–8, 141–3, 144, 182, 187, 190–1 *see also* individual works: *Dubliners*; *Exiles*; *Finnegans Wake*; *Giacomo Joyce*; "James Clarence Mangan"; *Portrait of the Artist as a Young Man*; *Stephen Hero*; *Ulysses*

Kenner, Hugh, 6n, 55n, 138, 139

lamps: and romanticism, 104–5; in *Ulysses*, 105, 114–25, 128–9
Lane, Jeremy, 102
Lawrence, Karen, 7, 138

Index

letters, of Joyce, 31, 92, 166
Litz, A. Walton, 137, 138
Lucifer, see Christ and Lucifer

MacCabe, Colin, 195–6
Marxism, 14
Merrill, James, 55
Miller, J. Hillis, 187, 190
mirrors: and classicism, 104–5; in Portrait of the Artist as a Young Man, 106; in Ulysses, 105–14, 128–9

Nietzsche, Friedrich, 185
notesheets, for "Circe," 107

O'Brien, Darcy, 139–40
Odyssey (Homer): gender roles in, 202–6; logic of, 193; and Ulysses, 5, 8, 16–17, 194, 206
Orsini, Abbé, 206–7

Pater, Walter, 145–6, 188, 189
Picasso, Pablo, 129
Plato (Platonism), 91–2, 93
Portrait of the Artist as a Young Man, A (Joyce): age in, 63; authority in, 53–62, 102–3; Christ and Lucifer in, 15–16, 53, 75–6, 79–83, 85; Christianity in, 71–5, 79–80, 83–5, 90; classicism and romanticism, 85–96; clothing in, 156; criticism of, 55–6n; doubling in, 50, 55n, 56, 57–8, 60, 62, 69, 83, 93, 99, 102; dualism in, 63, 69, 102; and Dublin, 50, 67–8, 96–101; gender roles in, 100; lamp metaphor, 123, 125; paternal authority in, 12, 16, 103; puns and language games, 55, 59–62, 71–73, 94, 99n, 153; reading in, 54, 56, 63–6, 69–70, 73–5, 83, 88, 97, 99–101, 135; reflection in, 106; sensual imagery, 76–9, 81–2, 87, 94–5; social criticism in, 4, 28, 96–101
post-structuralism, see deconstruction
puns and language play: in Dubliners, 29, 31, 69, 71; in Finnegans Wake, 2, 4, 10, 14–15, 19, 54, 61, 182–4; in Portrait of the Artist as a Young Man, 55, 59–62, 71–3, 94, 99n, 153; in Ulysses, 10, 15–16, 19, 61, 93, 142, 173–4, 179–80
Pythagoreans, 40–1

reading: and authority, 192–4 (see also deconstruction); and dualism, 6, 9, 60; in Dubliners, 31–2; in Finnegans Wake, 14–15, 37–8; in Portrait of the Artist as a Young Man, 54, 56, 63–6, 69–70, 73–5, 83, 88, 97, 99–101, 135; in Ulysses, 9–10, 11, 141–2, 155–6, 178–9
Rich, Adrienne, 208
romanticism, see classicism and romanticism

Scott, Bonnie, 138
Senn, Fritz, 6n
sexual anatomy, in Finnegans Wake, 32–4, 36–9, 43, 147; see also gender roles
Shakespeare, William: clothing in works of, 162, 210; in Ulysses, 5, 31, 47, 111, 113, 135, 165, 193, 194–5
Shelley, Percy Bysshe, 87–94, 95
Solomon, Margaret, 33n
Stephen Hero, 1, 69, 86, 92, 120, 121, 141; see also Portrait of the Artist as a Young Man
Stevens, Wallace, 12–13, 23, 44–5, 52, 161, 174–5
styles: female, 19, 187, 189, 190, 201, 206, 208–9, 211–12; Joyce's various, 1–2, 27–8, 56, 61, 96–7, 136–8, 141–3, 144, 182, 187, 190–1; male, 201, 206, 210–11; see also clothing; gender roles

textiles, see clothing

Ulysses (Joyce): age in, 62–3, 151–3; anti-Semitism, treatment of, 115, 116, 117, 129; authority structures in, 7–12, 174; and the Bible, 142, 147, 195, 199; Christianity in, 15–17, 46–7; classicism and romanticism, 104–5, 114, 128–9; clothing in, 141, 143–4, 148–9, 151–62, 165–72, 176–8, 181–2; criticism of, 2–4, 108, 117–18, 119n, 128–9, 136–9, 167; departure and return in, 133–6; division of, 6–7, 106n; doubling in, 8, 49, 109, 126–8, 136, 165; dualism in, 10–11, 15–17, 105, 108–9, 116–19, 127, 128–30, 134, 140–1, 164–6, 169–70; and Exiles, 150–1; fatherhood in, 8, 16, 47, 48; and Finnegans

221